HUBRIS

BY THE SAME AUTHOR

But What Do You Actually Do?

Kissinger's Year: 1973

The French Revolution

Age of Napoleon

Friend or Foe

Seven Ages of Paris

Telling Lives (editor)

How Far from Austerlitz? Napoleon 1805–1815

The Lonely Leader: Monty 1944–45 (with David Montgomery)

A Bundle from Britain

Harold Macmillan: Volume II, 1957–1986

Harold Macmillan: Volume I, 1894–1956

The French Army and Politics, 1870–1970

Napoleon, Master of Europe, 1805–1807

A Savage War of Peace: Algeria 1954–62

Small Earthquake in Chile

The Terrible Year: The Paris Commune 1871

Death of a Generation

To Lose a Battle: France 1940

The Fall of Paris: The Siege and the Commune, 1870–71

The Price of Glory: Verdun 1916

Canada and the Canadians

The Land is Bright

Back into Power

HUBRIS

The Tragedy of War
in the Twentieth Century

ALISTAIR HORNE

WEIDENFELD & NICOLSON

First published in Great Britain in 2015
by Weidenfeld & Nicolson

1 3 5 7 9 10 8 6 4 2

Copyright © Alistair Horne 2015

Maps by John Gilkes

A CIP catalogue record for this book
is available from the British Library.

ISBN: 978 0 297 86762 3

Typeset by Input Data Services Ltd, Bridgwater, Somerset

Printed and bound by CPI Group (UK) Ltd, Croydon, CRO 4YY

The Orion Publishing Group's policy is to use papers that
are natural, renewable and recyclable and made from wood
grown in sustainable forests. The logging and manufacturing
processes are expected to conform to environmental
regulations of the country of origin.

Weidenfeld & Nicolson
The Orion Publishing Group Ltd
Carmelite House
50 Victoria Embankment
London EC4Y ODZ

An Hachette UK Company

www.orionbooks.co.uk

For Nicholas Berry,
acute student of military history,
and the most supportive of patrons,
in the finest tradition

I'm not a theoretical historian, seeking to guide the reader to a general conclusion. I'm quite content to be a narrative chronicler, a slave of the facts.

Sir Martin Gilbert, *The Jerusalem Report*, 1996

CONTENTS

ILLUSTRATIONS

Watercolour painting of the Battle of Tsushima by C. Schön, 1905 *(Mary Evans/Alamy)*

Sketch of Heihachiro Togo visiting Zinovy Rozhestvensky in hospital *(Ann Ronan Pictures/Print Collector/Getty)*

Georgy Zhukov and Russian commanders, 1939 *(RIA Novosti/ akg-images)*

Soviet postage stamp featuring Richard Sorge *(Keystone France/Getty)*

Soviet soldiers inspecting a Japanese tankette at Nomonhan, 1939 *(RIA Novosti)*

Masanobu Tsuji *(Yomiuri Newspaper/AFLO)*

Georgy Zhukov presenting the Soviet Order of Victory to Bernard Law Montgomery, 1945 *(RIA Novosti/Topfoto)*

Soldiers on guard west of Moscow, 1941 *(Falkmart/Creative Commons)*

Women digging tank traps, 1941 *(US Information Agency)*

Wehrmacht transport carriage horses *(Bundesarchiv)*

Raymond Spruance *(US Navy/LIFE Picture Collection/Getty)*

Isoroku Yamamoto *(LIFE Picture Collection/Getty)*

USS *Yorktown (US Navy)*

English soldiers surrendering to Japanese forces, 1942 *(Mondadori/ Getty)*

Douglas MacArthur and Harry S. Truman *(LIFE Picture Collection/ Getty)*

Henri Navarre, Christian de Castries and René Cogny *(Press Association)*

Viet Minh soldiers at Dien Bien Phu *(AFP/Getty)*

Viet Minh victory parade, 1954 *(Pictures from History/Bridgeman)*

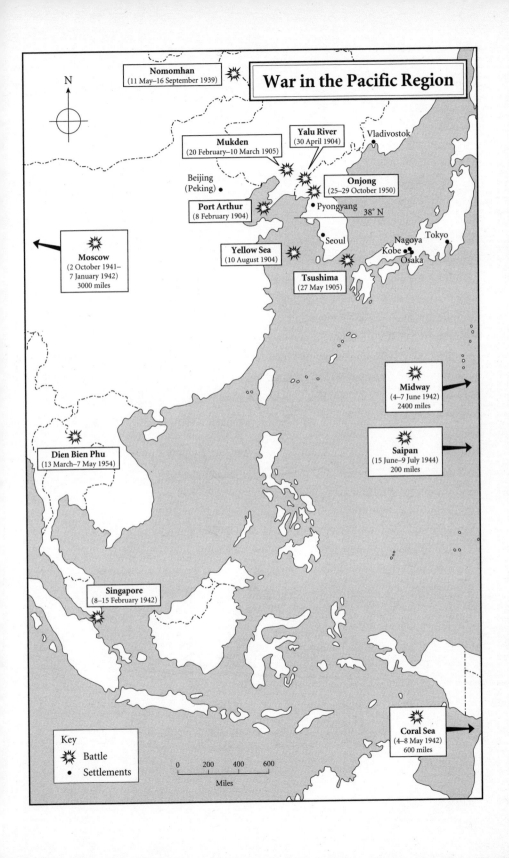

N

Nomomhan
(11 May–16 September 1939)

War in the Pacific Region

Mukden
(20 February–10 March 1905)

Yalu River
(30 April 1904)

Vladivostok

Beijing
(Peking) •

Onjong
(25–29 October 1950)

Port Arthur
(8 February 1904)

• Pyongyang

38° N

Moscow
(2 October 1941–
7 January 1942)
3000 miles

Yellow Sea
(10 August 1904)

• Seoul

Nagoya   Tokyo
Kobe ••   •
  Osaka

Tsushima
(27 May 1905)

Midway
(4–7 June 1942)
2400 miles

Saipan
(15 June–9 July 1944)
200 miles

Dien Bien Phu
(13 March–7 May 1954)

Singapore
(8–15 February 1942)

Coral Sea
(4–8 May 1942)
600 miles

Key
✳ Battle
• Settlements

0   200   400   600

Miles

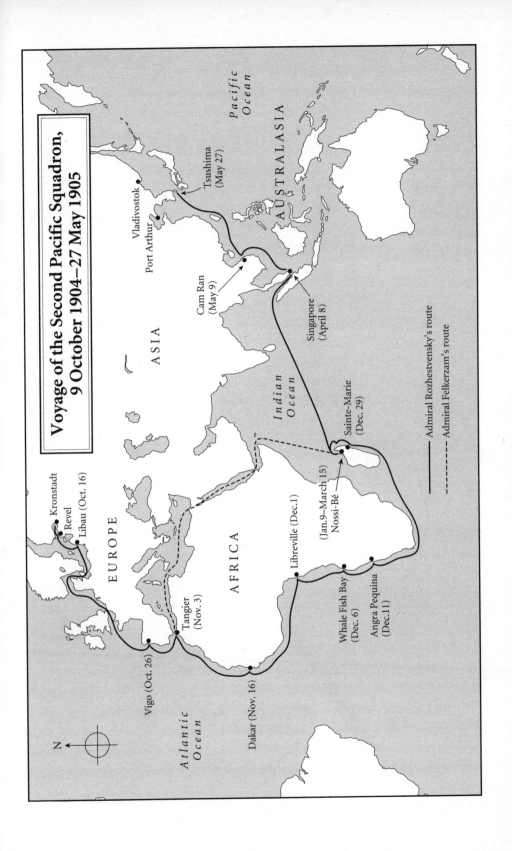

Voyage of the Second Pacific Squadron, 9 October 1904–27 May 1905

N

Atlantic Ocean

EUROPE

Kronstadt
Revel
Libau (Oct. 16)

Vigo (Oct. 26)

Tangier (Nov. 3)

AFRICA

Dakar (Nov. 16)

Libreville (Dec.1)

Whale Fish Bay (Dec. 6)

Angra Pequina (Dec.11)

Nossi-Bé (Jan.9–March 15)

Sainte-Marie (Dec. 29)

Indian Ocean

ASIA

Cam Ran (May 9)

Port Arthur

Vladivostok

Tsushima (May 27)

Singapore (April 8)

AUSTRALASIA

Pacific Ocean

——— Admiral Rozhestvensky's route

- - - - - Admiral Felkerzam's route

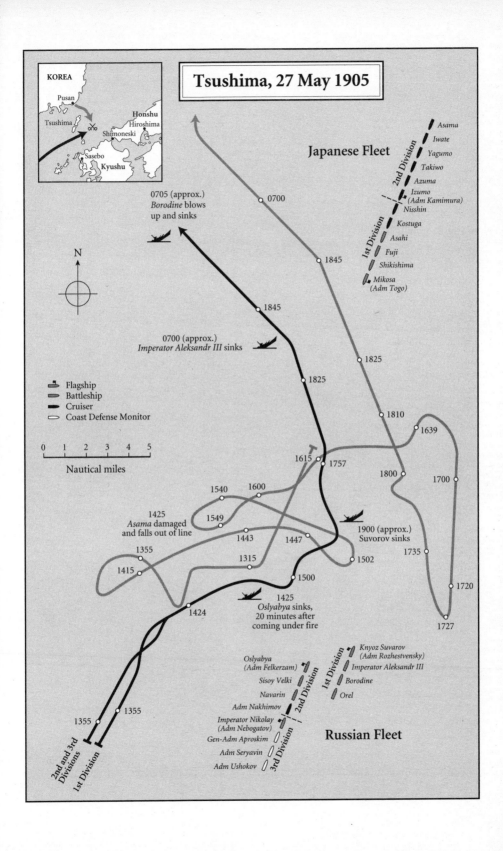

Tsushima, 27 May 1905

KOREA

Pusan

Tsushima

Honshu
Hiroshima
Shimoneski

Sasebo

Kyushu

Japanese Fleet

Asama
Iwate
Yagumo
Takiwo
Azuma
Izumo
(Adm Kamimura)
Nisshin

2nd Division

1st Division

Kostuga
Asahi
Fuji
Shikishima
Mikosa
(Adm Togo)

0705 (approx.)
Borodine blows
up and sinks

0700

1845

1845

1825

0700 (approx.)
Imperator Aleksandr III sinks

1825

1810

1639

N

1615   1757

1800   1700

Flagship
Battleship
Cruiser
Coast Defense Monitor

1540   1600

1549

1425
Asama damaged
and falls out of line

1443   1447

1900 (approx.)
Suvorov sinks

0 1 2 3 4 5

Nautical miles

1355

1415

1315

1502

1735

1720

1500

1727

1424

1425
Oslyabya sinks,
20 minutes after
coming under fire

Oslyabya
(Adm Felkerzam)

Sisoy Velki

Navarin

Adm Nakhimov

Imperator Nikolay
(Adm Nebogatov)

Gen-Adm Aproskim

Adm Seryavin

Adm Ushokov

2nd Division

3rd Division

1st Division

Knyoz Suvarov
(Adm Rozhestvensky)

Imperator Aleksandr III

Borodine

Orel

Russian Fleet

1355   1355

2nd and 3rd
Divisions

1st Division

Nomonhan, 11 May–16 September 1939

Halha River

N

USSR

Nomonhan •
MONGOLIA

MANCHURIA

KOREA

CHINA

JAPAN

Fui Heights

Soviet Northern Force

MANCHURIA

Bain Tsagan

Japanese Defences

Nomonhan

to Hailar 200 miles

Soviet-Claimed Border

MONGOLIA

Holsten River

Soviet Bridge

Soviet Central Force

to Tamsag Bulak 100 miles

Soviet Southern Force

Japanese-Claimed Border

Halha River

→ Soviet Advances

▪▪▪▪ Japanese Defence

0   2.5   5
Miles

Moscow, 2 October 1941–7 January 1942

N

Northwestern
Front
(Kurochkin)

Leningrad
• Kalinin
• MOSCOW
Baltic Sea
Smolensk •
• Orel
• Kiev

0   200   400
Miles

Black Sea

Kalinin
Front
(Konev)

Velikie Luki

Staritsa

Kalinin

Klin

Smolensk

Army Group
Centre
(von Kluge)

Partisans

Partisans

Mozhaisk

• MOSCOW

Naro Pominsk

Malosaraslavets

Western
Front
(Zhukov)

Livdinovo •

Kaluga

Kozelsk

Briansk
Front
(Cherevi-
chenko)

Tula

Briansk •

Delev

Stalinogorsk

Chern

Briansk
Front

• Orel

Front Lines
———— 5 December, 1941
– – – 16 December, 1941
· · · · · 1 January, 1942
Russian movements
German Counter-attacks

Army Group
South
(Reichenau)

Southwestern
Front
(Kosienko)

0   50   100
Miles

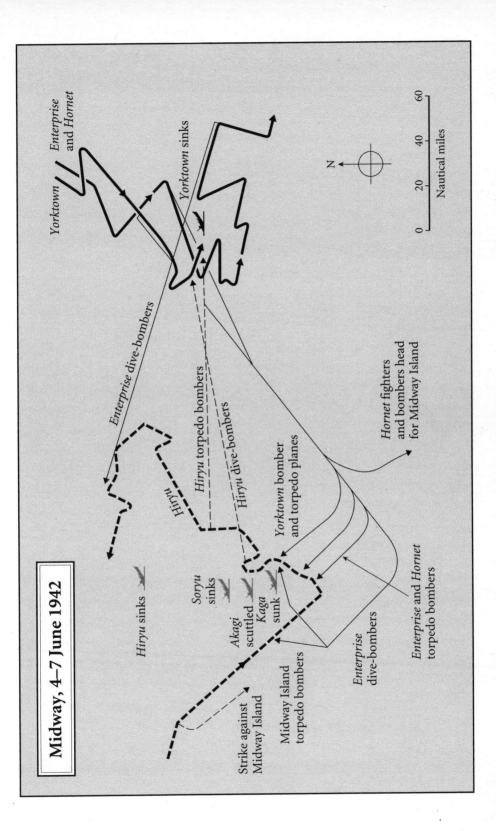

Midway, 4–7 June 1942

Yorktown

Enterprise and Hornet

Yorktown

Enterprise and Hornet

Yorktown sinks

Enterprise dive-bombers

Hiryu

Hiryu torpedo bombers

Hiryu dive-bombers

Hornet fighters and bombers head for Midway Island

Hiryu sinks

Soryu sinks

Akagi scuttled

Kaga sunk

Yorktown bomber and torpedo planes

Strike against Midway Island

Midway Island torpedo bombers

Enterprise dive-bombers

Enterprise and *Hornet* torpedo bombers

N

0 20 40 60

Nautical miles

PROLOGUE

The ancient Greeks defined hubris as the worst sin a leader, or a nation, could commit. It was the attitude of supreme arrogance, where mortals in their folly would set themselves up against the gods. Its consequences were invariably severe. The Greeks also had a word for what usually followed hubris. That was called peripeteia, meaning a dramatic reversal of fortune. In practice, it signified a falling from the grace of a great height to unimaginable depths. Disaster would often embrace not only the offender, but also his nearest and dearest, and all those responsible to him.

Having written, over the course of fifty-odd years, numerous books and articles on warfare in its various shapes, some time ago I sat down to reflect on what might be the common features of warfare that stood out over the ages. One that emerged pre-eminently was hubris: wars over the ages have generally been won or lost through excessive hubris on one side or the other. In modern military parlance it might also be dubbed 'overreach'. So this is the genesis of the current work. Wars and battles seldom happen in isolation, in a vacuum. Each has its causes from the past, and each has its often baneful consequences in a subsequent period. To study them the good historian needs to be able to scan backwards, and forwards, as well as sideways. Thus I have focused on those conflicts which affected future history powerfully in ways that transcended the actual war in which the conflict was set.

I chose to limit my study to the first half of the twentieth century, the bloodiest in history, and a century which indeed could be called the century of hubris – during which humans were slaughtered in numbers to exceed those of any other century, all at the whim of one or two warlords or dictators.

One immediate effect of hubris was often complacency, a first step on the path to ruin. As the German Chancellor Otto von Bismarck once remarked, in an axiom that might be seen as a prediction of the eventual fate of his own country: 'A generation that deals out a thrashing is usually followed by one which receives it.'

Two battles which I have already written about, the Siege of Paris (1870–1) and the gory Battle of Verdun (1916),* provide good examples of the validity of Bismarck's warning. Out of their victory in 1871, the Germans emerged so well stuffed with arrogance that defeat in the next war, if not the one after, seemed all but certain. Nearly half a century later, the French heirs to the terrible pyrrhic victory of Verdun, on the one hand, felt that they could never repeat such a sacrifice and, on the other, had been impregnated with hubristic self-confidence that they would be safe behind the super-Verdun-like fortress of the Maginot Line, and that the hereditary German foe *ne passera pas*. The shibboleth of their fathers' heroism was enough. Or was it? Six weeks in that summer of 1940 would prove that it was not.

The book is divided into five parts. I begin with the Battle of Tsushima, and the sinking of the Russian fleet at Port Arthur – an event that shocked the world. Bracketed within that, there is a look at the triumph of Japanese ambitions. In the second part, the little-known Battle of Nomonhan in Mongolia in 1939 illustrates the rise of Soviet power and the first check on Japan. Third, after Hitler had overreached himself with his invasion of the Soviet Union, there is the Battle of Moscow in 1941, which takes us to Pearl Harbor and to the fourth part, the turning point of the Pacific War with the Battle of Midway. Key episodes from the Korean War, in Part Five, provide a perfect illustration of the hubristic folly of not knowing when to stop. I end with the French disaster in Vietnam at Dien Bien Phu, last of the old-fashioned colonial wars in the Far East.

My choice of subjects may well be challenged as capricious: it is certainly idiosyncratic and personal. Deliberately, the First World War is left out. It seemed to me that the whole war began, and was caused by, various sublime practitioners of hubris in conflict with each other. Secondly, it would be difficult to identify any one battle more than another which held calamitous consequences for the future. The whole war did that.

---

* See Horne trilogy: *The Fall of Paris*, *The Price of Glory* and *To Lose a Battle*.

I would hesitate to write anything to belittle British prowess in either world war. But where was the battle in which hubris displayed by the leadership affected post-war events? El Alamein? Caen? Arnhem? Montgomery was certainly a candidate for hubris in the eyes of his allies. But, as I tried to show in my biography *The Lonely Leader*, Montgomery had his special reasons. He had inherited a battered army, which had been defeated almost incessantly since the beginning of the war, and had reason to be truly alarmed by the Wehrmacht; in consequence he had to infuse it with massive doses of what he called 'Binge' – the right spirit for victory. Then again, without belittling British arms, El Alamein, designated by Churchill 'the end of the beginning', was indeed a small affair compared numerically with the troops arrayed before Moscow in 1941 – over ten to one in comparison to Alamein – and could there be found in any of Monty's battles issues that would affect post-war history?

To my mind Moscow 1941 was more definitively an 'end of the beginning', added to which, probably more than any other salient victory, it was to have an influence on Soviet conduct in post-war events. Even today the scale of the fighting, and the numbers, before Moscow in 1941 stun the imagination. It was a true turning point in the war, seen from this distance, more significant even than Soviet Marshal Georgy Zhukov's great victory of the following year at Stalingrad. It marked a decisive moment in warfare, as the first time that the apparently invincible Panzers were stopped, defeated and then forced to retreat. It marked Hitler's final loss of confidence in his generals, displaced by belief in his own star – with the disastrous consequences which remain familiar to history. More than that, the victory, and its cost to the Russian people, established in Stalin's mind the shape of the post-war map of Europe under a Soviet aegis. More immediately, it confirmed him as the irreplaceable, omnipotent Russian war leader. As far as overall Allied strategies were concerned, so much after Moscow seems to have been dancing to Stalin's tune. Certainly, for the next unhappy forty-five years the shape of Europe would be the shape that Stalin had dictated.

Much of this book concerns the Pacific, and Japan. It's not an area I've written about much before. Perhaps I may plead, in part, the enticement for a historian, and the sheer excitement of uncovering fresh green fields, their consequence to world history perhaps not adequately explored in depth. Over the years I have written, in one form or other, about most of the battles in this book, from Verdun to Dien Bien Phu, to Pearl Harbor, and Korea 1950. But I have never before studied the Japanese side of things in depth. It has been instructive. My argument is that this is where it all began, with Admiral Togo's far-off victory over the Russians at Tsushima in 1905. In their invasion of Manchuria in 1931, Japan's warlords showed the way to aggression two years before Hitler came to power. A great deal subsequently flowed from this, in terms of the huge imbalance it caused in world affairs. And, of course, it was in the Pacific area, within a few miles of Tsushima, that the sword of Damocles descended on Japan with such catastrophic force in 1945. If one can read the tea leaves correctly, the Pacific theatre may well be the arena for future disputes between the major world players.

Characters in history often carry within them hooks and eyes which can provide a certain linkage. For instance, Japanese Commander Yamamoto, who as a lieutenant after the Battle of Tsushima went to comfort the humiliated Russian Admiral in his hospital bed, would be the leader appointed to inflict a copycat defeat on the American fleet a generation later at Pearl Harbor. At the Battle of Midway in 1942, Yamamoto would be roundly chastised for his hubris in attacking Pearl Harbor six months previously. Midway clearly marked a peripeteia in Japan's imperial pretensions, a harbinger of the doom that would overtake them three years later. With parallel congruence, one of the US leaders most responsible for Yamamoto's eventual defeat, General Douglas MacArthur, would live to see a hitherto triumphant career plunged into disgrace following one act of hubris in the ensuing Korean War.

As one who would mete out the punishment prescribed by hubris, Zhukov, on the Mongolian battlefield of Nomonhan in 1939, would emerge as one of the Soviet leaders responsible for beating back Hitler's armies on the outskirts of Moscow in December 1941. Zhukov, appropriately, would then go on, through the triumph of Stalingrad, to inflict the ultimate destruction of the Führer's evil dreams in the ruins of Berlin.

Thus, all of the conflicts I have chosen have links with each other, as do many of the players. One of the most depressing facts about military history is how very little the great warlords ever learn from

the mistakes, indeed calamities, of their predecessors. A thread running all the way through my selection is a kind of racist distortion
whereby one power would persist in writing off its foe because of the
colour of their skin or the slant of their eyes, or the supposed back-
wardness of their culture. Thus we may note the Russians' contempt for
the little yellow men; and, in reverse, the Japanese tendency to relegate
the Chinese to the rank of *Untermenschen*, much as Hitler regarded
the barbarian Slavic hordes during Operation Barbarossa. Before and
even after 7 December 1941, American indoctrination was persuading
pilots that the 'Japs' couldn't fly because of their poor eyesight. It was
a racial legend that would pursue the US into the Korean War, with
the denigration of the 'dumb gooks', and on into Vietnam. That sturdy
notion of occidental superiority would influence the French defenders
of Dien Bien Phu and even beyond: the heroic Para survivors of the
final colonial debacle in South-East Asia would carry the fatal mys-
tique on into the Algeria War.

One of the incidental questions prompted by this study is: why don't
successful generals know when to stop? A good general should know,
unlike those of the Western Front constantly battering away at an illu-
sory target regardless of the human cost. How different world history
might have been if MacArthur had had the good sense to stop on
the 38th Parallel. The answer of course is that it is hubris itself which
blinds generals. But we students of history should not succumb to our
own arrogance in supposing that hubris is easy to avoid. It arises out
of success. In the aftermath of triumph, anything seems possible. And
that, as this book tries to show, is when so many calamitous decisions
are taken. If a leader is successful, why hold him back? This book tries
to provide an answer.

PART ONE

TSUSHIMA, 1905

CHAPTER ONE

THE NEW CENTURY

As new centuries are wont to do, the opening years of the twentieth seemed generally full of promise – of a continuation of Victorian peace, prosperity and progress. Certainly there was no hint that might lead the most pessimistic of Cassandras to predict the horrors that would lie ahead, making it the most savage century in the history of mankind. Back in another untroubled summer, that of 1870, the British Foreign Secretary Lord Granville, gazing up from Whitehall, could detect 'not a cloud in the sky'. Yet a month later Europe would be torn asunder by a conflict, the Franco-Prussian War, that would mark the ending of a century of *Pax Britannica* and all its optimistic assumptions. But this was just the sort of dirty trick that history plays to confound historians – and the architects of grand policy.

The century had also opened on a note of melancholy and uncertainty, as well as optimism. Britain, as the Victorian Age ran to its end, was subjected to unheard-of humiliations at Ladysmith and Spion Kop in the Boer War which had broken out the previous October. It would be a year before the British Army could reassert its superiority. In the Far East fear and confusion among Europeans spread with the outbreak of the Boxer Rebellion, while in mid-Pacific the new American imperialism put down its marker by annexing Hawaii.

In England, on 22 January 1901 the old Queen, who had stamped her name on most of the previous hundred years, died. The uncertainty in every Briton's mind was – without her, would things go on, pursuing their same comfortable course? Reassuringly, a vast area of the inhabitable globe was tinted a friendly pink; in terms of mass, the only area to compete, generally shaded a cold green, was the Russian colossus, which stretched unmanageably from the eastern frontiers of Germany to Vladivostok. But, apart from the little-seen skirmishes in the 'Great Game' regularly taking place on the barren fringes of Central Asia

3

where the pink and the green met, backward Russia presented little threat to the pink areas. Of comfort was the fact that, almost as the old Queen's life ebbed to its close, the unpleasant Boer War was ending. Britain, however, having suffered a series of shocking defeats inflicted on her regulars by a bunch of armed farmers, had emerged with nil distinction, moral or military. Humiliating reverses had been dished out with an ease similar to that administered at Concorde, Massachusetts, over a century earlier. Jealous nations among Kipling's 'lesser breeds', such as Kaiser Wilhelm II's Germany, could not help but sit up and take notice. And so too, across the world, on the fringe of China and the Pacific, did the newly emerged nation of Japan.

In June of 1900, the European powers, comfortably established in their concessionary enclaves carved from the decaying body of China, were rocked by the outbreak of the Boxer Rebellion. A sudden eruption of the suppressed Chinese proletariat, led by the so-called Society of Righteous and Harmonious Fists outraged by the unequal treaties which the 'foreign devils' had imposed, massacred hundreds of Europeans in Peking, including the German Ambassador. Overstretched in Africa, Britain found itself having to fall back for help on a new ally, Imperial Japan, an unknown quantity only so recently released from its centuries-long hibernation from the world scene behind its self-imposed lacquer screen. Within a few months the Boxer Rebellion leaders were executed in Peking, and the Rebellion ended with the signature in September 1901 of the Peking (or Boxer) Protocol, which permitted the 'powers' to resume their bad old greedy ways. The difference was that now there was a new player on the scene: Japan. Some with the gift of prognostication might have deemed that the lid of Pandora's box had been lifted.

In terms of the technology of warfare, though undetected at the time, there were certainly pointers in the century following the epic struggle against Napoleon with which the nineteenth century had begun. There was the American Civil War, as well as various minor wars, to suggest what modern soldiery could do to each other on a land battlefield. But since Trafalgar in 1805 there had been no major battle at sea to suggest that warfare there too might have moved on. Ever since the invention of the cannon and its installation aboard ship, since before the Spanish Armada of 1588, the basics had remained little changed. Great wooden ships, studded with massive guns and propelled by acres of sail, hammered away at the enemy at almost point-blank range, 300 yards at most, until one or other was reduced to a mastless hulk, or blew up. It was all about weight of broadside. Tactics too had little altered; every midshipman would dream of one day 'crossing the T' of an enemy column as Nelson had done at Trafalgar, manoeuvring a line of ships to sail across the front of the Franco-Spanish fleet and so enabling them to fire broadsides while the enemy could deploy only his forward guns.

Yet there was one engagement, a very minor and inconclusive one, which gave an indication that, though out of sight, a most fundamental sea-change in naval warfare might be under way. That, too, took place in the western hemisphere, right at the beginning of the American Civil War. At Hampton Roads, Virginia, on 9 March 1862, two strange-looking craft, contoured like horseshoe crabs, one called the *Merrimac* and the other the *Monitor*, engaged each other. They were the first 'ironclads' in the history of naval warfare. They hammered away for about three hours, without being able to inflict significant damage, then backed off. The two American ironclads did not fight again, but a notable point had been reached. The days of the 'sides of oak' were henceforth numbered. Vanished almost overnight were the awe-inspiring ships-of-the-line like Nelson's *Victory* or the lithe greyhound-like frigates that had harried Britain's Royal Navy during the war of 1812. Navies the world over hastened to refurbish their fleets at immense cost. The two major naval powers, Great Britain and France, had already halted construction of wooden-hulled ships, and others followed suit. In 1859 France launched a new iron super-ship, properly called *La Gloire*, the world's first ocean-going ironclad, a steam-driven behemoth of 5,630 tons and a crew of 570. The next year Britain followed up with a mammoth twice its size, HMS *Warrior*.*

The world's first arms race was on. Fortunately there was no conflict in sight to lend it particular urgency and neither *Warrior* nor its French rival would ever see action. Navies would from now on protect the vitals of their ships with great slabs of cast iron of ever-increasing thickness. Even more challenging was the development of the long-range, rifled, breech-loading guns of monster calibres that could hit

* Superbly reconditioned, *Warrior* lives on today in Portsmouth harbour.

and destroy an enemy ship with huge high-explosive shells at 7,000 and even 10,000 yards' range, the guns themselves now protected in revolving armoured turrets. No more the murderous eyeball-to-eyeball grappling of Nelson's day. In October 1901 the Royal Navy launched its first submarine, a weapon that was to prove deeply disadvantageous to the progenitor nation.

If it challenged navies of the established world powers to compete, the new naval race also offered newcomers an entrée hitherto closed to Kipling's 'lesser breeds'. One such was Kaiser Wilhelm II's Germany, and another Meiji Japan.

Nevertheless, to the amazement of most of the world, not only of the injured party, this peaceful scene was scarred on 8 February 1904 when little Japan suddenly launched a surprise attack on the Russian base of Port Arthur (or Lüshun, as it was known by its previous, and perhaps rightful, owner, China), at the tip of a Manchurian promontory in the Yellow Sea. Three weeks later there followed reports of Russian troops retreating from Korea into Manchuria, pursued by an army of 100,000 Japanese.

Initially, not much occured to upset the applecart in the rest of the world. Then, suddenly, on 22 October, Great Britain was rocked by news that the Russian Baltic Fleet, appearing off the Dogger Bank, had attacked a British fishing fleet and sunk a trawler, killing members of its crew. The Russians' excuse was that they had mistaken the trawlers for Japanese torpedo boats which they believed were hunting them. Japanese torpedo boats in the North Sea? There was consternation and outrage in the clubs of St James's. Calls were made to declare war instantly on Russia, or at least to demand extensive reparations.

But what *was* this war all about? Who were they, these Japanese, anyway? And what did they think they could possibly achieve against the might of Imperial Russia, all that green on the map stretching from the Pacific to the Vistula? Where had these Japanese come from? What most people in the West knew of Japan was more or less limited to its skill in the decorative arts. Hokusai's woodblock print *The Wave*, for example, influenced the French Impressionists, from Manet to Renoir, and Art Nouveau in Germany. There were also netsuke, but awareness of these minute treasures was limited to the more refined occidental collectors. In 1885 there came Gilbert and Sullivan's *Mikado*,

6

or The Town of Titipu, a rather cruel send-up of pre-Restoration Japan. Though it was intended as a farce on contemporary England, some Japanese critics saw the setting of a medieval Japan as deeply disrespectful of the revered, and very modern, Meiji Emperor. Neverthless it ran at the Savoy Theatre for 672 performances, the second-longest run for any operetta. Then came Puccini's *Madama Butterfly*, hardly flattering of Japan's harsh social customs, and equally offensive to its modern sensibilities. (*Butterfly's* first night at La Scala took place within days of the outbreak of the Russo-Japanese War; it was a major flop.)

If Western views of Japan at the turn of the century were not flavoured by ignorance and condescension, they were downright contemptuous. The Tsar dismissed the Japanese as 'little yellow men from whom Europeans have nothing to fear', or simply as 'monkeys'. His cousin and fellow monarch Kaiser Wilhelm, ever the *provocateur*, sympathized with his views on the 'Yellow Peril': it was Russia's divine mission 'to defend Europe from the inroads of the Great Yellow Race'. The views privately expressed in the clubs of St James's would probably not have been dissimilar.

Nevertheless, here was a small nation, imbued with extraordinary discipline and aggressive spirit, which had emerged only recently from self-imposed obscurity. Tucked away in the isolation of its island strongholds, the Japanese nation had, from time immemorial, developed its own myths and beliefs, alien and largely incomprehensible to the rest of the world. To begin with, whereas monarchs in medieval or Renaissance Europe could claim to be God's Anointed, the Emperor of Japan was divine in his own right.

Thus ordinances issued by ministers in the emperor's name had to be regarded as coming directly from God. This would go some way to explain the fanatical bravery of Japanese combatants through the ages. By legend, the first Japanese were descended from the brother of the Sun Goddess, a contentious and violent figure called Susanoo-no-Mikoto. In a direct line from him came the first Emperor, Jimmu Tenno, who, after a great deal of combat and bloodshed, set up court in the central province of Yamato. The date when he established his throne, often given as 660 BC, is still celebrated to this day, thereby according to the current imperial dynasty by far the longest bloodline of any royal family in history.

7

Through the ages Japan tended to regard its neighbours with a mixture of fear and covetousness. The huge, shambling mass of China just across the East China Sea was always its principal worry – real or imagined. Twice in the thirteenth century Japan was threatened with invasion by the dread Mongol hordes of Kublai Khan, operating out of a vassal China. On the second occasion, in 1281, the Mongols had amassed an army estimated at 150,000. They established a toehold on Kyushu Island. Then, suddenly, the Mongol fleet was hit by a typhoon and virtually destroyed. Japanese history recorded it as the 'Divine Wind', or *Kamikaze*. It was a term that would gain fateful significance in the latter, desperate days of the Second World War, as the name accorded the imperial suicide bombers that attacked the US fleet. But, historically, the typhoon reinforced the legend of the nation's divine origin, something which would always protect it when confronted by disaster.

To meet foreign threats like the Mongols, in similar fashion to that other island kingdom, Britain, Japan built up its navy, a tradition that would survive through the centuries. In 1592, Japan used its navy to invade Korea, possibly as a prelude to attacking China proper. There followed a bitter campaign, lasting six years, and the establishment of an appallingly harsh and cruel regime which left an imprint of enduring hatred among the Koreans, who also would never forget the name of the *daimyo* or feudal warlord Hideyoshi.

Inevitably, with the advent of the Renaissance in Europe, the West came in contact with Japan. First, it was Portuguese merchants, and Jesuit fathers. Shortly after his arrival in Japan in the sixteenth century Father Francis Xavier wrote effusively: 'The people whom we have met so far are the best who have yet been discovered, and it seems to me that we shall never find among heathens another race to equal the Japanese. They are people of very good manners, good in general, and not malicious; they are men of honour to a marvel, and prize honour above all else in the world . . .'

Perhaps the good Father was lucky in his contacts. At any rate the honeymoon lasted some fifty years, reaching a point where the Jesuits seemed to have good prospects of converting the whole of Japan to Christianity. Then, by the end of the sixteenth century, a reaction set in. Twenty-six Christians were martyred, by the *daimyo* tyrant Hideyoshi

– acting, of course, in the name of the Emperor. English and Dutch traders who had set up commerce with Japan became almost as unpopular among the Japanese. By the 1630s, Japan's rulers decided that they had had enough of foreigners and their interference in domestic affairs. Abruptly all interaction with the outside world was cut off. In 1647 a draconian edict decreed that any Japanese leaving the country would do so under pain of death, and the same fate would await him if he returned. Foreigners attempting to enter would be similarly at risk. So Japan's self-isolation continued for two centuries, with consequences felt until the mid-twentieth century. On the other hand, as historian Richard Storry remarks, 'the Japanese lived in peace . . . with themselves and with the world, for two and a half centuries – a record that most nations, reviewing their own history over a similar period, must surely envy'.

At the same time, an unpleasant manifestation known as *bushido* was allowed to take root among the samurai. Achieving a semi-religious status, it was best described as 'a Spartan devotion by a warrior class to the arts of war, a readiness for self-sacrifice'. Its full unpleasantness would be demonstrated in the Second World War, and earlier in the invasion of China.

The aim of the ruling Tokugawa shogunate was, simply, to maintain the status quo of antiquity. But then, in the mid-nineteenth century, came a rude awakening. On 8 July 1853, four sinister black warships, commanded by US Commodore Matthew Perry (and accompanied by Puccini's fictional 'Pinkerton'), forced their way into Uraga Harbour, near Edo (modern Tokyo). Two of Perry's squadron were steamships, a novelty never before seen in isolated Japan. The Commodore rejected demands to leave, insisting instead that he present a letter from President Millard Fillmore, who probably did not know exactly where Japan was. Perry threatened force if the Japanese resisted. The presidential letter contained a demand that the Japanese regime open up trading relations – the first display of 'Yankee Imperialism'. Perry announced that he would return the following year for an answer. He was back in February, this time with seven warships, but in the interval the ruling shogunate had undergone a remarkable about-face. Antiquated Japan was more than ripe for change, and by 1857 Japan was telling the US, 'Intercourse shall be continued for ever.' Two centuries of isolation was abandoned almost overnight. A new, modern-minded oligarchy thrust aside the feuding *daimyos* and the Tokugawa shogunate, restoring centralized power to the new Emperor, the fifteen-year-old Mutsuhito, in 1867. He took on the name of Meiji, meaning 'enlightened rule'. Historians of Japan would dub the astonishing renaissance that followed the 'Meiji Restoration'.

In January 1869, the following declaration was issued from the new capital of Tokyo:

> The Emperor of Japan announces to the sovereigns of all foreign countries and to their subjects [that permission has been granted to the Shogun Tokugawa Yoshinobu to return the governing power in accordance with his own request]. We shall henceforward exercise supreme authority in all the internal and external affairs of the country. Consequently the title of Emperor must be substituted for that of Taikun [the shogun], in which the treaties have been made. Officers are being appointed by us to [sic] the conduct of foreign affairs. It is desirable that the representatives of the treaty powers recognize this announcement.

Shortly thereafter the young Emperor (he would rule for forty-five years) boarded a Japanese naval vessel for the first time, and the next day gave instructions for studies to see how Japan's navy could be strengthened. There followed an extraordinary, indeed miraculous urge to join the modern world. It is true that upon so proud a nation Perry's brutal forced entry would leave a scar which time could never efface. However, for the foreseeable future Japan, abandoning all national pride, would learn and copy from the West in every possible direction. In 1868 the young Emperor himself spelled out in a Charter Oath his determination that 'Knowledge shall be sought for all over the world and thus shall be strengthened the foundation of the imperial polity.'

A new, compulsory educational scheme would create 54,000 primary schools – or one for roughly every 600 inhabitants; this would lead eventually to the Japanese becoming the most highly literate people in Asia. Within one generation Japan subjected itself to an astonishing industrial revolution, designed to catch up with two centuries of Western progress. The mantra for Japanese industry and learning became henceforth, unashamedly and in general successfully, 'copy, improve and innovate'.

Inevitably, these developments acquired a military, and naval, flavour. Popular was the slogan: 'Rich country, strong army'. Envoys scoured Europe for the best models to emulate. Initially it was the France of Louis-Napoleon, which was reckoned to have the world's finest army – just returned from the Crimean War. French shipyards were filled with orders for Japanese naval vessels. Then came the sudden debacle of 1870, and France's humiliation at Sedan, at the hands of Bismarck and Moltke. Prussian military advisers were soon on their way to Meiji Tokyo, while British shipyards would shortly receive orders for the Emperor's new model navy. Naval officers, like the future Admiral Togo, were sent to Plymouth to study and train. Togo spent seven years with the Royal Navy, returning aboard one of the three new warships delivered to Japan. Hand in hand with this martial renaissance went thoughts of imperial expansion. As little Japan watched the land-grab for Africa, led by the forces of another small island power, Britain, and in which even a newcomer like the upstart Kaiser could claim outposts as far away as the northern coast of China, an element of 'me-too-ism' crept in. Predictably, this would bring Japan into conflict with the two neighbouring imperial colossi, first China, then Russia.

At that time, Japan could cite demographic excuses for becoming expansionist. Its population in 1873 totalled nearly 35 million, roughly the same as Great Britain. (By 1904, it would be approaching 47 million.) They were crammed into islands roughly the same size as the British Isles, but much of their mountainous terrain was as resistant to the plough as the Grampians. And Japan had no outlets for expansion as did the much envied Britain in India, Canada, Australia and the newly acquired colonies in Africa. The Japanese looked across the 100-mile Straits of Tshushima to the fertile fields of Korea, and beyond to the huge empty plains of Manchuria, rich in the mineral wealth, timber and raw materials that their country lacked. Both were vassal provinces of China's groggy Manchu empire.

In 1894 Japan went to war with China. The nominal excuse was the assassination, and quartering, in Shanghai of a pro-Japanese Korean revolutionary, Kim Ok-gyun. But in fact the Sino-Japanese War was one of more or less straightforward colonial acquisition, and gave the young resurgent Japan an opportunity to flex its muscles and demonstrate its newly acquired martial hardware. The war lasted only eight months. Japan won virtually every round – especially at sea, where its modernized fleet (eight of whose ships were of British origin, to three French and two Japanese-built warships) sank eight out of China's ten warships, and inflicted disproportionately brutal losses upon the sluggish Chinese ground forces. Most of the Japanese dead had succumbed to disease. Japan ended up in possession of Taiwan (Formosa) and with a degree of control over a Korea removed from fealty to Peking. For the first time in over 2,000 years, dominance in East Asia shifted from China to Japan. In China the humiliating loss sparked an unprecedented revolt against the tottering Manchu dynasty, leading eventually to the Sun Yat-sen revolution. In the harsh Shimonoseki Treaty that followed, China also had to pay war reparations of 200 million silver Kuping taels. According to the Chinese scholar Jin Xide, the Manchu government paid a huge sum of silver to Japan for both the reparations of war and war trophies, equal to about 6.4 times the total Japanese government revenue.

In addition – and it was a vital concession – China agreed to cede the strategically important Liaotung Peninsula, with its key naval base that later became known as Port Arthur* (now Lüshunkou), a superb and well-protected natural harbour on the extreme southern tip of the peninsula. Among other things, it was an imposing sign of how far Japan had come since the Meiji Restoration, within only one generation. The European powers, consisting of Russia, France and Germany, all with their own colonial interests, and their own enclaves on the coast of China, however, were shocked by the draconian terms exacted by this upstart minor nation. They were also incensed by the Japanese troops' brutal massacre of Chinese soldiers and civilians in conquered Port Arthur – a glimpse of the future. The powers expressed concern that the port, in Japanese hands, would present a 'constant menace' to the Chinese capital, which lay less than 300 miles to the north-west.

Russia, Germany and France (Britain, keen to sell warships to Japan, was conspicuously absent from this imposing line-up) intervened to

* Port Arthur was named after a humble Royal Navy lieutenant, William C. Arthur, who in 1860, during the Second Opium War, had towed his crippled frigate into the harbour of what was then an unfortified fishing village.

demand a revision of the Shimonoseki terms. Under threat of war against overwhelming force (all Russian ships in Japanese ports received orders to be ready to sail at twenty-four hours' notice, in preparation for hostilities), Japan, though allowed to hang on to Taiwan, was forced to cede Port Arthur back to China – which promptly leased it on to Russia for a period of twenty-five years. In return Japan was granted a further bribe of 30 million taels. It would be enough to re-equip its navy, and start up its own munitions industries, instead of having to depend on European imports: all in time to prepare its war machine for the next round – which would come in ten years' time.

However, not for the first or last time, the proud Japanese deeply resented this interference by the powers, and their 'disrespectful' condescension. In Tokyo the hand of the nationalists and expansionists was notably strengthened. The significance of Port Arthur's proximity to Peking, as an assurance against any future threat from the traditional foe, had certainly not escaped the strategically minded Japanese either. But not only that: the port was an ideal base from which to control Korea, or to launch any future venture into Manchuria just across the Yalu River. And what was more, Port Arthur, sheltered within the embrace of the Yellow Sea, offered the most northerly ice-free port on the mainland.

This is what now brought Russia on to the scene. As of the turn of the century, Tsarist Russia was both the largest and the most aggressively imperialist nation on the globe. Its advance across Siberia to the Pacific had begun with Yermak Timofeyevich, a freebooter Cossack, as early as the late sixteenth century, at the time of Ivan the Terrible. Yermak was eventually murdered by the exploited Tartars, and it was not until 1860 that a firm foothold was established on the Pacific, where a modest town was built at Vladivostok, opposite the northern Japanese island of Hokkaido. But the trouble with Vladivostok, though it was an excellent port capable of holding the whole of the Russian Pacific Fleet, was that it was iced in for three to four months in the year. In contrast, Port Arthur, protected by the almost landlocked Yellow Sea, was not – hence the Russians' passionate interest in acquiring it as a base, equalled only by Japanese determination that they should not. Apart from its winter limitations, Vladivostok was at the end of the world's longest, most attenuated and most tenuous railway line, the

Trans-Siberian, single-tracked from Moscow for 7,000 miles. In the event of war in the Far East the railway might be logistically disastrous: railway trucks had to be ferried for sixty miles across the vastness of Lake Baikal before performing a great loop around the north of Chinese Manchuria.

In 1896, a year after the Sino-Japanese War had ended, Russia wheedled rights from the battered Chinese to build a spur-line straight across Manchuria, via Harbin, to Vladivostok. This line, the Chinese Eastern Railway, shortened the route by about 400 miles. Only two years later, the Russians started to push through another spur-line, the South Manchuria Railway, from Harbin, a new Russian-built town, through to Port Arthur – thus connecting it by rail to Moscow. Under the dynamic lead of Sergey Witte, son of a German Baltic baron, a railways expert and the Tsar's Minister of Finance, work on the railways went ahead at phenomenal speed, unprecedented in shambling Tsarist Russia – although Witte himself was said to have been strongly opposed to Russia's commitment to constructing a naval base at Port Arthur.

An anxious Tokyo seethed with rage over the Russian rail enterprises. Understandably, it looked as if the Russians, deploying a substantial armed force to protect the railway workings, were pulling off a *de facto* take-over of Manchuria; and then, with the second line – the South Manchuria Railway – entrenching themselves permanently in Port Arthur. Towards the end of 1903, Japan prepared for war against the Russian colossus. Most observers in the West thought it would never happen, that this upstart oriental David could not possibly prevail against St Petersburg's imperial Goliath. Certainly the Tsar's generals didn't think so. But, at the beginning of February 1904, the Japanese Chief of Staff, Field Marshal Iwao Oyama, told the Emperor that it was essential for Japan to strike first if it wished to avoid the loss of its 'birthrights' in Korea and Manchuria.

CHAPTER TWO

PORT ARTHUR

On 6 February 1904, Vice-Admiral Heihachiro Togo, aged fifty-seven, Commander-in-Chief of Japan's Combined Fleet, summoned his commanders aboard his flagship, the 15,000-ton *Mikasa.*[*] They were greeted by an unsheathed *sambo*, the short sword used traditionally by the samurai for the rite of *seppuku*, or *hara-kiri*, lying on the table in his cabin. It was a clear signal that war had been decided upon. Togo told his officers with great solemnity, 'We sail tomorrow, and our enemy flies the Russian flag.' He then proceeded to hand out detailed orders. Aboard his British-built flagship, Togo led his force of six battleships (all of them also British-built), ten cruisers, thirty destroyers and forty torpedo boats out of Sasebo naval base on the southern tip of Japan. They headed into the Yellow Sea: direction Port Arthur. Before the fleet sailed, Japan's efficient spy networks on the mainland had supplied Togo with every detail of the location of the Russian fleet anchored safely in Port Arthur, as well as alerting him each time there was a change of berth.

Meanwhile another naval force escorting transports that carried 3,000 army troops was directed towards the Korean port of Chemulpo (later called Inchon).[†] They were to create a bridgehead from which Field Marshal Oyama's ground forces could threaten Port Arthur from the rear and advance northwards into Manchuria, with the objective of pre-empting Russian land reinforcements arriving via the Trans-Siberia rail networks. Timing was everything, and neither time nor numbers were on the side of the attacker. The assault had to be carried

---

* *Mikasa*, built by Vickers in 1900, with four twelve-inch guns was then one of the most powerful battleships afloat, the last of the pre-*Dreadnought* era. The Russians had nothing comparable.
† Inchon entered its name in the history books once again, when – in 1950, during the Korean War – General MacArthur took the North Koreans by surprise with an amphibious landing there in their rear.

out before the ice melted around Vladivostok, which would allow the Russian fleet iced in there to sortie into the Yellow Sea to reinforce that at Port Arthur. And certainly it had to be concluded before the new Russian railways across Manchuria could come into play.

Togo despatched ten fast destroyers (again, several of them British built) streaking ahead of his main force to deliver a surprise torpedo attack on the Russian fleet, insouciantly anchored in the security of Port Arthur. The first Japanese torpedoes, in what was in effect the earliest successful torpedo attack in the history of naval warfare, were fired just before midnight on 8 February. As no declaration of war had yet been received, St Petersburg, as well as the Russian fleet, was taken completely by surprise. Here was a new style of diplomacy and warfare. Certainly it took the Chancelleries of Europe by surprise; none had believed that the Japanese pygmy would really dare attack the Russian giant – least of all the giant itself.

At least it might have furnished a warning for the US Navy at Pearl Harbor a few decades later. The similarities were remarkable (the main difference being that on 7 December 1941 Admiral Yamamoto's force dropped their torpedoes and bombs from carrier-borne aircraft). In both incidents the element of surprise was achieved in that war had not been declared, and diplomatic negotiations were still under way. As Commander Fuchida, the dashing leader of the attacking squadrons at Pearl Harbor, exclaimed in amazement: 'Have these Americans never heard of Port Arthur?' But, to the dismay of us historians, our leaders tend not to read history; or, worse, they pay no attention to its lessons. Yet it does seem extraordinary that – in 1941 with tensions rising between the USA and Japan – Franklin Delano Roosevelt did not seem aware of the dangerous precedents: after all, he had himself been Assistant Secretary of the Navy in the First World War, only a decade after the attack on Port Arthur, and was well read in history.

What of the Japanese commander on this momentous night in February 1904? Heihachiro Togo was born in 1848, the son of a samurai living in the city of Kagushima in feudal, pre-Meiji Japan. It was an area from which came the notorious Satsuma samurai, as a breed of dedicated militarists perhaps comparable to the Prussians in history. The Satsuma were a clique that stuck closely together. Togo received his first taste of battle at the age of fifteen when the Royal Navy bombarded the city in gunboat justice for the killing of a Briton the previous year. The following year he and two brothers enlisted in the *daimyo*'s navy, which fought in the last of pre-Meiji civil wars, serving in a paddle-wheel warship. Despite his early blooding by the British, in 1871 Togo went for seven years to England as an apprentice officer, together with a group of other Japanese students. He thought London a strange city and was amazed by the 'abundance of meat', but found his own cadet rations 'inadequate': 'I swallowed my small rations in a moment. I formed the habit of dipping my bread in my tea and eating a great deal of it, to the surprise of my English comrades.' His British comrades, ignorant of the difference between Asiatic peoples, called him 'Johnny Chinaman'. Occasionally such affronts would end in blows; nevertheless, Togo graduated second in the class.

In 1875, Togo went round the world as an ordinary seaman on the British training-ship *Hampshire*, staying seventy days at sea without a port call until reaching Melbourne, and eating only salted meat and ship's biscuits. By the time he returned to Britain, he had sailed 30,000 miles. Young Togo then suffered a strange illness which severely threatened his eyesight, but was cured by Harley Street ophthalmologists after suffering a great deal of discomfort, a development which left him with an additional sense of gratitude to Britain. He subsequently went to the Royal Naval Academy in Portsmouth, followed by the Royal Naval College, Greenwich. While in Britain, he was able to inspect the construction of the *Fuso*, one of the warships being built for Japan at the Isle of Dogs. He returned to Japan in 1878 aboard another British-built ship, the *Hiei*. During his time in Britain he was described as a slender, pale-faced lad with conspicuously big lips, who showed 'no promise of distinction but exhibited no weakness that might bar it'. His captain reported: 'Togo was an excellent fellow. He was not what you would call brilliant, but a great plodder, slow to learn, but very sure when he had learnt; and he wanted to learn everything! . . . one of the best sailors the *Worcester* has ever turned out.'

In 1894, at the beginning of the Sino-Japanese War, now a captain of the cruiser *Naniwa*, Togo sank a British transport ship, the *Kowshing*, which had been chartered by the Chinese to transport troops. The sinking almost caused a diplomatic incident between Japan and Great Britain, but it was finally recognized by British jurists as being in conformity with international law. It also gave rise to unpleasant reports of what today might amount to war-crimes charges committed by Togo, involving the killing of the Chinese crew while they were struggling in the water. But all through history the Japanese would be known for their contemptuously brutal treatment of the Chinese. After the end of the Sino-Japanese War, Togo was successively commandant of the Naval War College (Japan) and commander of the Sasebo Naval College; then, in 1903, he was given command of the Standing Fleet. Because he was relatively unknown in imperial circles, Togo's appointment caused some surprise. The Minister of the Navy, Gonnohyoe Yamamoto, had to explain it to Emperor Meiji: 'Because Togo is a man of good fortune.' Napoleon, with his insistence that his generals be 'lucky', would doubtless have understood.

Contemporaries describe Togo as being 'temperamentally incapable of lifting a finger to gain the slightest preferment for himself', and found him to be 'modest and unassuming'. Yet he could write in the privacy of his diaries (in English), 'I am firmly convinced that I am the reincarnation of Horatio Nelson.' This was before his Tsushima triumph. As of 1904, he was a short, stocky man with a stubbly King George V beard and a thin greying moustache. He had a wide forehead and enormous ears, but was only five feet three inches in height. The war correspondent and artist H.C. Seppings Wright described him as having 'a kindly face . . . marked by lines of care . . . the eyes are brilliant and black, like those of all Japanese, and a slight pucker at the corners suggests humour, a small drooping nose shades a pursed-up mouth with the under lip slightly protruding. He has a large head which is a good shape and shows strongly defined bumps, and the hair is thin and worn very short . . .'

On the night of 8 February 1904, rather than a Nelson, Togo possibly bore a closer resemblance to a more cautious British admiral, Jellicoe. Of Jellicoe it was said by Winston Churchill that, in 1914, he was the only leader who could lose the war in an afternoon. So could Togo. As well as time, numbers were against Japan, which had a population of only 46.5 million against Russia's 130 million, a population that – in theory – could provide limitless reserves. Russia could mobilize 1.1 million men, plus 2.4 million reservists, to Japan's standing army of only about 380,000 (of whom only a fraction were instantly available in the Far East). By 1904 Russia's Pacific Squadron boasted seven battle-ships, seven cruisers, twenty-five destroyers and twenty-seven smaller ships. Japan's total fleet then numbered six battleships, ten cruisers, forty destroyers and forty smaller craft, and these ships – almost all British built – were superior in quality and speed. Yet in time of war Japan could count on no replacements; its shipyards had no facilities for building capital ships and were capable of only limited repairs. The Russians could draw, eventually, on substantial reinforcements from their home fleet, which included a class of five powerful battleships, though neither Port Arthur nor iced-in Vladivostok had any dry dock for substantial repairs. Both in 1905 and in the 1940s, the Japanese navy admirals were to show themselves habitually, and by tradition, more cautious than the army generals. So too now in the surprise attack of 8 February 1904: Admiral Togo could not afford to lose a single one of his precious capital ships.

On acquiring the lease to Port Arthur, Tsar Nicholas had exulted in his diary: 'At last an ice-free port!' That was about the best that could be said of it. In February 1904, in the words of one writer, Port Arthur resembled Chicago at its worst: 'rough, immoral, and vulgar. A Kansas barnyard, one visitor called it ... From the bay, Port Arthur looked picturesque, but it was derelict and decaying, a collection of jerry-built stone houses, temporary warehouses, and equally temporary adminis-trative buildings ...'

An American goldminer from the Klondike gold rush of 1897 might equally have found similarities with the Alaskan port of entry of Skag-way. Port Arthur was a town of whores and booze, with one hotel, the Effimiev, possessing only twenty-four beds in a dark, dingy and filthy shed-like building that was described by a contemporary traveller as the meanest ever provided for civilized men. But it was also a garrison town populated by some 18,000 soldiers and about 20,000 sailors and dock workers, and housing Chinese coolies in miserable conditions, upon all of which the Russians had imposed their own peculiar brand of squalor.

Yet above the slum the Tsar's personal envoy, the sixty-year-old Vice-Admiral Yevgeny Alexeyev, presided the grand vice-regal lodge. An incompetent and venal figure, Alexeyev almost certainly owed his rank to the fact that he was the illegitimate son of Tsar Alexander II,

'The Reformer', grandfather of Nicholas II. Between 1895 and 1897 he commanded the Russian Pacific Fleet, initially at Vladivostok, until it moved to Port Arthur in 1897. Next Alexeyev became Governor of the newly leased territory, and then C-in-C of the Pacific Fleet again. He was regarded in Tokyo as a hard-liner most hostile to Japan, so his appointment in August 1893 as plenipotentiary Viceroy, in charge of both military and civil functions over the whole of Russian-held territory in the Far East, had been taken as another omen that negotiations would bring no favourable concessions. It was the first time an admiral had been appointed to such high office, and Nicholas's able ex-minister Serge Witte considered Alexeyev 'a nincompoop', and certainly 'not an army man' because he could not even ride a horse. At least he had every reason to know the area extremely well; in consequence he personally could be held responsible for much of the extreme dilapidation of the Port Arthur defences.

Most serious was the failure of the Russian defenders under the indolent Alexeyev to keep the key harbour of Port Arthur, that which had been so coveted in St Petersburg (the tsarist capital), properly dredged. In consequence all seven of the Russian capital ships on the night of the attack were actually riding at anchor outside the port, in the roadstead. There, even though supposedly protected with torpedo nets, in their three parallel lines they were much more vulnerable to attack.

In Port Arthur the night of Togo's surprise attack, all was merry insouciance. The town and the Russian warships were brightly lit up. The Russian commander, the fifty-eight-year-old Vice-Admiral Oskar Stark, described as 'an affable old sea dog, growing weary and absent-minded', had an English nurse tending his children while he was celebrating a birthday party for his wife on the deck of his flagship, the *Petropavlovsk*. Most of the fleet's officers were aboard. On shore 'a gay atmosphere pervaded the streets, one could see people staggering tipsy along the streets . . .' Many ships' crews were prowling the bars on Pushkin Street, or carousing in brothels such as one called the American Legation.

Togo had ordered his destroyers to approach without lights, and with engines damped down so that their presence would not be betrayed by sparks belching out of funnels. Nevertheless some witnesses saw the approach of the Japanese destroyers coming in as a long line of moving lights, like fireflies. Ten minutes before midnight, the historic attack commenced. At first guests at the Admiral's party thought the exploding Japanese missiles were being fired in honour of the birthday. A witness wrote:

> The band was playing loudly, and the most honorary guest, Admiral Alekseyev, the viceroy, glided along the parquet with the heroine of the day with surprising grace for his rather obese figure. When the dance reached its apogee ... the windowpanes suddenly shook from the thunder of the cannonade. Everyone applauded, surprised by such a timely salute, and the overall excitement increased. The ball continued to the accompaniment of the orchestra and artillery fire.

After the first torpedoes had struck, wild firing came from the Russian ships, many shooting at each other in the confusion. The Japanese attack was swiftly over. There were also moments of panic among the inexperienced crews aboard the attacking destroyers, but nothing compared to the chaos that reigned both on the Russian ships and in the town. On the other hand there were people like the *Times* correspondent, asleep on a ship in the harbour, who knew nothing of the attack until the morning. When the Russians, licking their wounds, came to count their losses, they found that two battleships, the *Retvizan* and the *Tsesarevich*, the most powerful in the fleet, had been holed and were sitting on the bottom in shallow water, and the cruiser *Pallada* had been sunk with coal bunkers afire. *Retvizan* had a hole in her side measuring 220 square feet. Yet this was only two out of seven, and both battleships would be refloated. Considering the risks involved of an undeclared war against mighty Russia, the results looked pretty poor.

That night, Togo, though his fleet had practised the operation several times, through inexperience and excessive caution committed several cardinal errors. In the destroyer attack he failed to have at least one ship provided with a radio to inform him of results. Faulty reconnaissance resulted in four of his precious battleships being hit, suffering sixty casualties, despite the wildness of the Russian shooting. At the same time, with exaggerated fears of the danger presented by the Russian batteries, he withdrew after making only a single pass. In fact, such was the shock of the attack that the batteries were largely unprepared for action. Captain W.C. ('Willie') Pakenham RN, the fearless and perceptive British observer who was at Togo's side right through the war, excuses this on the grounds that, to Togo, it would have been 'incomprehensible that he would find everything in such a state of unpreparedness'. One biographer of the Admiral, Edwin A. Falk, reckons that, had Togo deployed all his available force with full vigour, 'the Port Arthur squadron could have been wiped out' and 'the control of the sea virtually would have been won before the war had commenced'.

Criticism should perhaps be levelled against Togo as the first twentieth-century naval commander to have the advantage of striking such a surprise blow. In contrast to the Americans at Pearl Harbor, Togo was faced by a somnolent, incompetent and lethargic enemy, inert in its supreme self-confidence. Admiral Yamamoto has been criticized for his excessive caution in December 1941 for not following up on his first success by destroying the Pearl Harbor oil depots and ground installations. He had also failed to catch the aircraft carriers commanded by US Admiral William F. Halsey Jr, which were then out at sea and were to prove the decisive weapons in the war to follow. But, by comparison, Togo in his caution, if not pusillanimity, seems to deserve more severe castigation. He had better intelligence than his successor; he knew the positions of every single Russian capital ship; with both the factor of complete surprise and weapon superiority, should he not have been able to sink the lot? Did he in fact prove, in this operation, to be a less successful admiral than Yamamoto? On the other hand, he was a green commander, in charge of new weaponry, in a novel form of offensive warfare.

So Togo's surprise pre-emptive attack proved at best a qualified success; indeed, it could easily have ended in disaster for Japan. The Western press did not on the whole react with disfavour to Japan's ungentlemanly attack. The London *Times* robustly endorsed it as 'stunning' and 'masculine'. 'Our ally', it declared, 'put her navy in motion with a promptness and courage that exhorted the admiration of the world ... this [was a] dashing and courageous exploit'. After all, the Russian fleet had been inviting attack by standing in the outer roadstead. These were hardly the words that would be used on the 'day of infamy' thirty-seven years later; but then the brutal, autocratic country of the Tsar of 1904 was hardly the flavour of the day with liberal Britain. Suddenly Europeans began to revise their opinions of the 'little yellow men'. Only France, dependent upon its own alliance with Russia, was swift to criticize.

Upon the Russian navy crews at Port Arthur the psychological impact was grave; little effort was made to venture out and confront the attackers. When Russian warships were sent out, on 11 February, disaster struck. A minelayer, *Yenisey*, and a destroyer, *Boyarin*, both ran on to mines which *Yenisey* herself had just laid, and two Russian destroyers were damaged in a collision. *Yenisey* sank at once; *Boyarin* stayed afloat, despite two risibly incompetent Russian attempts to torpedo her to keep her out of Japanese hands. The following day a boarding team was sent to salvage the wardroom silver, and she sank during a storm that night. The captain was duly court-martialled, and deprived of command for a year.

The fortunes of war swung back and forth, with the Russians mining the entrance to Port Arthur to prevent the Japanese entering again, and the Japanese also laying down mines to deny to the Russian warships access to the open sea. At Chemulpo, in contrast, where the Japanese launched a diversionary attack on the Korean coast, a heroic fight was fought by *Varyag*, a modern US-built cruiser commanded by a Captain Vsevolod Rudnev. Refusing Japanese calls to surrender while anchored in the port, Rudnev put out to sea to face overwhelming odds, declaring to his crew, 'Let us put our trust in God, and go bravely into battle for the Tsar and for the Motherland – Hurrah!' He then sailed towards the enemy, with the ship's band playing the national anthem, 'God Save the Tsar'. *Varyag* fired 1,105 rounds from her various guns, though not one found a target. Hammered into a wreck, with Rudnev wounded and with thirty-one of her crew dead and another ninety-one seriously wounded, *Varyag* was scuttled. Reaching Odessa, Captain Rudnev was accorded a triumphant welcome with parades and banquets, as the only hero of the war so far.

Meanwhile the Japanese 12th Division had successfully established its bridgehead in Korea and was thrusting northwards for the lower reaches of the Yalu River at Antung – names that would become ominously familiar to the UN armies during the 1950 Korean War.

On 24 February, Togo, reckoning he could no longer count on sinking the Russian capital ships outright, endeavoured to block them in Port Arthur. To this end he sent five old merchant ships full of ballast to be sunk in the harbour mouth. This meant more or less imposing a death sentence on the ships' skeleton crews, all volunteers. Apparently 2,000 applications were submitted, some of them 'earnestly written in blood'. But the attempt was thwarted by heavy shellfire from Russian shore batteries, and from the brand-new battleship *Retvizan*, aground in the mud but able to bring her powerful twelve-inch guns to bear. All five of the blockships were destroyed before they could be positioned. A second abortive attempt to block the harbour was made on 27 March; and Togo attempted yet a third on 27 April. Russian morale had been vastly improved in the meantime, though only temporarily, by the arrival of a new admiral to replace the disgraced Stark.

Vice-Admiral Stepan Makarov was the ablest of all Russia's admirals, one among few. On hearing of his appointment, across the Pacific Squadron there were cries of 'Makarov is coming! Makarov is coming!' To the demoralized sailors he was 'the closest thing to a saviour'. Ironically given the Japanese choice of weapons in their surprise attack, Makarov – a prolific inventor – had been one of the progenitors of the deadly torpedo boats. In January 1878, during the Russo-Turkish War, he had been the first in the world to launch torpedoes from a 'fastboat', against an Ottoman Navy ship, *Intibah*. He was highly decorated for his services during that war.

It is hard to tell from portraits what manner of man was Makarov, gentle or harsh, intelligent or insensitive. In the style of the times his face was covered with an impenetrable fuzz – a vast moustache and bifurcated beard, not dissimilar to those of his exact contemporary and fellow admiral, Germany's Alfred von Tirpitz (also an exponent of torpedo development). Makarov was a huge man, 'with self-confidence and a prestige second to none'. He soon became known, affectionately, to every officer and seaman in the fleet as 'Old Beardy'. After Russia took over Port Arthur in March 1898, Makarov wrote to the Naval Minister, 'The fall of Port Arthur would be a terrible blow for our position in the Far East. Port Arthur should be made impregnable.' He also suggested that forty torpedo boats should be disassembled and sent to Port Arthur by the Trans-Siberian Railway. Unfortunately for

Russia, few such measures were ever pursued before the outbreak of hostilities in 1904.

Makarov arrived to take over command in Port Arthur on 7 March. Unlike any other Russian leader in the war, he was aggressive and innovative, and reportedly had a rare ability to 'inspire confidence in his subordinates'. He at once stepped up activity in the Russian squadrons, as well as improving the defences of Port Arthur. Shipwrights were set to work repairing the ships damaged in the initial Japanese torpedo attack. Because Port Arthur lacked a dry dock big enough to take the battleships *Retvizan* and *Tsesarevich*, Makarov had cofferdams laboriously constructed, large wooden boxes that fitted against the ship's hull. Once in place, the cofferdams were pumped out, giving the shipwrights a dry working space right down to the bottom of the ship. The valuable battleships were refloated; in terms of numbers, Togo's surprise attack had been all but annulled.

Up till then the Russian fleet had done virtually nothing but exist on the defensive, as a fleet in being. A riddle made the rounds: 'Why do Russian squadrons need two admirals? Answer: One to take the ships to sea, and one to order them back.' Under Makarov's leadership, his ships now put to sea nearly every day, and so were constantly on the move, ensuring that they were never taken by surprise outside the protection of Port Arthur's shore batteries. Unlike his predecessor, Makarov energetically sought engagement with the Japanese, and when Japanese cruisers bombarded Port Arthur from the Yellow Sea in March, his cruisers returned fire with such efficacy that the Japanese ships were forced to withdraw. Rather than risking a major engagement, Makarov's objective was more to build up technical competence, and morale. Eventually his aim was to break out of the cul-de-sac of the Yellow Sea and sail with his fleet to Vladivostok, the more effectively to harry Togo's fleet, disrupt Japanese lines of communication and strike at the Japanese homeland.

In the middle of one briefing, Makarov was told that the destroyer *Steregushchy* was pinned down in action with Japanese destroyers outside the port. Without saying a word, Makarov left the conference. Minutes later, it was observed that the small cruiser *Novik* was leading the ships out of harbour and now flying the Admiral's flag. Cheers went up from those watching; and even though it was too late to save

Steregushchy, Makarov had decisively demonstrated that he intended to lead from the front.

But his new command troubled him. 'Oh, to know what to do!' he wrote. 'Truly our men are in need of everything. They do not know how to walk in the night. Mismanaged and confused, they continue to elbow each other near Port Arthur. Incapable of identifying themselves they hesitate to return [to port] for fear of being mistaken for the Japanese. Complete misfortune!' That same month, nonetheless, when the Japanese made their second attempt to seal the port's entrance with blockships, Makarov's cruisers vigorously attacked the escorting Japanese warships and put them to flight.

Then, on 13 April, providence deserted the reanimated Russians. A Russian destroyer, *Strasny*, returning from patrol, tried to re-enter Port Arthur but was intercepted by Japanese destroyers. An engagement began between the opposing destroyers, and Makarov immediately sent the cruiser *Bayan* to assist *Strasny*, while he himself led a force of three battleships, four cruisers and some destroyers into the Yellow Sea to seek battle with the surrounding enemy warships. The Japanese warships withdrew out to sea, with Makarov in pursuit. With the arrival of enemy heavy units upon the scene, Makarov, now out of range of gunfire support from the shore, turned about and headed back to Port Arthur. The Japanese fleet did not pursue. The dashing Makarov had fallen into a trap. The previous night a Japanese minelayer, *Koryu Maru*, had laid a field outside the harbour. The Japanese destroyers covering *Koryu Maru* were observed by Makarov, but the minelayer herself went undetected. As his flagship, the battleship *Petropavlovsk*, moved closer to the harbour's entrance, she struck one or two mines in the newly laid field; moments later, her forward magazines exploded, with such violence that the entire forward turret was thrown into the air.

Captain Vladimir Semenov aboard the cruiser *Diana* described the scene graphically. He heard a violent explosion, then a second.

Suddenly cries of horror arose: 'The *Petropavlovsk*! The *Petropavlovsk*! Dreading the worst, I rushed to the side. I saw a huge cloud of brown smoke. In this cloud I saw the ship's foremast. It was slanting, helpless, not as if it was falling, but as if it were suspended in the air. To the left of this cloud I saw the batttleship's stern. It looked, as always, as if the awful happenings in the fore-part were none of its concern. A third explosion! White steam now began to mix with the brown cloud. The boilers had burst! Suddenly the stern of the battleship rose straight in the air ...

Petropavlovsk sank within two minutes; some observers said they saw the Admiral kneeling in prayer on the bridge as the ship went down. Word spread that Japanese submarines were near by; the Russian ships began firing wildly in all directions. Witnessing the sinking from the Japanese battleship *Asahi*, William Pakenham RN recorded that 'the silence of the Japanese fleet was broken by an involuntary burst of cheering ...' Destroyers sent to search the site of the disaster found only fifty-eight survivors from *Petropavlovsk*; over 680 officers and men had been lost with the ship, among them most of Makarov's staff, and his close friend the famous war artist Vasily Vereshchagin, noted for his paintings of Napoleon's retreat from Moscow. Of Admiral Stepan Makarov himself, the searchers found only his overcoat. Throughout Russia, 'a grief-stricken nation', there was sombre mourning for the death of the Admiral. Tolstoy criticized the regime bitterly for sending innocent sailors to their deaths.

The Japanese fleet paid handsome tribute to a fallen enemy hero, such as would not be repeated in a later, less chivalrous and more brutal Pacific War. Togo himself ordered all flags to be flown at half-mast, and a day's mourning for the Russian. In Port Arthur morale plummeted. The fleet once more sat locked in harbour. Outside in the Yellow Sea Togo's cruisers prowled, like cats waiting for a mouse to venture out from its hole, ready to pounce. Togo further enhanced the growing competence of his young navy by sending a task force north to bombard Vladivostok and the Russian units trapped inside. He then mined its approaches, thus further separating the two Russian naval units. It was all good training for the Japanese, while Russia's frustrated sailors gained nothing but further humiliation. At least for the time being, Japan had assumed command of the seas. In St Petersburg contempt for the 'little yellow monkeys', and the belief that their threats would never amount to anything, was replaced by a certain sense of alarm. The despatch of army reinforcements, led by General

Alexey Kuropatkin, down the long tube of the Trans-Siberian Railway was urged on and there was discussion about sending naval reinforcements from the Baltic; but, as was normal in Tsarist Russia, nothing happened except vacillation.

Supposing, however, that Makarov had not gone down with *Petropavlovsk*, might the Russo-Japanese War have taken a different turn? One of the more recent historians of the war, J.N. Westwood, remarks: 'Although Makarov was subsequently credited with a genius which he may not have possessed, he was certainly Togo's equal, and perhaps more . . .' One thing was certain; Tsarist Russia could not field anybody better. Nevertheless, in Tokyo celebration of the sinking of *Petropavlovsk* and the elimination of a redoubtable foe was muted. It was not only the wise heads of the anti-war lobby who recognized that the longer the war went on so did odds against a Japanese victory lengthen.

CHAPTER THREE

INTO MANCHURIA

The focus of the war now moved from sea to land as Japan's armies pushed northwards from Chemulpo, into north Korea and the bleak landscape of southern Manchuria. Now may be a good place to compare the quality of the opposing armed forces, and notably their most essential ingredients: the fighting soldiers and sailors. A Russian epigram of the time about postings for newly commissioned officers ran, 'Drinkers to the fleet, dimwits to the infantry,' and there was more than an element of truth to it. Because of the iced-in conditions, Russian Baltic sea crews spent six months ashore, boozing; the same applied to forces at Vladivostok. Little time could be spent on gunnery. The contrast between the shipboard living conditions of officers and those of men was far worse than in other navies. The officers often showed little concern about distributing rotten meat to the crews. Consequently morale in general was poor. By comparison, Japanese crews lived well. Under their British instructors, they spent much more time out at sea, and trained harder. Most Japanese sailors had been raised on or near the coast: many were fishermen. On the other hand, few Russian sailors had ever seen the sea prior to conscription; few were literate, in contrast to the Japanese. And these days of steam and big-gun technologies placed heavy demands on the ill-educated.

On land the Russian *muzhik* or peasant would fight sullenly and die stoically for his Tsar. In contrast, under the ethos of the samurai, to the Japanese fighting man dying for his Emperor was rated the highest achievable honour. The *British Official History of the Russo-Japanese War*, for instance, speaks admiringly of Japanese values, not least 'that wonderful spirit of self-sacrifice which animates the heart of every man – soldier or sailor – and makes him feel it a privilege to give his life, if by that means the welfare of the nation may be advanced ...' In marked contrast was the Russian serviceman, for whom 'The

dull surroundings of his village home deaden his imagination and produce a stolid nature which, even after frequent defeats, is usually proof
against sudden panic or disorganization.' Out in the field Russian infantry commanders would be averse to deploying in 'extended order'
– because it increased the difficulties of command. This was a mentality which was to cost the Russians dearly as the land battles developed.
Thus infantrymen on both sides in 1904–5 were ready to accept heavier
losses than would their Western equivalents.

As regards intelligence and spying, the Japanese also had a distinct
advantage. Both sides treated the indigenous Koreans and Chinese
with contemptuous brutality; pictures of the times show Russian soldiers hanging recalcitrant locals from the trestles of railway bridges,
and the Japanese lopping off their heads with ceremonial swords. But
by and large the Japanese came out ahead; they paid their spies better.
Apart from his first serious misjudgement, Togo was consistently well
informed about the moves of the Russian fleet. To the intense dismay
of the Russians the Japanese could also boast a highly well-placed
and informed intelligence and disinformation network inside Europe,
and indeed inside Russia itself. Paranoia about an infestation of spies
swiftly spread among the Russian forces, uncovering networks everywhere across Manchuria, and provoking excessive alarm.

By coincidence, both opposing generals in 1904, Field Marshal
Oyama and General Kuropatkin, had been present at the historic
Battle of Sedan, in September 1870, to witness the cataclysmic,
dynasty-changing defeat of France by Moltke's Prussians. Born in
Kagoshima, and like Togo of Satsuma samurai blood, Oyama had instantly fallen for the martial virtues demonstrated by the Prussians,
though he was only twenty-eight at Sedan. He later became one of
the founders of the Imperial Japanese Army. (He was also, incidentally,
the first recorded Japanese customer for Louis Vuitton, having pur-
chased some luggage during his stay in France.) Under his influence,
and true to the 'copy and improve' principles of the Meijis, the Japanese Army had then selected Prussians to advise and train its forces.
The Prussian General Jakob Meckel had taught the Japanese how to
establish an efficient general staff. The Prussian doctrines of discipline,
Gehorsamkeit, and opportunism, the *Auftragssystem*, together with the
bark of the bullying *Feldwebel*, were not unsuited to the ethics of the

samurai and *bushido*. For better or for worse, they would remain at the heart of the Japanese Army for decades to come. In consequence, one observer with the Japanese Army in 1904–5, the future General Sir Ian Hamilton, later of Gallipoli fame, regarded them as 'the world's best infantry'.

During the Sino-Japanese War of 1894–5, Oyama, then a general, had led the seizure of Port Arthur – for which triumph he was made a marquis and, three years later, a field marshal. In 1904, a venerable sixty-two-year-old, he was nominated Commander-in-Chief of the newly formed Manchuria Army, though he had been among those who had opposed the war. His operative Chief of Staff was a tough nut called General Gentaro Kodama, who had worked with General Meckel,* and then went on to be Military Attaché in Berlin. An anti-Russian hawk, Kodama had also served as a hard-line Minister of the Army, under Prime Minister Ito Hirobumi. Not unlike the Ludendorff–Hindenburg relationship, the German command on the Western Front in the First World War, it was Kodama rather than Oyama who laid down the strategy of the whole land campaign of 1904–5.

The Russian General, the fifty-six-year-old Aleksey Kuropatkin, however, perhaps groomed in Tolstoyan tenets and convinced that all Germans were innately stupid, paid little heed to the lessons of the victors at Sedan. The son of a minor noble from Pskov Province, Kuropatkin has been described as 'a bureaucrat's general'. Appointed War Minister in 1898, his priority was to improve conditions for both officers and men, as well as the quality of the officer corps. None of his reforms achieved much success. Though counted as an expansionst, a believer in railways, he opposed war with Japan, deeming that southern Manchuria was untenable by Russian arms. A trip in June 1903 to Japan, where he was impressed by the state of the Imperial Army, strengthened these views. He arrived in Manchuria to take overall command of the Tsarist land forces in March that year, with something

---

* Although his period in Japan (1885–8) was relatively short, Meckel had a considerable impact on the development of the Japanese military. He is credited with having introduced Clausewitz's military theories and the Prussian concept of war games (*Kriegsspiel*). His reforms were also considered to have played a role in Japan's overwhelming victory over China in the 1894–5 Sino-Japanese War.

of a fatalist, if not defeatist, view. If he had a strategy, it was decidedly defensive. Arriving at the chief Russian base at Liaoyang, just south of Mukden, on the crucial railway line, Kuropatkin prepared to sit it out and wage a war of attrition. He would avoid any offensive action until the Trans-Siberian Railway had brought in decisive reinforcements in troops and matériel. But the Japanese were not going to give him the time he needed. His command would be marked by caution and inde-cision, which would lead to repeated Russian defeats.

Once Togo had been assured that the Russian Navy, bottled up in both Port Arthur and Vladivostok, could not interfere, on 16 February Kodama landed the rest of the 12th Division at Inchon. Despite the bitter winter weather, it swiftly occupied the Korean capital, Seoul, some twenty miles inland. Nine days later Japan imposed the status of a Japanese protectorate on Korea, though it was not officially annexed until some six years later. Thus was completed the work of Hideyoshi four centuries earlier. Korea would remain a colony of Japan, often sav-agely repressed, until 1945. Two further Japanese divisions were landed between 14 and 21 March, and were grouped together with the 12th Division into the Japanese First Army, under the command of General Tamemoto Kuroki. Without waiting for the end of the spring thaw, which made the primitive Korean roads all but impassable, Kuroki thrust north towards the lower reaches of the Yalu River, that strate-gic and historic river which over its 500-mile length demarcated the frontier of Korea and Manchuria. Early European visitors to Korea remarked that the country resembled 'a sea in a heavy gale' because of the many successive mountain ranges that crisscrossed the peninsula. Some 80 per cent of northern Korea is composed of mountains and uplands, bitterly cold in winter, divided by deep and narrow valleys. In the west, however, the coastal plains are wide and flat. It was to these that Kuroki's invading force wisely stuck in 1904.

Brushing aside a feeble Cossack force that arrived from Manchu-ria, weary and travel-stained, Kuroki, with some 42,500 men backed by 10,000 Korean coolies and porters, reached the Yalu in mid-April. Strategically and tactically, it was not an overwhelming task for the Japanese Army; it followed exactly the same route as a decade previ-ously, in the Sino-Japanese War. Many of its senior commanders, such as General Maresuke Nogi (who had commanded the 1st Infantry

Brigade), had accompanied that expedition and remembered it well. With admirable intelligence and deception measures (the Russians were constantly hamstrung by an almost total lack of intelligence about the enemy), Kuroki built a fake timber bridge conspicuously across the wide lower Yalu, to attract Russian fire; meanwhile ten further pontoons were being laid out upstream. Sketches of the time show troops crossing in sampans towed by steam launches, or lashed together and propelled by oars over the stern. Fabricated by Krupp of Essen, Kuroki's 4.7-inch howitzers, heavier than anything in the Russian armoury, were used with devastating effect on the defenders. The Russian commander, General Mikhail Zasulich, was urged by his staff to pull back to a more defensible position. However, also ignoring General Kuropatkin's orders for a phased withdrawal, Zasulich stubbornly refused, even sending a telegram to the Tsar in St Petersburg informing him that victory was at hand. On 1 May 1904, remnants of the Russian Eastern Detachment either surrendered or escaped northwards.

Thus the Battle of the Yalu River, the first major land campaign of the war, ended in victory for the Japanese. It had cost them a thousand dead and wounded, while the Russians suffered some 2,700 casualties overall, including about 500 killed, and the loss of twenty-one out of twenty-four field guns. The defeat of the Russian Eastern Detachment finally removed any remaining notion that the Japanese would be an easy enemy, that the war would be short and that Russia would be the overwhelming victor. The major achievement was that the attackers were now across the main river obstacle separating them from the back door to Port Arthur.

Four days later General Nogi's Third Japanese Army, 90,000 strong, landed at the base of the narrow Liaotung Peninsula, on whose tip sat Port Arthur. These troops swung left, towards Port Arthur, while the rest of the Japanese forces, three armies, the Fourth, Second and First, under Generals Nozu, Oku and Kuroki, combined to push northwards up the railway to deny Kuropatkin any chance of coming down to relieve Port Arthur. The outlook for Port Arthur began to look distinctly grim.

Then, in the way of the unpredictable fortunes of war, disaster suddenly hit Togo's blockading squadron. Two of the Imperial Japanese

Navy's capital ships, the battleships *Hatsuse* and *Yashima* (built in Newcastle), struck mines laid by the Russians in the open approaches to Port Arthur. To lay mines in neutral waters was a serious offence against the existing rules of war, and was completely unexpected by Togo. Both ships sank; and to add to the catastrophe the cruiser *Yoshino* was sunk after a collision in the fog. At a stroke, the IJN had lost one-third of its capital force; the Russians now boasted a notable superiority in Pacific waters – at least on paper. With their habitual flair for secrecy, the Japanese managed to hide the sinking of one of the battleships till after the fall of Port Arthur. But, had Russia still had a Makarov at hand, the pendulum of war might easily have been made to swing in a decisive reversal of fortune against Japan. With a superiority now of 6 to 4, an audacious commander could well have broken the blockade and chased off the surviving capital ships. In this event, the huge land force which the Japanese Navy was now protecting and supplying in Korea and Manchuria would surely have been left to dry out on its long and exposed lifeline. One cannot imagine Allied navies in the Second World War missing such an opportunity, let alone the Japanese themselves.

But there was no Makarov now available to Russian arms. In his place was the inept and slothful Viceroy of the Far East, Admiral Yevgeny Alexeyev, a pet of the Tsar, whose first reaction to Togo's surprise attack on Port Arthur had been that it was 'impossible'. Though he had been a leading hawk before war started, early May saw the Viceroy and his entourage prudently pulling out of Port Arthur before his escape route could be cut, to Ying Kou in Manchuria.

The absconding Alexeyev then placed his junior, Vice-Admiral Wilgelm Vitgeft, born in Odessa but – like so many of the Tsar's leading sailors and soldiers – of German descent, to take over command of the Port Arthur fleet. Vitgeft is described acidly by Togo's biographer Edwin A. Falk as 'qualified by temperament and long hours of duty ashore to entwine the propellers with red tape and inertia', and, when Vitgeft finally flew his flag aboard the *Tsesarevich*, as 'a worried desk-sailor very much at sea'. Vitgeft consistently rejected the now safely land-bound Viceroy's urgings to break out of port. His cautiously modest view was to await the arrival of the Baltic Fleet from St Petersburg and the stream of reinforcements coming in at a snail's pace along the railway. But the hawkish Viceroy, so far misguided in all his actions, constantly prodded Vitgeft to break out of the Japanese head-lock and hit their depleted fleet. Had it been Makarov, Alexeyev might have been right. But Vitgeft sat tight, with his six capital ships to Togo's four.

The situation on land was becoming critical, turning decisively against the Russians. On 26 May, at the Battle of Nanshan, General Oku's Second Army had cut the narrow, vital isthmus that connects Port Arthur with the Manchurian hinterland. Other Japanese Army forces were rolling the rest of the Russian Army up northwards, up the railway towards Mukden, before Kuropatkin's reinforcements could intervene effectively. As Port Arthur's predicament became grimmer, its isolation definitive, Alexeyev at last appealed to the Tsar to force Vitgeft to move. Faced with imperial censure, early on 10 August 1904 Vitgeft, flying his flag in the *Tsesarevich*, led his fleet from the harbour. Almost apologetically he signalled to his ships: 'The Tsar has ordered our squadron to sail to Vladivostok.' It was make or break, Vladivostok or bust, and smash impertinent Togo on the way.

The Russian fleet consisted of an impressive array of battleships: *Tsesarevich*, *Retvizan* (both refloated since their sinking in February), *Pobeda*, *Peresvet*, *Sevastopol* and *Poltava*; the cruisers *Askold*, *Diana*, *Novik* and *Pallada*; and fourteen destroyers, plus a similar number of torpedo boats. But, once out of Port Arthur, under prevailing wartime law as combatants they could be prevented from recoaling anywhere else. From his advanced outpost in the Elliott Islands, conveniently tucked just off the Liaotung Peninsula, Togo spotted the massive belch of black smoke as Vitgeft stoked up his boilers. He was on to him in a trice. His aim was to head off the Russian in a Nelsonian 'crossing of the T' before he could leave the Yellow Sea.

There would now follow an historic encounter, the first ever between the all-steel, all-steam behemoth capital ships that would set the pattern of naval warfare for the next two generations. Since that first encounter of the *Monitor* and *Merrimac* half a century previously, progress in naval weaponry had been meteoric. The combination of electric power and hydraulics enabled battleship designers to install hugely heavy armoured turrets that could traverse and elevate vast guns at speed. But they had so far been untried; so far the war had been fought largely with the new deadly weapons – the mine and the torpedo. Thus neither of the combatant navies, Russian or Japanese, could have any conception of the damage that would be inflicted by the monster cannon of 305mm (twelve-inch) calibre, which had a range of 15,000 yards, more than eight miles, firing a massive shell weighing 850 pounds (each gun alone weighed nearly fifty tons). Nor could they conceive of the punishment that these high-explosive projectiles could inflict on their own ships. And how would the new cannon perform after repeated firing? The two fleets were steaming into an unknown – and rather frightening – world.[*]

Shortly after midday there was some tentative firing between the two fleets at a long range of over eight miles. No hits were scored. Relying on his ships' superior speed, Togo adopted an elliptical course south-eastwards, moving out of sight of the Russians, but dogging them all the way with his light and fast cruisers. He came close to losing them. Many Russian sailors must have breathed sighs of relief as the Japanese capital ships disappeared. Perhaps after all Togo was not going to risk a further encounter against a superior foe? Meanwhile, down in the hellish boiler-rooms the sweat-drenched stokers in both fleets were being pressed to supreme efforts: the one to escape to open sea, the other to prevent that escape. Indeed, at that point it was very much what was dubbed a 'stoker's battle'. Under such pressure ships of both fleets faced the danger of a boiler-burst, which would have scalded the crews to an instant death, or a major engine breakdown. *Poltava* was already limping. For Togo, whose fleet could maintain sixteen knots to Vitgeft's fourteen (with luck), the race was also one against the day's remaining light. With only a few hours to go, the Russians might well elude him in the dark, or turn unexpectedly and maul his outnumbered capital ships. With the two Russian fleets combined at Vladivostok substantially outnumbering Togo's IJN, the outcome would determine the whole course of the war.

By mid-afternoon, Togo was overhauling, and his leading ships getting in range. The risk of 'T-crossing' is that the lead ship – which is likely to have the Admiral himself on board – initially takes the

[*] At the last fleet engagement, Trafalgar, almost exactly 100 years previously, Nelson's biggest gun could fire projectiles weighing only sixty-eight pounds, while ranges were generally seldom more than a murderous 200 yards.

heaviest damage. Contrary to expectation, Russian gunnery on 10 August 1904 turned out to be extremely accurate, if not superior to the enemy's, especially at long range. So reported Britain's fearless observer with the Japanese, Captain Pakenham RN.* Togo's *Mikasa*, in the van, took several hits. Splinters from one heavy shell exploding on the mainmast narrowly missed Togo, who refused to take cover in his ship's armoured conning-tower but insisted he remain on the exposed compass-bridge.† When the battle was over, it was noted that *Mikasa* had been hit twenty times; more than was sustained by all but one of Vitgeft's ships. Worse still, no fewer than five out of sixteen of Togo's twelve-inch battleship guns had been knocked out by their own armament in the course of the action, shells exploding in super-hot breeches with disastrous consequences. It appears that either the excessively sensitive Japanese-designed fuses or their own explosive called *shimose* tended to 'cook off' inside the gun-tube. This could easily have cost Japan the battle – and the war. As it was, however, by an extraordinary twist of fortune it may have caused the opposite to occur.

Shortly before dusk on the 10th, Vitgeft's flagship, *Tsesarevich*, was hit by two Japanese twelve-inch shells in quick succession. Instead of being armour-piercing shot designed to penetrate the vitals of a ship and then explode, with often mortal consequences, these seem to have been filled with *shimose* explosive and detonated by super-sensitive fuses that were touched off by a ship's superstructure, or even by the rigging. One blew to pieces the unfortunate Admiral Vitgeft, of whom only one leg was ever found. He had so far that day performed better than expected, but – given his limitations as a commander – the consequences of his demise were far surpassed by the second shell which burst on the slit of the conning-tower, its blast killing or knocking out all its occupants. Jammed by dead bodies, the wheel of *Tsesarevich* remained immovably stuck at 'hard-over', with the result that the Russian flagship performed a tight circle, nearly ramming two other battleships and disrupting the line she had been leading. Wrote Edwin

* Ironically for the nation which, in later years, was to excel in the manufacture of precision optical equipment, the Japanese capital ships were equipped with British Barr & Stroud range-finders, with a serviceable range of only 6,600 yards.

† Observation from warship conning-towers was through narrow, protective slits, not unlike that of a closed-down army tank. Hence commanders in both world wars tended to eschew them as being too limiting to their overall vision of the battle scene.

A. Falk: 'No one remained above decks to report below what had happened or to send a signal. So far as the rest of the fleet could tell, there was nothing particularly significant about those two puffs of smoke on the *Czesarevich* at a time when the entire line was sustaining hits.' The rigging that carried her semaphore flags had been shredded, as well as her nerve centre destroyed, so none of *Tsesarevich*'s subordinate capital ships could perceive what had happened; and, presuming that Vitgeft was pursuing some deliberate course of his own, like good obedient Russians they attempted to follow his strange course. Chaos swiftly ensued. The Russian line was broken, its separate units 'moving independently like parts of a severed earthworm', in Falk's vivid phrase, with Togo pouring in devastating fire at close range, from his secondary armament as well as his heavy weapons. 'Had the shells pierced the deck and burst in the bowels of the ship,' concludes Falk, 'the *Czesarevich* might have been destroyed, but the result would have been less decisive than it was. The other Russian ships would have observed and understood what had happened ...'

As it was, the coherence of the Russian squadron was shattered, and – as dusk gathered – so it scattered. Five battleships, a cruiser and nine destroyers escaped and crept back to Port Arthur; however, the damaged *Tsesarevich* and three escorting destroyers sailed to Tsingtao, where the Germans were obliged to intern them. The cruiser *Askold* and a destroyer reached Shanghai, where the Chinese interned them, while the *Diana* ran all the way to Saigon, and French internment. The extraordinary thing about this ferocious seven-hour engagement, the first gunfire battle between iron leviathans, was that not a single ship was sunk. Though the damage to the *Tsesarevich* proved far and away the most critical in the battle, Togo's *Mikasa*, hit twenty times, had her aft twelve-inch gun turret knocked out, and she suffered 125 casualties – by far the heaviest of the day. Togo has been criticized for squandering his initial position of advantage, while young hawks in the IJN might grumble about his failure to move in at dusk and sink what remained of Vitgeft's ships. But he didn't need to. It had been a clear-cut strategic victory for Japan. Without a ship being lost, 10 August was a defining day in the war. Thenceforth Russia's proud First Pacific Squadron, like Admiral Scheer's German fleet after Jutland in 1916, would not venture out of port again. It would sit in Port Arthur until scuttled, or sunk by the Japanese land batteries that were steadily moving in. There would be no question now of these ships linking up with the Vladivostok forces. Dismounted, their heavy guns were moved ashore as entrenched batteries to face the approaching Japanese armies.

With the Russians now effectively neutralized in Asian waters, the focus of the war once more returned to the land. On 16 August, following the defeat of Admiral Vitgeft, Togo and Nogi jointly signed a letter to the Russians, inviting them to surrender in the hopes of avoiding a 'useless sacrifice on a large scale of lives and property'. The invitation was refused. The slaughter on land now began to escalate. The veteran General Nogi landed with the 90,000-strong Third Army at the root of the Liaotung Peninsula, after the Russians had been pushed back into it at the key Battle of Nanshan. He had done it all before in the Sino-Japanese War of ten years earlier and the terrain was familiar to him. His express role was to advance down the peninsula and lay direct siege to Port Arthur. Meanwhile the First, Second and Fourth Japanese Armies, under Generals Kuroki, Oku and Nozu respectively, would carry on pushing the Russians northwards up the railway towards Mukden, to interdict Kuropatkin's Trans-Siberian reinforcements arriving to relieve Port Arthur. For the Japanese, perpetually on the offensive, it was, as always, a race against time before superior Russian numbers could swing the tide of battle. As Russian resistance mounted, with the well-known stoicism of the Russian soldier fighting on the defensive, so Japanese casualties soared. Two of Nogi's own sons were to die in the battle.* Tactical over-reliance on the use of infantry attacking frontally, as taught by the Prussian Meckel, was later considered to have contributed to the large number of Japanese casualties in the subsequent actions.

New levels in the intensity of infantry warfare, where the Maxim machine gun and field artillery dominated, were experienced daily. For the first time in the history of war, the Russian defenders would introduce the barbed-wire entanglement to stop the massed Japanese infantry. They would also develop the field telephone, though its value

---

* Attempting to console Nogi's bereaved wife on the loss of her two sons, Togo received a reminder of samurai stoicism: neither of her children, she said, had 'brought disgrace on the true name of a soldier and this gave her sufficient consolation ...'.

would become somewhat limited when frost-bitten Russian troops cut down the telegraph poles for firewood. There were many such harbingers of the First World War, just ten years away, and Western observers like General Sir Ian Hamilton were there alongside the Japanese commander to take note. The lessons didn't seem to sink in; Hamilton would lose his reputation, as well as many thousands of British and Anzac lives, at Gallipoli only eleven years later under not dissimilar conditions. Yet the Russo-Japanese War on land was rightly to become regarded as the first 'modern' war – if only military minds in the West could have taken serious note of it.

The Japanese commanders discovered that infantry attacks in massed formation, as taught them by their Prussian instructors, were prohibitively costly. The Russians in turn realized that their much vaunted Cossack cavalry were useless. Six massive eleven-inch Krupp howitzers, destined for Nogi's siege forces, were sunk at sea by Russian raiders creeping out of Vladivostok, and their loss would be felt bitterly by the attacking Japanese, as they were forced to reduce one fiercely contested strongpoint after another. All through September, and into October and November, as the autumn rains turned the battlefield into a bog, like Passchendaele in the First World War, Nogi's men clawed their way forward, in relentless and sometimes suicidal frontal assaults. To replace the losses, an extra 16,000 reinforcements had to be shipped in. But the defenders, now isolated, could count on neither reinforcements nor food supplies.

Then, in October, disturbing news from Europe reached Tokyo. After endless vacillations, the Tsar had finally despatched the bulk of his home naval forces (the Baltic Fleet), imposingly renamed the Second Pacific Squadron, to the Far East to reinforce what remained of Makarov's and Vitgeft's First Pacific Squadron and relieve beleaguered Port Arthur. The new squadron would face an 18,000-mile world cruise to reach the battle zone; it was indeed late in the day, if not far too late. But, with his numerical superiority still at risk, the news that one of the major naval forces in Europe was on its way could not fail to cause Togo deep concern. If this Russian fleet could break his battle line, and then seal off the four Japanese armies in Korea and southern Manchuria, the nation would face extinction. Nogi was instructed to press ahead with the seizure of Port Arthur at top speed, and regardless of cost. There was talk among the Tokyo 'doves' about proffering peace terms, before the tide of battle truly turned.

The battle swayed back and forth for the possession of a modest height known as 203 Metre Hill, which dominated Port Arthur at less than three miles from the harbour. It had a clear view for almost point-blank fire on the surviving vessels in it. One by one these were sunk by Nogi's heavy siege guns. Rations in the beleaguered city began to run out, with horses and donkeys being eaten. Because of the shortage of vegetables and fruit, cases of scurvy proliferated, as did acrid recriminations between the defeated navy and the army that continued to fight. Of the army commanders themselves, Lieutenant-General Stoessel – another German, described as an 'uncouth-looking man with a stentorian voice' – countermanded every order given by his rather more effective subordinate, Smirnov, and in turn fell out with the C-in-C, Kuropatkin. He was denounced by both as 'not a fighting general'. Those other handmaidens of the misery of siege warfare, dysentery and typhoid, began to take hold. The Japanese meanwhile suffered from shortages of rice, crucial to their rations.

Winter was beginning to blow in from the cruel uplands of Manchuria. Nogi moved in over 400 guns; he had the advantage of bringing them up under the superb cover of fields of millet, which had been allowed to grow ten feet tall, but which the defenders had neglected to cut down. Still Port Arthur held out. There were even reverses, as when the Japanese attempted to board the battleship *Reshitelny*, only to be repulsed with the Japanese commander chucked overboard. Morale sank on both sides; there were cases of Russian regiments firing on each other, and even reports of Japanese units, having suffered very heavy losses, refusing to leave their trenches. One Japanese regiment, thrown into the assault 1,800 men strong, emerged four days later with only 200 alive. Two attempts to seize 203 Metre Hill were beaten off at huge cost, and it was finally taken only in late November. Surging back and forth, with tunnelling and counter-tunnelling, the bitter fighting presented a foretaste of what the Western Front a decade later would be like.

So did the butcher's bill. In two days, the Japanese would lose another 10,000 men with little gain. Feelings against General Nogi become intense on account of his terrible casualty lists, as the Japanese had to storm uphill over open ground. There were proposals that he should be replaced. Then his second, and favourite, son was killed on the deadly hill. Officers were authorized to kill those men who, without proper reason, straggled or retreated. In a weird custom, instead of identity discs Japanese officers would send home to families of the killed the dead soldier's Adam's apple.

On the Russian side, their best and bravest commander, Colonel Nikolai Tretyakov, put up a desperate defence comparable with that of the defenders of Stalingrad in 1942, using home-made grenades in hand-to-hand fighting. Frostbite, lice and scurvy were as much the enemy as the Japanese. Terrible was the stench of the wounded – though, in the arctic cold, they mainly froze to death. By the end of November, every inch of the ground of 203 Metre Hill had been ploughed by the shells from the eleven-inch Krupp howitzers that Nogi had brought up, manhandled into position by teams of 800 soldiers: 'rocks were ground to powder . . .' reported correspondent-cum-artist H.C. Seppings Wright. On the 30th, the courageous defenders finally gave up. From the captured hill, Nogi's howitzers now completed the final destruction of the fleet at their mercy in the harbour below. The once noble Russian Pacific Squadron at last succumbed to shore fire and torpedo attacks. A total of 120 torpedoes were fired at *Sevastopol*; she survived, only to be scuttled ignominiously by her crew.* The *Retvizan*, sunk on 8 February but resuscitated by Makarov, was sunk again by the Japanese howitzers.† It was indeed a 'messy end to the fleet that had once been the late Admiral Makarov's pride'.

Meanwhile in the besieged town conditions had become intolerable. Hospitals had run out of soap, bedpans and mattresses. Dysentery was universal. The Cossacks took to treating the Chinese inhabitants with unbridled brutality. Stoessel asked the Tsar for permission to surrender. On 2 January 1905, the battered and starved port finally caved in. On occupying the port, Nogi was surprised to find large stores of food and

* Its remains still lie outside the entrance to Port Arthur.
† After the surrender of Port Arthur in January 1905 the Japanese raised and repaired her. She was commissioned in the Imperial Japanese Navy as *Hizen* in 1908. When the Japanese declared war on Germany in 1914 she was sent to reinforce the weak British squadron in British Columbia. She was disarmed in 1922 in accordance with the Washington Naval Treaty, and sunk as a gunnery target in 1924.

ammunition, suggesting that Stoessel had surrendered prematurely. Now the Russian looters took over. Upon returning to St Petersburg, Stoessel was court-martialled and sentenced to death, though this was later commuted to ten years' imprisonment. Over 30,000 Russian soldiers and seamen surrendered their arms, and about 15,000 sick and wounded remained in the squalid hospitals. The siege had cost Japan 57,780 in killed and wounded; while dysentery, beri-beri and other diseases brought the total to around 100,000, losses that this small nation could ill afford. The Russians were estimated to have lost at least 31,000 men.

Though his two sons had died in the fighting, Nogi's terms for the defeated were chivalrous – they would stand in marked contrast to the treatment of British and US troops surrendering to Japanese arms in 1942. Together with Togo, Nogi clambered to the top of Hill 203, still strewn with bodies. Nogi invoked the 'Spirits of the Dead' to share his victory, begging the Emperor for forgiveness for the excessive number of soldiers' lives he had lost. At the war's end, in contrition he asked his permission to commit *seppuku* by way of atonement. 'Not while I'm alive,' came the response. But by and large the fall of Port Arthur was greeted with jubilation and immense outbursts of patriotism. 'Of all the news which reached Tokyo during the war,' wrote the British correspondent Ellis Ashmead-Bartlett, 'there was none which caused such intense joy.' A new generation was coming along, too: a Lieutenant Hideki Tojo was celebrating his twentieth birthday at military college the day before the fall was announced. Three decades later he would lead Japan into its most disastrous war, and end on an Allied gallows.

In the world outside, the fall of Port Arthur caused the credit of Russia to fall, and that of Japan to rise. In St Petersburg there were the beginnings of revolutionary grumblings; Lenin would write that the capitulation was 'the prologue to the capitulation of Tsardom'.

Notable among Japanese intelligence agents there was the ex-Military Attaché in St Petersburg, Colonel Motojiro Akashi, who on the outbreak of war moved his quarters to Stockholm. From there he acquired an extraordinary field of contacts among Russian dissidents and revolutionaries bent on the downfall of the regime; these included Lenin, for whom Akashi would provide funds for the first issue of his newspaper, in January 1905. To the High Command in Tokyo Akashi was reckoned to be worth ten divisions.

A short while later Akashi would be in London, arranging shipment to Russia of arms for the revolution that was would explode in 1905. In December a strike broke out at the important Putilov plant, supplier of munitions to the armies in the Far East. High among the workers' demands were calls that the war should stop. Such a strike was unprecedented in Tsarist Russia. But it spread swiftly until 800,000 workers were out.

Then, on Sunday 22 January 1905, the real trouble began. A mysterious but charismatic priest, Father Gapon, led an entirely peaceable crowd of several thousands to the Winter Palace to present petitions to the Tsar (who in fact was out at Tsarskoe Selo). After warning shots, the panicky troops guarding the Palace fired directly into the crowd, killing an estimated 1,000 innocent demonstrators – men, women and children. After 'Bloody Sunday', the gauntlet was down. In February the Tsar's uncle, Grand Duke Serge Alexandrovich, would be assassinated. For Tsarist Russia these were the first steps towards revolution; more would follow as further bad news came in from the Pacific.

At Port Arthur this first, most terrible battle of the twentieth century where so many thousands had died did indeed seem like the ugliest harbinger of the horrors that would begin in so few years in Europe: at Verdun, on the Somme, in Galicia, on the Piave. But, taking place in this far-off corner of the globe only a few would see it, and even fewer note its awful significance, its warnings of what heavy artillery, the Maxim machine gun, the bolt-action rifle, the land mine, barbed wire and a determined defence could do to humanity.

Port Arthur having surrendered, to its north in Manchuria, along the railway lifeline to Mukden, Oyama's armies – totalling 128,000 men to the Russians' 158,000 – hammered all the time at Kuropatkin's forces. Several times Kuropatkin, now named Supreme Commander in place of a disgraced Alexeyev, launched counter-attacks in the bitter Manchurian weather – conditions in which Russian troops traditionally excelled. At last major reinforcements were funnelling in over the creaking railway system. But, despite their growing numerical superiority, the Russians in Manchuria suffered from a variety of handicaps. Kuropatkin and his subordinate commanders were wedded to defensive doctrines (two of them, Generals Samsonov and Rennen-kampf, would find themselves commanding armies in East Prussia at the beginning of the First World War – with disastrous consequences). In contrast, Field Marshal Oyama instructed his generals to attack constantly – before Kuropatkin's reinforcements could reach the front. As all through the war, Japanese intelligence proved superior; Russian commanders arrived in southern Manchuria without any up-to-date maps of the area. The Russians' communications could hardly have been worse; not knowing their own positions, there were frequent cases of 'friendly fire'. Morale was little better, with reports of broken units raiding vodka stores. And transport remained chaotic, with en-gineless goods wagons sometimes being pushed by squads of sixteen coolies. Each time, the Russian offensives were repulsed, but at enor-mous cost to both sides. Japan was rapidly reaching the bottom of the barrel in terms of manpower reserves. As Hitler would find in the Second World War, Russia's seemed to be limitless.

The bitter winter conditions imposed a lull in the fighting. But by the end of February 1905 both sides were squaring up for the decisive battle, for the key centre of Mukden. Acting with their customary ag-gression and vigour, the Japanese armies – now at their peak strength – struck to pre-empt the counter-stroke that Kuropatkin had been so sluggishly preparing. Given the superiority he had assembled, espe-cially in artillery, with a total of more than 1,400 pieces to the Japanese 924, his opponent Oyama had to move swiftly and adroitly. He chose a copybook 'pin-and-hook' strategy of which Napoleon would have approved. Coming out of the hilly country to the east, General Kawa-mura's newly formed Army of Yalu, whose strength was unknown to Kuropatkin, always short of reliable intelligence, attacked energetically to give the impression that this was the main assault. With the Rus-sians pinned down in that direction, Nogi's army, released from the siege of Port Arthur and now a highly experienced, battle-toughened force, was 'looping boldly' to the west. It would cut the railway nearly ten miles north of Mukden, and well to the rear of Kuropatkin's Gen-eral Headquarters.

An attempt by Kuropatkin to meet the challenge, by splitting off portions of General Alexander Kaulbars' Second Manchurian Army, was disrupted by a fierce blizzard on 2 March. Panic spread, with demoralized Russian soldiers rushing to loot the vodka stores. Even so the Japanese remained at risk, with Nogi's army not seeming strong enough to close the jaws of the trap. A more talented commander than Kuropatkin might have seen an opportunity there. But the opening was missed. On 7 March, with the railway north of Mukden cut, Kuropatkin was telegraphing St Petersburg tersely: 'I am surrounded.' With that, he cut his losses and abandoned Mukden.

It was a disorderly and disgraceful retreat. Much of Kuropatkin's munitions and transport was lost. Discipline collapsed, with Russian troops turning on their officers and drunken men roaming the streets. There were many self-inflicted injuries. The *British Official History* recounts: 'There were carts in matchwood, wagons with their wheels in the air ... every kind of baggage lay crushed by the horses' hooves or by the wheels of vehicles which had passed over them ...'

Kuropatkin was sacked by the Tsar, and replaced by another incompetent general, Linievich. The army withdrew to a safe point 200 miles north of Mukden. The whole of valuable southern Manchuria was lost to Russia. But it was not a rout; Oyama's forces were too exhausted to follow. They had lost more than a quarter of the troops committed to the battle. General Gentaro Kodama admitted, 'it was never thought possible by us that we could surround the Russians and bring about a second Sedan'. Indeed, had the Russians been capable of mounting a strong counter-offensive at that moment, Oyama's army would have been caught dangerously exposed.

The cold was crippling in its intensity, tougher on the unacclimatized Japanese than on Kuropatkin's Siberians. Losses had been horrendous on both sides, far higher than had been experienced in any one of Napoleon's battles, or for that matter even on killing fields like Gettysburg in the American Civil War.* At the Battle of Mukden, in 1905, out of sight of most of the world, Japan lost 15,892 in dead and 59,612 wounded; Russia 40,000 killed or missing and 49,000 wounded – equal to about one-third of each side. Many of the wounded would not survive. The Russians had also lost most of their heavy weaponry. Mukden was rightly judged to be the bloodiest battle in history up to 1905. By the end of the battle, both sides were ready for a settlement,

---

* Leipzig, in 1813, Napoleon's costliest battle, resulted in 38,000 French casualties to 54,000 of the Allies. Gettysburg cost a total of 51,000 for both sides.

for a negotiated peace. It marked the end of any serious fighting on land in the Russo-Japanese War. Although, on paper, Japan had been the winner on both sea and land all along, in fact it was the more in need of an end to the fighting. Having relied on a short war, it had lost too heavily, in terms both of blood and of wealth. And Russia could always mount another offensive from the Trans-Siberian Railway. As it was, its mighty new fleet, the Second Pacific Squadron, was already nearing the end of an 18,000-mile expedition to avenge, or reconquer, Port Arthur.

But revolt was simmering in European Russia.

Meanwhile, in southern Manchuria, as the spring thaw brought an end to campaigning, both sides sat down and licked their wounds. For Japan, at least, Mukden and the territory captured in southern Manchuria, plus of course Port Arthur, would be valuable bargaining counters when it came to a peace settlement.

As both sides gasped for breath, the final and most dramatic act of the war, the battle with which it would forever be identified, remained to be played out, at sea once again.

CHAPTER FOUR

ODYSSEY, FOLLOWED BY ILIAD

We now approach the last, melodramatic act in the extraordinary saga of the Russo-Japanese War. The climactic battle, for which Russia's newly formed Second Pacific Squadron would spend more than half a year voyaging 18,000 miles round the world, was to be fought and won within a span of roughly half an hour. As Admiral Togo reflected afterwards, pondering the uneven-handedness of fate, was there not something gross in the fact that a great battleship could take several years to construct, and train up, and yet it could be destroyed completely in that same half-hour? Thus, similarly, the destiny of nations.

The man the Tsar chose to lead the Second Pacific Squadron on its epic voyage around the world, to defeat Togo and recapture Port Arthur, was Vice-Admiral Zinovy Rozhestvensky. The Tsar, as usual, was unerring in his ability to make the wrong choice – though, since the demise of Makarov, the Russian list of available candidates was not overwhelmingly large. The question is: could any naval commander have done better than Rozhestvensky, on a voyage that was to prove an almost impossible task, all but a death sentence? In the struggle just to keep his crews together, maybe no one could have performed better than he.

Rozhestvensky was born the same year as Togo and had begun his career as a gunnery officer with the Baltic Fleet. During the Russo-Turkish War of 1877–8, as a lieutenant, his torpedo boat, equipped with spar torpedoes,* had been caught up in the nets deployed to protect the enemy ships, and his formation had had to withdraw without success. In 1891 he spent three years as Naval Attaché in London, where he gained a somewhat grudging respect for the Royal Navy, then regarded as without rival, and in 1894 he served under Makarov in Russia's

---

* Spar torpedoes, attached to the bowsprit, required the ramming of the enemy ship, and thus close combat, which in turn necessitated a great deal of courage.

Mediterranean Squadron. But promotion was slow. Aged fifty in 1897 Rozhestvensky had been a mere captain in command of the gunnery school of the Baltic Fleet, with retirement looming. It was at this point that he caught the eye of the Tsar. The occasion was a review in honour of the Tsar's cousin, Kaiser Wilhelm II of Germany, on 24 July 1902. At a naval review off Reval (now Tallinn in Estonia), Captain Rozhest-vensky laid on a brilliant display of gunnery, which greatly impressed the naval-minded Kaiser. The rapidity and accuracy of the big gun sal-voes, the result of weeks of fiercely tough training, were outstanding. The Kaiser lavished praise on the Russian commander: 'I wish I had such splendid admirals as your Rozhestvensky,' and as he departed he offered a typically arrogant compliment: 'The Admiral of the Atlantic bids farewell to the Admiral of the Pacific.'

Rozhestvensky was a martinet with an explosive temper. He was nicknamed, very much in private, 'Mad Dog'. In a rage he was given to throwing his binoculars overboard. A huge figure of a man, with an impressive bearing, his trim pepper-and-salt beard made him resemble the Tsar's other eminent cousin, King George V – except for the arch-ing, very Russian eyebrows.

As a consequence of his performance and the Kaiser's praise at the 1902 manoeuvres, Rozhestvensky had caught the Tsar's attention. From then on his promotion was meteoric. That same year he emerged as a vice-admiral, and Chief of the Naval Staff. Proposing a plan to send most of the Baltic Fleet round the world to reinforce the em-battled ships in the Far East, suddenly he found himself in command of it. Was he up to it? This unprecedented task would be fateful and ultimately fatal. One historian regarded him as 'the right man for the job, for it would take an iron-fisted commander to sail an untested fleet of brand-new battleships ... and new untrained sailors on the long-est coal-powered battleship fleet voyage in recorded history'. Another historian, rather less charitably, regarded Rozhestvensky as 'a scream-ing imbecile, promoted well past his abilities ... suffering from a near mental breakdown', even before the battle he was going to be sent to face. Most of his officers were reputed to 'tremble before him like thieves before the constable. He treats them worse than a bad master treats servants.'

Typical both of the vacillations of the last Emperor of All the

Russias and of the poor state of his warships, week by week, month by month, as the odds lengthened against the survival of Port Arthur, the departure of newly rechristened Second Pacific Squadron – originally set for June 1904 – had been delayed. Part of the trouble, despite the presence of the new battleships, was the poor state of some of the other ships, which had seen service during the Russo-Turkish War of a generation earlier; it also reflected the haphazard way in which sailors were recruited by an essentially non-maritime nation. Ships' complements were largely made up of a mix of Germans, Poles, Balts, Jews and Finns; many had no naval training whatsoever; and there were also a substantial number who brought vehement revolutionary sympathies, if not tracts, on board with them. Driving himself as rigorously as his crews, Rozhestvensky had to work eighteen hours a day, often going without sleep for three nights in a row, to get his ships ready for their Iliad, roaring at his staff and terrifying the commissary merchants that came on board. As well as ammunition, shells, torpedoes and mines by the ton, food for his 12,000 seamen had to be provided, along with clothing for both tropical and arctic conditions. Herds of cattle were driven on board to provide meat, while dried biscuits and vegetables, and vodka and champagne for the officers' ward rooms, were loaded.

Most critical were the vast quantities of fuel, in an era before the oil-fired boiler had arrived, which had to be stocked – thousands of tons of coal. With no Russian base en route, the whole issue of coaling would remain Rozhestvensky's most constant headache throughout the seven-month cruise. No other nation in history had undertaken such a voyage.

The Admiral raised his flag on the new, Russian-built *Knyaz Suvorov*, named after the great general of the eighteenth century, a *Borodino*-class juggernaut that displaced over 15,000 tons. One of the most modern warships afloat, built in a Russian shipyard to French design, she had been in commission only a matter of weeks, and had had few comprehensive sea tests. For no very clear reason her twin funnels were conspicuously painted a bright canary yellow. Eventually the fleet's departure date would slip to 9 October. It was late in the day, if not too late. Russia's best admiral, Makarov, had been killed, likewise his successor Vitgeft; and all attempts to break through the Japanese blockade of Port Arthur had failed. By land the Japanese Army divisions were relentlessly moving in on the port. Even the crucial hub of Mukden was under threat. The day Rozhestvensky finally sailed, with cheerful military bands and gay bunting along the waterfront, both the Tsar and Tsaritsa came to watch the fleet up-anchors. They could not help but be impressed by the bearing and 'rock-like authority' of the newly appointed C-in-C. He would go far to restore Russia's battered reputation in the Far East. He also sailed with the additional blessing of the Kaiser: in the web of alliances and counter-alliances that was building up in the years before 1914, Wilhelm II calculated that either Japan, the naval ally of his arch-enemy Britain, would be humiliated, its British-built warships shown to be defective; or Russia, the best friend in Europe of his traditional foe France, would be trounced. It must have looked like a no-lose situation.

As the historian Richard Hough notes, 'Never before in the whole annals of naval warfare had a Commander-in-Chief sailed forth on such a long, such a dangerous and difficult mission with such an ill-assorted selection of vessels.' The mighty flotilla, fifty ships strong, was built around four of the navy's latest battleships and three older ones. The voyage began inauspiciously. Unable to count on resupply from neutral or unfriendly ports anywhere along its route, all Rozhestvensky's ships started off critically overloaded. The battleship *Oryol*, laden down to her gunwales with victuals, ammunition and coal, ran aground on a sandbank. It was a humiliating and unhappy omen. A few days later, the *Suvorov* also ran aground at Libau (then a leading port in the Russian Baltic, now in Latvia). To superstitious Russians these were bad signs. Among the farewell speech-making at the send-off one of the commanders, Captain Bukhvostok of the *Alexander III*, struck a grimly prophetic note: 'we know why we are going to sea. We also know that Russia is not a sea power and that the public funds spent on ship construction have been wasted. You wish us victory, but there will be no victory . . . But we will know how to die and we shall never surrender . . .'

Meanwhile Rozhestvensky alarmed his officers by ordering them to show extra vigilance, as there were reports of Japanese torpedo boats lurking in the North Sea, disguised as trawlers. Any suspicious ships were to be sunk on sight. This was all good 'disinformation' work by

Japan's astute Naval Attaché, Motojiro Akashi – who had been re-located to Stockholm on the outbreak of hostilities. Akashi's false intelligence was picked up by Russian reports out of Copenhagen, which appeared to substantiate rumours about the torpedo boats being at large. Consequently tension, if not alarm, aboard the flotilla was high: noted one officer, Chief Engineer Politovsky of the *Suvorov*, 'we must be on our guard ... panic prevails on board. Everyone examines the sea intently.'

On the night of 21/22 October 1904, as the great fleet plunged on towards the English Channel, Rozhestvensky's worst fears crystallized just off the Dogger Bank. It was a typical North Sea night for that time of year: black, spectral, with limited visibility. While still in Danish waters the repair ship *Kamchatka*, lost in fog, suddenly radioed that she was being attacked by about eight torpedo boats, coming from all directions. Rozhestvensky's nervous commanders promptly stood to, and in short order the sea was ablaze with searchlights, and with heavy guns firing in all directions. The *Oryol* alone fired off some 500 shells. Great spouts of water were sent up close to the *Suvorov*. The enemy appeared to be attacking from every point of the compass. In the mêlée, one Russian cruiser, the *Aurora* (later to become famous in the 1917 Revolution), was hit by friendly fire; her chaplain lost a hand and subsequently died of blood-poisoning – the fleet's first casualty. But the engagement seemed to be going Russia's way. Three enemy ships had been hit; one was listing heavily. Then the dreadful penny dropped: the Japanese 'torpedo boats' were in fact small, 100-ton trawlers, of the British Gamecock Fleet, out on its business from Hull – and, of course, unarmed. Aboard the *Crane* most of the crew had sustained wounds, the captain had been decapitated and the trawler was sinking. Many of the other British trawlers had also been hit.

When the news reached England, outrage swept the country. A fierce editorial in *The Times* denounced the Russians unsparingly: it was 'almost inconceivable that any men calling themselves seamen, however frightened they might be, could spend twenty minutes bombarding a fleet of fishing boats without discovering the nature of their target ... butchering poor fishermen with the guns of a great fleet without endeavouring to rescue the victims of their unpardonable mistake ...'

Anger spread electrically. Trafalgar Square was filled with protesting crowds; the Russian Ambassador was booed as he left his Embassy; there were deputations to Downing Street and to Parliament, calling for action. To many in liberal Britain the authoritarian Tsarist regime was anathema anyway, and few wanted the pending extension of the Entente Cordiale to embrace Russia too.* Japan was Britain's ally. Moreover, the offence was exacerbated by the fact that it had taken place on Trafalgar Day, of all days, the centenary of which was to be celebrated in exactly a year's time. The King, Edward VII, deeply angered, summoned the Foreign Secretary, Lord Lansdowne, to the Palace. He donated 200 guineas for the victims, and pencilled in the margin of the report to Parliament: 'A most dastardly outrage.' Even the German press, then normally favourable to the Russians, damned Rozhestvensky, questioning whether his fleet should be permitted to be at sea at all. In St Petersburg the Tsar wrote privately to his mother that the English 'are very angry and near to boiling point. They are even said to be getting their fleet ready for action. Yesterday I sent a telegram to Uncle Bertie, expressing my regret, but I did not apologise ... I do not think the English will have the cheek to go further than to indulge in threats.'

Yet, by 25 October, momentarily it did indeed look as if Britain was on the brink of war. 'The mind of the government, like the mind of the nation, is made up,' thundered *The Times*. The Home Fleet, commanded in the North Sea and with guns loaded and at the ready, was despatched to Portland. Fast cruisers were alerted to shadow the Russians out of the Channel. By the evening of the 26th there were twenty-eight battleships, with steam up, ready to destroy Rozhestvensky's squadron at one word from the Admiralty. Gibraltar was put on a war footing, and British warships were recalled from foreign ports. The Russians were closely shadowed, almost escorted, all the way to the coast of Africa.

Until the Russians arrived at Vigo Bay, in north-west Spain, Rozhestvensky seems to have been sublimely unaware of the storm he had precipitated – until, among other British journalists, Edgar

---

* The Triple Entente alliance between France, Britain and Russia followed in 1907 and was thought by many historians to have been among the contributory causes of the First World War.

Wallace, the detective writer, then a reporter for the *Daily Mail*, interviewed members of his fleet. They were still convinced they had genuinely come under attack by Japanese torpedo boats disguised as trawlers. Then the truth came home to the Russians: the Japanese 'torpedo boats' were in fact small, 100-ton, British trawlers. The crisis ebbed. Amends were made. Rozhestvensky admitted his errors; Russia agreed to pay compensation of £65,000 to the families of the dead and injured fishermen. It had been a close-run thing. But being shadowed all the way by the cruisers of Admiral Lord Charles Beresford 'as if they were prizes of war' caused the already jumpy nerves of Rozhestvensky's sailors to fray still further, as they could not help noting superior seamanship beyond anything of which they were capable. A dashing figure who commanded the Channel Fleet and was normally accompanied by a very British bulldog, Beresford teased the Russians by darting ahead and crossing their bows, then falling astern to steam past at full speed in perfect line-ahead formation, with humiliating closeness to Rozhestvensky's plodding fleet. Rozhestvensky himself observed gloomily to his subordinate, now Commander Vladimir Semenov: 'Those are a real squadron. Those are seamen. Oh, only if we—' He broke off in mid-sentence and hurried off down a companion ladder. But British anger over the Dogger Bank incident would pursue Rozhestvensky for the rest of his voyage.

The most immediate problem that the crisis imposed on the Russian commander was in the urgent matter of refuelling, coaling. The recoaling of warships was considered to be one of the most distasteful tasks, and was often dangerous. Until the fuel for capital ships was replaced by oil in the First World War, they had to be refuelled at regular intervals with vast quantities of coal. Every spare man and officer was brought in to do the coaling; stokers and ratings often died of heart failure in the heat. During the coaling the whole ship was filled with dust, which even penetrated the cabins and wardrooms of the officers. At a single recoaling, a battleship could take on over 2,000 tons of coal, which could add to the danger of the ship listing and ultimately overturning. Any ships caught when coaling in a time of war were sitting targets.

Before Rozhestvensky's departure, St Petersburg had skilfully done a deal with the Hamburg-Amerika line to provide coalers the whole length of the fleet's extraordinary voyage. With Kaiser Wilhelm anxious to distract European powers from his own naval designs, the Hamburg firm would faithfully fulfil its coaling contract. But the problem lay with the ports on the route; with Russia being a belligerent power, they could lawfully refuse Rozhestvensky access for the lengthy and tricky process that coaling entailed. In the open sea it was something all commanders would avoid like the plague. At Vigo, maximum pressure from London ensured that the port was closed to the Second Russian fleet; the fleet could even be interned. The Spaniards insisted on acting within their rights. And the Russians' fuel situation was critical. The fleet had steamed 1,800 miles and the coal bunkers were low. Finally the Port Commandant allowed a maximum of 400 tons per ship to be loaded, a half-load. This could signify a cruising range of perhaps no more than 1,500 miles – not much in terms of the total distance the fleet had to travel. There was also recognition in Whitehall of the superior claims of diplomatic amity with Russia, with that new tripartite European alliance in the offing, and tempers cooled down. Rozhestvensky set off for the west coast of Africa. Thence he would take his fleet round the Cape of Good Hope, and into the Indian Ocean, not risking the shorter passage through the British-controlled Suez Canal.

Nevertheless, more than problems of morale, or gunnery standards, or the depreciating condition of his ships, it was the problem of coaling which, right to the very end, would plague Rozhestvensky. Between the time when steam took over from sail and Winston Churchill, as Britain's First Lord of the Admiralty, switched the Royal Navy over to recently acquired Middle East oil, all ships were fuelled by coal – whole mountains of it, filthy and inefficient stuff. And not all coal was suitable. For instance, that which was mined in Japan was of too poor quality, so just prior to the outbreak of war, the Japanese Navy had providently stocked up with 650,000 tons of the best Welsh coal, topped up obligingly by Britain with another 650,000 tons as war began. But even so, with the fleet consuming 10,000 tons a week at even modest speeds, as the war dragged on into its second year, and as Togo waited anxiously for the arrival of Rozhestvensky's fleet, he had to watch his stocks carefully.

The situation was even more worrying for the Russians, never quite sure when, or how, their next delivery would arrive. Cruising at twelve knots, a modern battleship like the French-built *Tsesarevich* with its powerful Belleville engines would eat up three tons an hour; increase the speed to eighteen knots, as under battle conditions, and consumption would soar to fifteen tons. When, during the Battle of the Yellow Sea, the ship had its funnels riddled with shell fragments, consumption rose to twenty tons per hour; which was why, down to its last tons of fuel, *Tsesarevich* had been forced to seek refuge, and internment, in the nearby neutral port of Kiaochow. Similar rises in consumption would occur when ships suffered from hull-fouling and excess weight, both of which contingencies would inevitably affect Rozhestvensky's ships over their long cruise through tropical waters, as we shall see.

After leaving Vigo, the Russian fleet enjoyed a few days of relative calm. At Gibraltar Rozhestvensky ordered Admiral Dimitry von Felkerzam to take his division of older, slower ships through the Suez Canal, rather than risk the voyage around the Cape of Good Hope. They were to rejoin the main fleet at Madagascar. There was some controversy in the ward room as to the reasoning behind Rozhestvensky's decision. At Tangier the Russian fleet was treated royally by the Sultan of Morocco, who was uninterested in the extant state of war. There the sailors were overjoyed to welcome the delivery of a thousand tons of frozen meat. Less pleasing was the coaling from the waiting German colliers that took place in a sub-tropical rainstorm. Rivers of water poured down the mountains of good Welsh coal, turning into filthy streams on the decks of the warships. A dozen ships' bands blasted away to encourage the back-breaking manual work of shifting the heavy bags of coal, 'white teeth gleaming through black-stained faces'. Rozhestvensky offered a prize of 1,500 roubles for the crew loading the most coal in the shortest time.

Next stop for the Second Pacific Squadron was French-owned Dakar, on the bulge of Africa. With temperatures of up to 120°F (49°C) in October, and with hideous humidity of over 90 per cent, coaling became far more unpleasant. There were ten colliers waiting, bearing 30,000 tons, and there could be no delay because of the uncertainty of French hospitality. Rozhestvensky, with secret information that the French had forbidden use of the next port down the line, Libreville (in present-day Gabon), ordered that those of his battleships with bunker capacity of 1,100 tons, would each take on no less than 2,200 tons. His captains were dismayed; how could they conceivably keep their ships clean? Rozhestvensky refused to budge. Draconian instructions were issued: the excess coal should be stored 'in any spare place on the upper deck, lower deck, gun deck, poop and in the cockpit, over closed water-tight manhole covers, in the bath rooms, drying rooms . . . loose on the quarter deck, with some means to prevent it falling overboard . . .'

Even officers' cabins, up to the rank of commander, were not to be excluded. It would be hard to imagine the natty Captain Paken-ham RN, or an Admiral Beresford, accepting such conditions. But Rozhestvensky was ruthless, and cleanliness was about the least of his worries. In the gangways, mess decks and cabins there was an atmos-phere similar to that of a mine shaft in a heatwave. For the next four months the Russian crews worked and ate with the bitter fumes in their nostrils, and the filthy and irritant coal dust creeping even into their food. Under extreme pressure from the French colonial authori-ties, coaling at Dakar was accelerated so that it could be completed in twenty-nine hours. Men died of heat exhaustion, including the son of a Russian ambassador, young Lieutenant Nelidov. There were the first signs of mutiny, aboard the supply-ship *Kamchatka*, the rogue vessel responsible for the Dogger Bank incident. Like Bligh of the *Bounty*, Rozhestvensky threatened to cast the lot off in open boats. Mean-while their excessive gross tonnage left the warships verging on the unmanageable, 'like sluggish, overloaded river barges' in the words of one chronicler.

But there was worse to come, at Whale Fish Bay (in present-day Namibia) on 11 December. There, the Portuguese, Britain's 'oldest allies', were unfriendly. Then, because of the inadequacy of the harbour, the fleet had to carry out coaling in open waters, and in a heavy sea. Rolling and pitching, the plucky colliers repeatedly bashed against the sides of the warships as they struggled to come alongside. The barrels of *Suvorov*'s light guns holed the sides of her own collier, damaging guns and torpedo booms. Eventually the attempt had to be called off, and instead Rozhestvensky ordered that the coal be shifted by means of ships' launches. It proved a painfully laborious business, and even after working night and day only a few hundred tons had been loaded. With his notably short fuse, Rozhestvensky flew into a terrible rage, adding to the barely tolerable burdens of his staff. A young sub-lieu-tenant on the *Oryol* lost his mind and ran round the deck, sobbing: 'The Japs are waiting for us. We shall all be sunk! We shall all be sunk!' He was locked in his cabin under guard. His ravings and their dark forebodings could be heard throughout the ship, having a bad effect on the crew, who had now been at sea for two months without any news from home.

Then, as the storm died down and coaling could proceed, on 15 December Rozhestvensky received from an itinerant German officer the worst possible tidings from the Far East: Port Arthur's key height, 203 Metre Hill, had been taken. It meant nothing to Rozhestvensky; the German explained that it dominated the whole harbour and could well mean the end of Port Arthur. There was further bad news in the shape of reports that the Japanese had fitted out civil schooners with torpedo tubes, and that these camouflaged vessels might be lying in wait off Durban on the east coast of South Africa. Unrepentant about his Dogger Bank interlude, Rozhestvensky in a fury declared that he would 'ruthlessly destroy' all Durban fishing craft that might come within torpedo range. Thus concluded what was held to be the worst coaling episode of the entire Odyssey.

Amid further stormy seas the fleet ploughed on, round the Cape of Good Hope. It was almost halfway through its long saga. Nerves continued to be stretched, though the rumoured schooner attack never materialized. But *Kamchatka*, the albatross of the fleet, its worst ship, and cause of the Dogger Bank shoot-up, once again fell foul of Rozhestvensky, signalling that she had shipped bad coal and wanted permission to throw overboard 150 tons. Acidly Rozhestvensky signalled back: 'Find the guilty ones and throw them overboard instead!' A short while later *Kamchatka* followed up: 'Do you see the torpedo boats?' Action stations were called, officers roused from their sleep. Then *Kamchatka* followed up: 'Sorry.' The signalman had used the wrong signal, intending simply to say 'We are all right now'. Rozhestvensky's language would have been blistering.

Without further incident the fleet reached Madagascar, anchoring off Île Sainte-Marie, an insalubrious little island off its eastern sea-board used by the French as an overflow penal settlement for Devil's Island. It was here that Rozhestvensky was to be joined by Admiral

Felkerzam's detachment, after it had navigated the Suez Canal. But Felkerzam turned up at Nossi-Bé, some 500 miles round on the other, north-west side of the island, and announced that, on account of their 'tired machinery', his ships would be unable to sail for another two weeks. Rozhestvensky flew into another of his famous rages, shouting: 'If they are so old that they can't steam then they may go to the devil. We have no use for rubbish here ... However, I'll go there myself – I'll dig them out fast enough!' He set off to confront Felkerzam himself. Meanwhile, an ocean-going tug brought in calamitous news. Following the fall of 203 Metre Hill, the whole of First Pacific Squadron had been destroyed inside Port Arthur's basin, and Port Arthur itself was on the verge of capture. All of a sudden it seemed as if the whole purpose of Rozhestvensky's epic voyage had been rendered null and void: his squadron could no longer reinforce the First Pacific Squadron if it had ceased to exist; it could not save Port Arthur if it had already surrendered.

At the same time news came that, at home, a new fleet with the grotesquely ambitious title of the Third Pacific Squadron was being formed – out of all the slow, old ships that Rozhestvensky had expressly left at home. In command would be Rear-Admiral Nikolai Nebogatov. Rozhestvensky was to await their arrival in two to three weeks' time. It was the last straw. He despatched a signal to St Petersburg, asking to be relieved of his command; then, feeling suddenly old and ill, he retired to his cabin and locked the door. Needless to say, his request would be turned down by the Tsar.

A miserable Christmas was passed in wretched conditions off the Madagascan isle of Nossi-Bé (now its leading holiday resort), with its sweaty, well-named port of Hell-ville. Deep gloom settled in on the personnel of the battleship *Suvorov*, as recorded by Commander Vladimir Semenov. There was now harsh recognition of the realities of what lay ahead. What had appeared 'to be hopeless enough, was suddenly seen as suicidal. Nothing could save them now.' Fatalism gripped even the most loyal, such as Semenov, who wrote in his diary, '... St Petersburg had grasped how utterly hopeless – not to say criminal – our adventure was, and if they had sent us categorical orders to come back, I should have said "The Lord be praised."' The arrival of Felkerzam's ancient ships, which had enjoyed an easier cruise through the Suez Canal, did nothing to restore morale; lacking discipline, if anything they spread more gloom in the fleet.

Then, on Christmas morning, Rozhestvensky stood atop the aft twelve-inch turret and, champagne glass in hand, 'as if forcing himself out of a coma', delivered a clarion call to the assembled sailors. He exhorted them, 'what fine fellows you are', to do their duty – to Russia. In a voice broken with sobs, he added, 'May God help us to serve her honourably, to justify her confidence, not to deceive her hopes. To you, whom I trust! To Russia!' Such an appeal to patriotism, to love of Mother Russia, was sure to provide a shot in the arm. As Rozhestvensky sat down, there were loud cheers, caps thrown in the air and cries of 'We'll do it!', 'We won't give in!', 'Lead us!', 'Lead us!' The Russian fighting-man, exhausted and exploited as he might be, was still a formidable foe. But the new year brought further bad tidings: definitive news of the fall of Port Arthur.

Once again the agony of coaling began – the same killing heat, the same plague of coal dust pervading everything. Two seamen on the battleship *Borodino* died of the poisonous fumes. Sunstroke killed another rating, and knocked out dozens more. Dysentery broke out on several ships. On the *Ural* one officer was killed and another injured by a swinging crane. Ships broke down at regular intervals, causing the fleet to ease its speed on occasions to six knots. Then followed the more welcome activity of revictualling: 50,000 cases of potatoes from Cape Town; a thousand bullocks, flour, vegetables, chocolates and biscuits; and fancy foodstuffs and drink for the officers' messes. It would have to last for most of the rest of the journey north-eastward.

The state of Rozhestvensky's fleet was hardly improving. Ships stank from rotten food. The cold-storage supply ship *Esperance* had her refrigeration plant break down, and in consequence was forced to throw overboard 700 tons of bad meat. The windfall lured in swarms of sharks from miles around; they made life impossibly dangerous for underwater crews sent down to attempt to clean the ships' keels fouled by weed and barnacles. Several lives were lost, and this essential work abandoned. A supply ship, the *Irtysh*, arrived from Russia, supposedly bringing ammunition for the heavy guns; in fact she contained quantities of fur-lined winter coats and 12,000 pairs of heavy boots – a cargo that was hardly welcomed in the tropical heat of Madagascar. A vital firing exercise, badly needed by the untrained gunners, was a disaster: ships nearly collided, and the gunnery was wild. One of the battleships' munition hoists jammed; inside it a cobra's nest was discovered, the snake insouciantly coiled within. It appeared to have come aboard in a bale of hay for the livestock. To preserve valuable ammunition, which *Irtysh* had failed to bring, Rozhestvensky suspended the exercise, remarking savagely: 'by day the entire squadron did not score *one single hit* on the targets which represented the torpedo boats, although these targets differed from the Japanese boats to our advantage, inasmuch as they were stationary . . .'

'Unpardonably bad!' and 'Wretched performance!' were among the printable epithets that the fierce C-in-C would employ repeatedly – and with every reason. On one occasion a gun crew was reduced to tears when a poorly machined shell jammed in the breech. On a firing exercise with precious torpedoes, out of seven fired, one jammed, four darted off eccentrically at right angles either to port or starboard, and one went round and round in circles, 'popping up and down like a porpoise', and causing consternation throughout the fleet. That would be the last fleet exercise with live ammunition.

In the steamy idleness and boredom of Nossi-Bé, morale continued to plummet. Mutiny broke out on several ships because of the rotten food. Several leaders were hanged from yardarms. Men broke down and cried when they received infrequent letters from home. Drink took over, with lethal brews of *kvass* made from rye flour and malt. Men fell overboard from drunken orgies. 'Our men despaired of escaping from the war with their lives,' recorded the seaman Alexey Novikov-Priboy of the *Oryol*, 'so they drowned thought in drink, dicing, and drabbing.' To Hell-ville women flocked as if by magic from all over the island. Whore-houses and bars suddenly proliferated. The mixed-race owner of one such, called the Parisian Café, announced that he was retiring to Paris 'after you all leave'. But his joy was cut short.

Abruptly on the morning of 17 March 1905, after two months' enforced idleness waiting for Nebogatov and his collection of rust-buckets – *samotopy* in Russian, or 'self-sinkers' – the Russian fleet upped anchors and departed. Rozhestvensky had received a communication full of menace: the Japanese were threatening that 'any colliers discovered in the vicinity of the Russian squadron would instantly be fired upon and destroyed'. Reacting promptly the Hamburg colliers warned that they had signed on to sell coal, not to engage in naval warfare. This prompted Rozhestvensky to leave unhealthy Nossi-Bé forthwith and make a secret coaling rendezvous across the Indian Ocean. Four more colliers would meet him in distant Saigon, carrying a further 30,000 tons. That should suffice to take the fleet to Vladivostok. But weed and barnacles that had prospered in the tropical heat, fouling hulls, slowed speeds by at least two knots, at the same time increasing coal consumption at cruising speed by between 100 and 130 tons daily. That could prove critical.

Meanwhile details had dribbled through to the fleet of the appalling events in St Petersburg on Bloody Sunday, which would be but an overture to the bloodiest year ever experienced under Romanov rule to date. There were crew members who feared that wives and even children had been among the casualties. Mutiny broke out first of all on the armoured cruiser *Nakhimov*. Nominally it had been sparked by a lack of bread, and by mouldy biscuits, but it was more than that. Mutineers prepared to rush the bridge, then saw that *Suvorov's* guns were pointed at them. Fourteen ringleaders, chosen arbitrarily, were shot. Rozhestvensky was ruthless in his stamping out of the revolt. Court martials were held on board *Borodino*, *Alexander III* and the regularly miscreant *Kamchatka* (she had excelled herself once more in firing in error a live shell, which bounced off her neighbour, *Aurora*). The worst offenders were shipped home in miserable conditions aboard an ancient vessel Rozhestvensky wanted to be rid of, the *Malay*.

The biggest worry to loyal officers like Commander Semenov was the health of the Commander-in-Chief. Semenov noted how increasingly, after one of his fits of rage, Rozhestvensky would retire to his cabin for hours on end. Sometimes his leg seemed to drag; could he possibly have had a mini-stroke? And what would happen to the fleet if he collapsed or died? It was an unimaginable prospect. His successor by seniority would have been Rear-Admiral Nikolai Nebogatov, currently plodding along with the Third Pacific Squadron of rust-buckets, to join up shortly with Rozhestvensky's fleet and, in theory, replace the First Squadron, lost at Port Arthur. There could hardly have been a greater contrast between the two men. At fifty-six, Nebogatov was fat and small, with a chubby face suffering from chronic eczema, though partly concealed behind a short beard. Moving about his deck in little steps, he was an unimpressive figure, but quietly spoken, mild-mannered, approachable and tolerant of his crews to an extent incomprehensible to the fiery Rozhestvensky, to whom he was anathema. At Port Said he had telegraphed St Petersburg for instructions. Back came a vague response: 'You are to join up with Rozhestvensky, whose route is unknown to us.' Having crossed the Indian Ocean safely to reach Singapore, he received news there that Rozhestvensky had already passed through, on 8 April.

From when it had left Nossi-Bé until the evening of 8 April Rozhestvensky's squadron had in fact been lost to the world, as well as to the Russian Admiralty. Nearly fifty ships strong, it had steamed across the wide, lonely Indian Ocean for 3,500 miles without seeing another ship. It had only had faint sight of land at Sumatra, where it chose the narrow Malacca Straits to attain Singapore. To Semenov's expert eyes, their safe passage was 'unexampled in the history of steam navigation'. Overcome with depression and anxiety neurosis, several more sailors had thrown themselves overboard. Every four or five days there would be a halt for the back-breaking task of coaling from Rozhestvensky's own emergency colliers, and more frequent stops on account of breakdowns. The food situation was dire; long ago the fleet had run out of cabbage for making the soup which was essential to a Russian sailor (though hardly palatable to his Royal Navy counterpart). Ships' cooks had had to make do with manioc, a poor substitute. There were more cases of rotting meat and worm-ridden biscuits, and more angry murmurings.

When it arrived at Singapore on the evening of 8 April, literally out of the blue, the sight of the great fleet caused the utmost excitement. Even *The Times*, somewhat amending the hostile tone it had adopted after the Dogger Bank incident, rated it 'a splendid spectacle', as impressive as anything the British navy had ever presented. 'The smoke they made was visible for miles,' reported Reuters. 'The ships, magnificent but foul, were proceeding at about eight knots, and it took them fifty-five minutes to pass a given point. All the vessels showed signs of their long voyage in tropical seas, about a foot of seaweed being visible along the waterline, and the decks were laden with coal.'

Another London leader-writer declared that an account of the fleet's passage 'will send a thrill of admiration through all Englishmen who read it'. Would Togo, one wonders, on reading such reports, have been affrighted – or encouraged?

But Rozhestvensky, regarding British Singapore as essentially a hostile port, whence Togo would certainly receive detailed intelligence, decided not to tarry there. He stayed just long enough to receive some more unwelcome news, shouted at him through a megaphone by the Russian Consul aboard a steam launch: 'Mukden has fallen . . . General Kuropatkin has been dismissed.' Next came information of much greater immediacy: 'Admiral Kamimura's cruiser squadron called at Singapore three days ago, and is now believed to be on its way to North Borneo, and twenty-two more warships under Togo's flag . . . are now at Labuan* . . .'

Other news, of personal concern to Rozhestvensky, and indeed causing him great affront, was that, by an order from St Petersburg, on reaching Vladivostok he was to hand over command to an Admiral Aleksei Birilev, who was already trundling eastwards along the Trans-Siberian Railway. To have taken his great fleet safely halfway round the world, possibly yet to face a major battle with the enemy, then to be rewarded with the sack was hardly the way to treat a commander on the eve of his greatest challenge. Understandably, Rozhestvensky sank into the deepest Russian gloom. There were also rumours that the United States was putting pressure on the belligerents to end the fighting. The forceful President Theodore Roosevelt was hatching a peace plan; Japan was considering its terms. So what, Admiral Rozhestvensky and his brave Russians might have wondered, was now the point of sailing on to face a murderous battle when peace was already in the offing?

As they headed for Cam Ranh Bay through the South China Sea, the squadron now passed many ships, including more British naval vessels which they thought must be tailing them on behalf of their Japanese allies. Why, Commmander Semenov frequently asked himself, were the Japanese missing so many opportunities of a surprise attack? What was Togo doing? The answer was, once repairs to his damaged

* An island off the north-west coast of Borneo, and menacingly close to Rozhestvensky's onward route.

vessels had been completed, the Japanese leader – more or less at leisure – was training on, perfecting the manoeuvres of his fleet, carrying
out gunnery exercises such as Rozhestvensky had so noticeably failed
to achieve in the Indian Ocean. Cannily, to preserve his heavy ammunition and gun tubes, he had carried out firing by use of sub-calibre
adaptors, which allowed the use of lighter shells. Yet, like the Russians,
Togo too had to ration exercises; his coal supplies were also finite and
waning. But he had the unassailable advantage of time, fresh manpower and morale on his side. As Napoleon had once remarked, 'The
moral is to the physical as of three to one.'

CHAPTER FIVE

THE BATTLE AT SEA

On his last coaling and rest-up rendezvous before the final confrontation, Rozhestvensky assembled his fleet in the great natural harbour of Cam Ranh Bay in Indo-China. It was the first week of May 1905. In what is now Vietnam, during the war of that name Cam Ranh was host to many a US fleet, but in 1905 it still flew the flag of the French empire. Once again Rozhestvensky and his huge armada had disappeared from sight of reporters and other navies. Yet in April a resourceful editor of the London *Daily Telegraph* – in the best tradition of Evelyn Waugh's Lord Copper of *The Beast* – had wired his new man in Hong Kong, William Donald, a go-getting Australian with an instinct for a story: 'RUSSIAN FLEET REPORTED LOST SINCE LEAVING RED SEA STOP MAY BE SOMEWHERE YOUR AREA STOP GO FIND IT'.

Accordingly, acting on a hunch, Donald booked a steamer for Saigon. Passing Cam Ranh, he spotted the tell-tale forest of smoke-columns; pressing forward, he found himself confronted by the massive hulk of the Russian flagship *Suvorov*. On the flank, as if guarding the Russian fleet, lay a French cruiser, *Descartes*. It was 1 May; Rozhestvensky had arrived on 14 April. The *Telegraph* had a world-beating scoop, and Japan's loyal ally, Britain, a piece of prime intelligence. As Russia was in a state of war, Rozhestvensky's fleet was not allowed to remain in any port for more than twenty-four hours. Rozhestvensky was in the middle of his crucial coaling operation, but was ordered to leave forthwith by a reluctant France. This he did, but after a brief sortie he immediately returned. The pause at least enabled him to link up, finally, on 14 May with Nebogatov and his fleet of tired old 'flat-irons and galoshes'. There was a solemn though brief moment, as the two squadrons, now over fifty vessels strong and 16,000 miles away from home, steamed majestically towards each other. Briefly the leaders celebrated

Russian May Day with a crate of Mumm, toasting the health of the Tsar 'and victory'. It was, however, the coolest of encounters, this meeting of the two Russian admirals, who disliked and even despised each other. Nevertheless, news of this great event, reaching St Petersburg, gave the jingoists one last fleeting hope of a victory in the offing; despite all the setbacks, invincible Mother Russia was about to regain her rightful claim to be regarded as 'Mistress of the Pacific'.

In Cam Ranh, however, the triumphant juncture of the two Russian fleets was seriously diminished when the obese Admiral Felkerzam suffered a stroke. Rozhestvensky managed to keep this quiet. The significance of this mishap was that, if Felkerzam were eliminated, the despised Nebogatov as next in line would automatically become second-in-command of the whole enterprise. Rozhestvensky displayed his contempt for Nebogatov by receiving him with icy formality at Cam Ranh, refusing to discuss his plans: 'He gave me neither instructions nor advice . . . I only saw Rozhestvensky once in the whole course of the cruise.' Hardly a happy omen for the decisive engagement that must lie ahead.

Meanwhile the eagle-eyed Donald was not fooled: 'These ships', he reported, 'will be disgraced in their first engagement.' A second, follow-up story in the *Daily Telegraph* reported Rozhestvensky's return to Cam Ranh and the news that he had then been ordered by the French, definitively, to pack up and leave French waters.*

The interruption of Rozhestvensky's vital, final refuelling meant that he would now not have enough coal to take the longer and safer route to Vladivostok by sailing to the east of Japan, rather than through the perilous Scylla and Charybdis of the Tsushima Straits, which were narrow and commanded by the Japanese home fleet. A deciding factor here was that, through what seems like a foolish housekeeping error, probably a result of campaign-fatigue from the long, long journey, one of Rozhestvensky's most powerful units, the battleship *Alexander III*, which had consistently won the 'fastest coaling' prize throughout the previous weeks, at Cam Ranh loaded only 300 tons of coal, instead of 900. There was no way that would suffice to take the *Alexander III* on

---

* So impressive was Donald's reportage that the *Daily Telegraph* felt able to claim his forthcoming account of the Battle of Tsushima as an 'eyewitness's story', although it would in fact be written from the tranquil setting of Hong Kong, 1,200 miles to the south.

the longer, safer route to Vladivostok. It was a mistake which seemed to indicate the state of morale within Rozhestvensky's armada as a whole. Once again the awful, choking coal dust was everywhere. Day after day the number of suicides multiplied. Aboard *Oryol* drunk and mutinous crewmen broke open a case of liquor and attacked officers. Morale was hardly helped by the news trickling through of mounting discontent at home, and of the smashing defeat of Kuropatkin's army at Mukden. ('We shall have about as much chance as a game-cock would have in a battle with a vulture,' declared an engineer officer aboard *Oryol* on hearing the dire tidings from Port Arthur.) What, indeed, was the point of driving on into the jaws of death now? The remarkable thing, surely, was that there remained a single ounce of fighting spirit among Rozhestvensky's Pacific squadrons.

Aboard his flagship *Mikasa*, Togo was able to deduce from Donald's two despatches, with reasonable certainty, Rozhestvensky's course, and the timing. In tranquil Japanese waters, he waited anxiously – but with confidence. On 14 May the great combined fleet was reported to have left Cam Ranh Bay, heading north. With no radar, no spotter planes, and radio over only very limited ranges,* Togo had to depend on visual sightings and good intelligence analysis. Once again the elusive Rozhestvensky and his armada seemed to be swallowed up in the vastness of the ocean. Only on 25 May did a report of six Russian auxiliaries, including their colliers, arriving at Shanghai confirm to Togo that the enemy was heading for the Straits of Tsushima. Had it been either of the longer routes to Vladivostok, the La Pérouse Straits between Hokkaido and Sakhalin Islands, or the Tsugaru between Hokkaido and Honshu, Rozhestvensky would have been sure to keep the colliers with him as he sailed eastwards round Japan.

So Togo kept his fleet in waiting, undivided and concentrated, at

---

* In 1905, ship-to-ship radio communication was still in its infancy. The Russians had equipped their latest, *Poltava*-class battleships with the most up-to-date German-designed radio sets. But each weighed up to six tons and, with a fraction of the power of today's mobile telephone, could only communicate – intermittently – over a maximum of forty miles. Togo had equipped his fleet with the latest Marconi wireless sets, using Morse code, but they had limited reliability and a maximum range – on a good day – of fifty miles. Nevertheless Togo depended on them for locating and shadowing the Russian fleet as it sailed up towards Tsushima, thus giving the forthcoming battle the distinction of being the first at sea to be fought with electronic warfare.

the port of Masan, on the southernmost tip of the Korean peninsula. It was a secret base, in a deep and sheltered bay, which Togo had been developing for many months. Apart from a few light forces held back to defend the home ports, the whole of Japan's navy was concentrated there. The cautious Admiral delivered to his ships an uncharacteristically aggressive message on 15 May: 'If your sword is too short take one step forward . . . There is no need to think of defence. A positive attack is the best form of defence . . .' Admiral Hikonojo Kamimura was despatched to watch, and heavily mine, the approaches to Vladivostok, should any of Rozhestvensky's ships break through the Tsushima cordon. Only the battleship *Asahi*, with an impatient Captain Pakenham on board, champing for action, had been temporarily left in the Inland Sea, with damage inflicted at the Battle of the Yellow Sea still being repaired. But 'nothing could be better than the temper of the personnel of the Japanese Navy or the condition of their ships . . .' according to the last pre-battle report from the Royal Navy observers.

For the Russians, the night of 26/27 May (13/14 May on the Russians' Julian calendar) brought just the kind of North Pacific weather that they might have prayed for: thick mist and dense patches of fog. Every hour that it enveloped them brought the fleet another hour closer to Vladivostok and safety. In his Fleet Order No. 294, Rozhestvensky prayed 'that God may strengthen my right hand, and that if I fail to fulfil the oath I have sworn, He may purge my country from shame with my blood'.

He now reorganized his ships into three divisions, the first consisting of the four new *Borodino*-class battleships commanded by himself. Admiral Dimitry von Felkerzam, though mortally sick, commanded the Second Division of the battleships *Oslyabya* (flagship), *Navarin*, *Sissoi Veliky* and the armoured cruiser *Admiral Nakhimov*; while Nebogatov retained his ships as the Third Division. As just one more setback to hit the doomed fleet, the obese Felkerzam died on 26 May; but, in order to maintain morale, Rozhestvensky elected not to inform the fleet. So the Second Division nominally went into battle led by a dead admiral, though the captain of *Oslyabya* in fact became its commander, while Nebogatov had no idea that he was now the squadron's *de facto* second-in-command.

Approaching the Tsushima Straits, just thirty miles across,

Rozhestvensky ordered the vast column to swing round on a more north-easterly course, to north 23 degrees east, for Vladivostok. It was the 'home stretch'. The Russian fleet was now sailing in six separate columns, which, in conditions of severely restricted visibility, made command and control difficult. There were last-minute preparations for battle. Anything that was combustible (excepting the emergency stocks of coal), bedding, hammocks, furniture, was thrown overboard. The guns were sprinkled with holy water, letters written home, and the surgeons prepared for casualties. A welcome tot of vodka was issued to every man. It would not have been very different to last-minute preparations aboard Nelson's *Victory* a hundred years before, with prospects equally terrible for the losing side. That night before the battle, 'Hardly anyone slept; it was too clear we'd be meeting the enemy in full strength ... The orderlies secretly tell the officers that rats have appeared on the accommodation deck,' recorded Flag Captain Clapier de Colongue, Rozhestvensky's handsome and rather effeminate Chief of Staff aboard *Suvorov*.

On the Japanese side, as soon as he realized that the enemy was committed to taking the shorter, Tsushima route, Togo ordered all but the essential minimum of his precious stocks of Welsh coal too to be dumped overboard, to ensure the maximum speed and manoeuvrability of his ships. Together with the excess of weed fouling the hulls of the Russian ships after their 18,000-mile journey, and the weight of their extra coal supplies, this would give Togo at least a knot or more of extra speed over his adversary. On top of this Rozhestvensky's emergency supplies of coal rendered some of his battle-wagons so low in the water as to threaten the operation of his hull-mounted secondary armament in the event of heavy seas.

Suddenly, at 0245 Japanese time, on 27 May, there was a brief clearing in the fog. Through it a Japanese auxiliary cruiser, *Shinano Maru*, observed three lights twinkling on the distant horizon. She closed in to investigate. They were the lights of a Russian hospital ship, *Oryol* (not to be confused with the battleship of the same name). In compliance with the rules of war, the hospital ship continued to display them. Mistaking the *Shinano Maru* for a friendly vessel, she failed to notify the Russian command; instead, obligingly, she signalled *Shinano Maru* the useful information that there were other Russian vessels near by in the fog. *Shinano Maru* then made out the shapes of ten other enemy ships. The cat was out of the bag, the Russian Baltic Fleet discovered. At 0455 Captain Narukawa of the *Shinano Maru* was signalling Togo at his Masan base: 'Enemy is in Square 203.'*

On the Russian side, following this first contact, all was peace and tranquillity – for a few hours. No more Japanese ships were seen. Optimists hoped that, having thrown them off the scent in the fog, the Russian fleet had escaped. Intercepting the Japanese wireless traffic, Rozhestvensky knew better. At 0505 Togo was ordering his whole fleet, of over forty vessels, out into the Straits of Tsushima. He was in the lead, aboard his flagship *Mikasa*, with the ship's band loudly playing the Japanese national anthem on the aft deck. At 0634, the Navy Minister in Tokyo received the following signal: 'the enemy fleet has been sighted. Our fleet will proceed forthwith to sea to attack the enemy and destroy him. Today's weather is fine but waves are high.'

About seven hours later, at 1.40 p.m., the main fleets sighted each other and prepared for battle. At 1.55 p.m. Togo ran up his 'Z-flag', with the simple, Nelsonian message: 'The Empire's fate depends on the result of this battle, let every man do his utmost duty.' The two great fleets were set on parallel courses, heading towards the northeast. Togo with his advantage of speed was clearly aiming to overtake Rozhestvensky. For no very clear reason, Rozhestvensky decided to concentrate his First and Second Divisions into a single battle line, but poor training and signalling confusion led to a chaotic muddle. This was still being sorted out when the Japanese battleships appeared out of the mists, a long line of grey hulls streaming out black smoke. In contrast, the conspicuous bright yellow funnels of Rozhestvensky's battleships may well have helped the Japanese range-finders.

Cutting across the Russian line, with the clear intention of 'crossing the T' in the best tradition of Nelson at Trafalgar, at 1405 Togo ordered his ships to 'turn in sequence', doubling back across the Russian line so as to strike on its weaker flank. It was a breathtakingly bold move, which could be performed only by highly competent seamen. It meant

---

* Well in advance of the battle Togo had gridded the Tsushima area into squares, to help his gunners get precise ranges of enemy vessels and lock on to them. By chance '203' was also the number of the key strategic height dominating Port Arthur, whose capture had defined the fall of the base to Japan.

that for a period of roughly ten minutes each Japanese ship would be turning, pivoting, on precisely the same spot, making them easy, sitting targets for the enemy gunners. But when it was completed, it left the Japanese battleships in a powerful arc able to bring the full weight of their broadsides to bear on the Russian ships, which could deploy only their forward-pointing main armaments. The risk Togo was taking was immense, and had Rozhestvensky been a Makarov it might well have been disastrous. As it was it was his own ship, *Mikasa*, which, in the van, bore the brunt of the opening exchanges of fire. Clearly he was intending to purge any suggestion of the excessive caution he had shown in earlier engagements – such as the first surprise attack of February 1904, and the Battle of the Yellow Sea.

Initially the Russian shooting, at an unusually long range of 9,000 yards, was more accurate than anticipated. The first shots fell only twenty yards astern of *Mikasa*; thereafter it was hit fifteen times in the next five minutes with both six-inch and twelve-inch heavy shells. His staff urged Togo, who had already been wounded by a splinter in the thigh, to leave the exposed bridge for the safety of the armoured conning-tower; but he refused, saying, 'I'm getting on for sixty . . . and this old body of mine is no longer worth caring for.'

A sense of Drake-like coolness was manifest. Aboard *Asama* Captain Yatsushiro amazed his staff by playing the flute until it was time for the batteries to open fire. On *Asahi*, which had now just rejoined the fleet after being repaired, 'Officers gathered round the tobacco tray near the after turret, where an observer found them quite confident of victory, smoking cigars and listening to a gramophone.' Wrote one historian, 'a stranger seeing them would not, I think, have guessed that they were people who this very day were going into battle, a battle in which many perhaps were fated to die . . .'

No one aboard *Asahi* seems to have been cooler than Captain Pakenham RN, Britain's official observer. In the middle of the battle, he ordered a deckchair and sat on the exposed quarterdeck, taking notes 'as though he were aboard a committee boat keeping score at a yacht race'. Always immaculately dressed, almost a dandy, Pakenham with his trim beard and bushy moustache, monocle in one eye and telescope glued to the other, typified almost to the point of caricature a certain kind of Royal Navy officer of the Edwardian era. As a teenaged midshipman, he had been commended for gallantry for rescuing a coxswain who had fallen overboard. During the battle *Asahi* suffered nine hits from heavy shells, which killed eight and wounded twenty-three. Pakenham was hit by a flying human fragment, which he identified as 'the right half of a man's lower jaw, with teeth missing'. His uniform splashed with Japanese blood, Pakenham went briefly below, only to return to his deckchair post clad in an immaculate fresh white uniform. Like the Japanese C-in-C, Pakenham seemed to be immune to any sense of personal danger. His notes taken on board *Asahi* provide the best account of the Battle of Tsushima as seen from the Japanese point of view, before the fog of war and the smoke of battle confused everything. As well as publicizing the Japanese victory in Royal Navy circles, his reports confirmed the superiority of Togo's training and tactics. His observation of the dominance of big guns led, in part, to the adoption of the all-big-gun battleship in the Royal Navy, beginning with the 1906 *Dreadnought*, which under the aegis of Admiral Jackie Fisher was to become the backbone of the new, reformed Royal Navy by 1914.[*]

Based on Pakenham's reports, the Royal Navy's *Official Report* weighed up the moral fibre of the two opposing fleets as the battle began:

> on the one side were crews of veterans who had already shown magnificent fighting qualities, who had been handling the huge mass of material in their charge for over a year under war conditions, who were under the command of an admiral in whom they reposed the utmost confidence. On the other side were collections of men hastily assembled, who were deficient in gunnery training ... the Russian crews were half beaten before a shot was fired ...

Pakenham recorded the anxious moments when Togo first crossed the Russians' 'T', as his ships performed their tricky 'turns in sequence': 'It was possible to see down the length of the Russian Lines. In the

---

[*] In 1916 Pakenham, now promoted rear-admiral, under the dashing David Beatty, led the 2nd Battle Cruiser Squadron during the Battle of Jutland, and from 1917 on replaced Beatty as Commander-in-Chief of the Battle Cruiser Fleet. Retiring as Admiral Sir William Christopher Pakenham, KCB, KCMG, KCVO, a member of the Longford clan, he died unmarried. For his work during the Russo-Japanese War he was decorated by both the British government and the Emperor of Japan (Order of the Rising Sun (Second Class)).

right column the four biggest battleships loomed enormous, dwarfing all others into insignificance . . . It was not easy to realise that the battleships of Japan were probably producing at least equal effect on the minds of the Russians.' As the range closed to about 7,000 yards, part of the Russian fire continued to rain down on Togo's *Mikasa*, six-inch shells as well as the monster twelve-inch projectiles, but the main weight of shell-fire continued to converge 'on the Japanese turning point, and it is interesting to watch each ship approach and run through this warm spot, a feat all were lucky enough to accomplish without receiving serious injury . . .' The 'luck', judged Pakenham, was aided by the 'absolute confusion' of Rozhestvensky's battle line. Two Japanese cruisers were hit (surprisingly by Nebogatov's despised 'flat-irons') and forced to retire. Aboard *Mikasa* a twelve-inch gun turret was put out of action by an ammunition explosion caused by unpredictable *shimose* charges.

Nevertheless, with furious swiftness the tide of battle turned. Togo's ships, some capable of turns of speed up to five knots faster than Rozhestvensky's weed-clogged and overloaded ships, made it difficult for the Russians, with their outdated (1880s) Luizhov range-finders, to track them. The Barr & Stroud range-finders, introduced in 1903, a year before the war, were speedier and substantially more accurate. Then the Japanese had the advantage of Krupp armour-plate, and Krupp armour-piercing shells for their vast twelve-inch guns. And, of course, they had Togo. On the other side, as Richard Hough saw it, the battle was to be lost 'by the momentary hesitancy of a tired and wasted Admiral who could not make up his mind, and when he changed it, disregarded the consequences'.

A terrifying storm of steel and high explosive now poured down on the Russian battleships. Given the confusion and the smoke of battle, not to mention the lack of survivors, much of the blow-by-blow description of the Russian side of the engagement stems from Commander Semenov, aboard Rozhestvensky's flagship *Suvorov*. Many individual acts of great heroism, and cowardice, would go unrecorded. It was *Suvorov* that bore the brunt of the concentrated deluge of shells from Togo's battle line. Such was now the closeness of the two fleets, perhaps less than 5,000 yards apart, that even Togo's secondary, six-inch sponson guns could register. Soon Semenov described himself as 'slipping and sliding in pools of new blood'. One of the first shells exploded with deadly effect in the officers' quarters, starting a fire.

Semenov, veteran of the previous year's Battle of the Yellow Sea, noted, with concern, a kind of 'stupor which seems to come over men, who have never been in action before, when the first shells begin to fall ... The men at the fire mains and hoses stood as if mesmerized, gazing at the smoke and flames, not understanding, apparently, what was happening.' He galvanized them into action, to get the hoses flowing. Then he himself was hit and stunned. 'Shells seemed to be pouring upon us incessantly.' The Japanese shells, equipped with instantaneous fuses and filled with their deadly *shimose* explosive, 'burst as soon as they touched anything ...' Handrails and even funnel guy ropes '... were quite sufficient to detonate a thoroughly efficient air burst ... the splinters caused many casualties. Iron ladders were crumpled up into rings, and guns were literally hurled from their mountings ...' The exploding Japanese shells produced such a high temperature, he claimed, that:

> I actually watched a steel plate catch fire from a burst. Of course the steel did not burn, but the paint on it did. Such almost noncombustible materials as hammocks, and rows of boxes, drenched with water flared up in a moment. At times it was impossible to see anything with glasses, owing to everything being so distorted with the quivering, heated air.

Semenov tried to make his way to the conning-tower where Admiral Rozhestvensky and *Suvorov*'s captain were peering out through a chink between the armour and the roof. He realized they couldn't see what was actually happening aboard the ship, pride of the Russian Navy: 'What havoc! – burning bridges, smouldering debris on the decks – piles of dead bodies. Signalling and judging-distance stations, gun-directing positions, all were destroyed. And astern of us the *Alexander* and *Borodino* were also enveloped in smoke ...'

Men were falling 'faster and faster': 'The officer commanding the fire parties had had both his legs blown off and was carried below ... Over and over again the hoses in use were changed for new ones, but these also were soon torn to ribbons, and the supply became exhausted. Without hoses how could we pump water on to the bridges

75

and spar-deck where the flames raged?' One heavy shell had landed squarely on the ship's hospital, already full of wounded men: 'Between the wrecked tables, stools, broken bottles and different hospital appliances were some dead bodies, and a mass of something, which, with difficulty, I guessed to be the remains of what had once been men.'

The Russian ships nevertheless kept on firing with unflinching courage, that dogged courage of simple Russian servicemen, such as dignifies their history from time immemorial – men knowing that they were doomed, who would yet fight on like heroes. Unsurprisingly, considering their lack of training, their gunners' accuracy was considerably less than Togo's, with observers calculating that the Japanese registered 3.2 hits per hundred shells fired, while the Russians had a success rate of no more than 1.5. Moreover many of their 'hits' were by shells that proved to be duds. After the furious first half-hour it was reckoned that not a single Japanese ship received a hit. At about 1420 hours Togo's ships switched to armour-piercing shells, at increasingly close range, with horrendous results.

Aboard *Suvorov* the Japanese shells had also ignited the overloaded stocks of coal, causing dense smoke. When it cleared Semenov attempted to make his way through the wreckage to see what had happened to the *Suvorov's* after turret, 'but along the upper deck no communication between bow and stern was possible ...' It became evident that 'owing to our steering-gear being out of order, we had turned nearly 16 points'. At this juncture, in the smoke and general confusion of battle, accounts lose their coherence, become disconnected. But with the Admiral's badly battered flagship limping out of line, all notions of the brave Russian fleet as a fighting unit began to dissolve. The Japanese account recorded that *Suvorov* was:

> so battered that scarcely anyone would have taken her for a ship, and yet, even in this pitiful condition, like the flag-ship she was, she never ceased to fire as much as possible with such of her guns as were serviceable ... Her upper part was riddled with holes, and she was entirely enveloped in smoke. Her masts had fallen and her funnels came down one after the other. She was unable to steer, and her fires increased in density every moment.

Nevertheless she kept on firing with a courage which even drew admiration from the enemy seamen. It was at this point that Rozhestvensky himself was hit, several times, but most seriously with a shell splinter in his skull. He was 'carried into the turret and seated on a box, but he still had sufficient strength at once to ask why the turret was not firing ... none of us knew how badly he was wounded because, to all enquiries when he was hit, he angrily replied that it was only a trifle'.

Meanwhile, 'The engines had ceased to work. The electric light had given out for want of steam; and no one came up from below.' To Pakenham, 'Her condition seemed infinitely deplorable.' Aboard *Suvorov* it was all too clear that the great ship was dying, and the Admiral had to be evacuated by torpedo boat. Half-a-dozen seamen 'got hold of some half-burned hammocks and rope from the upper battery, and with these had begun to lash together something in the shape of a raft on which to lower the Admiral into the water ...' Rozhestvensky was then 'almost thrown on board the torpedo boat, at a moment when she rose on a wave and swung towards us.' The Admiral was then transferred to the destroyer *Buiny*.

To all intents and purposes *Suvorov* was abandoned. Yet one brave young midshipman, a German named Werner von Kursel, a humorous and eccentrically wild youth much loved in the officers' mess, insisted on manning a small-calibre gun on the stern, the battleship's last serviceable weapon, to the very end, endeavouring to keep at bay Togo's jackal-like torpedo boats: a midshipman left in charge of the Russian flagship.

The battleship *Oslyabya* had now been hit by heavy shells right on the waterline. 'Three shells, one after the other, almost in the same identical spot,' Semenov was told by an officer who survived. 'Imagine it! All of them in the same place! All on the waterline under the forward turret! Not a hole – but a regular gateway!' Her ten-inch guns were outranged by the twelve-inch weapons of Togo's fleet. The lethal Japanese shells struck her just fifteen minutes into the engagement, and immediately caused serious flooding. Forward motion exacerbated the flooding, so, forced to cut speed, she too had to fall out of line, while listing dangerously to port. Ill-advisedly the commander, Captain Ber, gave orders to flood the starboard magazine in an effort to correct the list. But this just added to the forward weight, with mortal consequences for the ship's stability. Suddenly she rolled over to port, until her funnels were touching the sea, and at about 1515 Captain Ber gave the order 'Abandon ship!' *Oslyabya* sank within minutes, her propeller still turning. Captain Ber and 470 crew members out of her complement of 770 went down with her.

Oslyabya was the first modern steel battleship to be sunk entirely by naval gunfire. It may well be that the speed of her capsizing had something to do with her bulbous 'tumblehome' hull* design, grossly overloaded as she was with coal stocks. The sight of her rolling over was deeply demoralizing to those in the rest of the fleet who witnessed it. For Pakenham, it presented 'a terrible spectacle'. The Russian fleet now lost any semblance of order: its line gone, each battleship now isolated from her sister ships. To some observers it seemed like a 'battle of shadows', with the Russian ships losing sight of each other altogether in the heavy seas and smoke. Similarly an overall account of the battle loses all cohesion as the engagement broke down into individual battles, often of great heroism on the Russian side. Even Pakenham from his strategically placed deckchair found it impossible to follow events. On *Mikasa* one twelve-inch gun turret had been knocked out, apparently by an internal ammunition explosion.

Togo now regrouped his battle fleet, and moved in for the kill, to a range of less than 5,000 yards. There was a two-hour pause in the battle while the Japanese Admiral was reordering his battle line. Then the Japanese battleships concentrated their fire on *Borodino* and *Alexander III*, both completed, like their sister ship *Suvorov*, between August 1903 and September 1904, making them the most modern ships in any fleet. But all the *Borodino* class suffered from instability because of a high centre of gravity, which was exacerbated by overloading. They were inherently in danger of capsizing. Some naval architects regarded them, in retrospect, as being among the worst battleships ever built. At Tshushima, already listing from their wounds, the two ships could only return feeble fire. At 1830 hours, a Japanese salvo hit *Alexander III*, which veered sharply to port and then abruptly keeled over. Half an hour later, she sank; from her 825-man crew there was not one survivor.

As twilight set in and light began to fail, Togo decided to call off

---

* Following the lessons of Tsushima, navies would discontinue use of tumblehome hulls.

the gunnery duel and pursue Rozhestvensky's crippled fleet with his plentiful torpedo boats. They circled like prairie wolves bringing down a great buffalo, scurrying about at high speed, with all the precision of months of hard training for this one engagement. If one can compare anything so barbaric and murderous as the destruction of a great fleet to a musical masterpiece, it was as if Togo were conducting a superbly rehearsed symphony, with all its components coming together in a thunderously magnificent last movement. Four boats from his Eleventh Torpedo Boat Division closed in on the blazing and abandoned *Suvorov*, where the heroic Midshipman von Kursel kept up his solitary fire from the one surviving small-calibre gun, attempting to deter the lupine torpedo boats. At about 1920, Rozhestvensky's brave flagship, hit by numerous torpedoes, finally capsized 'in a thick cloud of yellow smoke'. In all this mayhem, what deck officers like Semenov and Pakenham could not witness were the horrors down below on the stricken ships, as stokers and engineers were scalded to death by superheated steam from burst boilers, or – if they escaped that fate – trapped below in rising waters. From gallant *Suvorov* there were only twenty survivors. Kursel was not one of them.[*]

Borodino too was burning fiercely, but was managing to drive off the torpedo boats with her 75mm and 47mm quick-firing guns. At 1928 hours, however, as Togo signalled his battleships to cease fire with their main armaments, one of his commanders, Captain Matsumoto Kazu of British-built *Fuji* (one of the older Japanese battleships, commissioned in 1897), decided to loose off a last salvo that had already been loaded into his twelve-inch guns. That lucky parting shot struck *Borodino* just below a six-inch gun, detonating the ready ammunition. Fire spread rapidly to adjacent magazines, which exploded with monstrous force, blowing out the hull. According to Pakenham aboard the *Asahi*, it produced 'the sensation of the day . . . an immense column of smoke, ruddied on its underside by the glare of the explosion and from the fire abaft, spurted to the height of her funnel tops'. There was left only 'a dense cloud that brooded over the place she had occupied'. Hidden

---

[*] *Suvorov* had had a short existence, serving for less than nine months within the Imperial Russian Navy before being sunk at Tsushima. Completed only at the beginning of September 1904, she had had virtually no proper sea trials. As a result, her crew was newly assigned and largely inexperienced.

beneath the cloud *Borodino* swiftly capsized, the third modern Russian battleship to do so that day. There was only one survivor: Seaman 1st Class Semyon Yushin, rescued from the sea twelve hours later.

In one short afternoon the Second Pacific Squadron had lost four of the world's most up-to-date and powerful battleships. Rozhestvensky's achievement, his epic, record-breaking voyage, bringing a fleet of fifty ships, with often semi-mutinous crews, halfway round the world, then to fight a major battle, had ended tragically in one of history's worst naval disasters. As a fighting unit it now no longer existed.

But what of its leader, the unfortunate Zinovy Rozhestvensky? Before being transferred to the destroyer *Buiny*, he was last described aboard his flagship as 'sprawled in the disabled six-inch gun turret, his head, wrapped round and round with a blood-stained towel, nodding on his chest'. In the tumultuous seas it was a remarkable feat that such a badly wounded man, his body limp and heavy, could be transferred safely to a tossing small craft, already overladen with 200 survivors from the sunken *Oslyabya*. With a splinter of his skull embedded in his brain, the tough old sea-dog cheated death, drifting in and out of a coma, not ceasing to give orders in his moments of consciousness. He instructed that, with his flag of command, he be transferred to the destroyer, *Bedovy*, one of the few surviving ships with sufficient coal to reach Vladivostok, whither he now ordered it to head. By burning every inch of her wooden fittings, *Bedovy* could make the remarkable speed of twenty-two knots. Nevertheless, on the morning of 28 May, she was overhauled by Japanese destroyers and brought to a standstill.

In a scene more in keeping with Trafalgar, a Japanese officer, Lieutenant Ayiba, leaped aboard *Bedovy*, unsheathing his sword and declaring, 'I am now in command of the ship.' Semenov, the only member of the staff aboard the destroyer who could speak Japanese, explained that the Russian C-in-C was below, but in no condition to be disturbed. Ayiba apparently could not comprehend the extent of his capture: the fleet commander aboard so insignificant a craft! Nevertheless, efficiently and with notable dignity, *Bedovy*, bearing the stricken Rozhestvensky, was towed into the Japanese port of Sasebo, on the morning of 30 May.

Meanwhile, as Togo resupplied and reorganized his battle fleet that night, the action turned to one of flight, pursuit and humiliating round-up of the isolated, disconnected Russian ships which individually were still trying to reach Vladivostok. Safety lay just 300 miles away. The Japanese cruisers, destroyers and torpedo boats took over as the carnage continued. First to fall prey was the second-line battleship *Navarin.** Though she was third from last in the Russian line of battle on the 27th, little is known of *Navarin*'s actions, as there would be few survivors. She was hit late in the day by large-calibre shells, which caused serious flooding and forced the ship to stop for repairs.

Rashly *Navarin* switched on her searchlights to illuminate the attackers savaging her, but this served only to make a better target for the torpedo boats. They may have achieved one or two torpedo hits in the dark. *Navarin* managed to get under way again and damaged one torpedo boat badly enough that she sank later that night. Around 0200 on 28 May, the battleship was attacked again by Togo's Fourth Destroyer Division, which had laid six strings of floating mines ahead of her. Two of these mines struck *Navarin*, which swiftly turned turtle and sank. Three survivors were found alive sixteen hours later. The rest of her crew of 674 officers and seamen went down with their ship.

Next to succumb was *Sissoy Veliky*, a single-class ship planned to be the first of sixteen ocean-going battleships. Sandwiched between the doomed *Navarin* and *Oslyabya*, she survived the daytime artillery duel with Admiral Togo's forces, though badly hit. The crew managed to extinguish the resulting fires and prevented her magazines from exploding, but could not contain the flooding of the ship. During the night the Japanese destroyers scored a torpedo hit, blowing off her rudder. Unable to maintain way, in the morning her engines were shut down, and she was forced to surrender to a Japanese armed merchantman. The abandoned ship sank at 1005 on 28 May. Fifty members of the crew perished.

Meanwhile, unbeknown to the semi-conscious Rozhestvensky, just over the horizon his *de facto* successor in the command, the despised Admiral Nebogatov, was surrendering his even more despised Third Pacific Squadron, together with four more battleships. These

---

* Launched on 24 October 1891, the sixty-fourth anniversary of the Battle of Navarino in the War of Greek Independence, but completed only in 1896.

included the fourth of the five *Borodino* class, *Oryol*.* During the battle of the 27th, as the Japanese fleet concentrated its efforts against the Second Pacific Squadron, so Nebogatov's ships had escaped the fate of Rozhestvensky's battleships that first day. With Rozhestvensky seriously wounded, and most of the Second Pacific Squadron's warships sunk or disabled, command automatically devolved on Nebogatov. With daybreak on the 28th his squadron was still plodding, or limping, towards Vladivostok and safety, their speed sorely limited by boiler breakdowns and battle damage. He was commanding from *Nikolai I*, which, though hit five times the previous day, was otherwise virtually intact. With him was left only *Oryol*, two old coastal defence battleships, *Senyavin* and *Apraxin*, the lightly armoured cruiser *Izumrud* and a miscellany of lesser ships. Another elderly coastal defence battleship, *Admiral Ushakov*, had been left behind in the night but not discovered by Togo's torpedo-boat wolf packs. Acting independently, three cruisers, *Oleg*, *Aurora*† and *Zhemchug* had abandoned any attempt to reach Vladivostok and were instead heading south for the Philippines and interment.

Suddenly, by 0930 hours, Nebogatov realized that he was surrounded by Togo's battle fleet. During the night *Oryol* had managed to repair one of her twelve-inch gun turrets. These were the only two weapons available to Nebogatov that possessed the range to strike the Japanese. So Togo settled down to a long-range gunfight, to sink the Russian survivors without further risk to himself. It was obvious to Nebogatov that the Japanese intended to keep their distance and shell the Russians at leisure; and they had the whole day before them. Realizing that his ships were no match for Togo's, and that the Russian cruiser division under Admiral Oskar Enkvist would not arrive in time to prevent his destruction, at 1034 hours Nebogatov decided to surrender. He declared to his crews, in the knowledge that he might well be shot on returning home, 'You are young, and it is you who will one day retrieve the honour and glory of the Russian Navy. The lives of the two

---

* Of this class, only *Slava* now remained. Completed in June 1905, she was too late to accompany Rozhestvensky to the Pacific.
† *Aurora*, which had been a source of the trouble in the North Sea, would survive through to the First World War, when she allegedly fired the first shot in the 1917 Bolshevik Revolution in St Petersburg. She still sits as a prize exhibit in the Neva.

thousand four hundred men in these ships are more important than mine.'

Nebogatov then ran up the 'XGE' flags: the international signal of surrender. For a while Togo would not accept the appeal to surrender, it was so completely at odds with all the principles of *bushido*, and ruthlessly he continued his bombardment. 'It really was', he recorded, 'the strangest occurrence, and we were astonished, and somewhat disappointed.' Eventually he accepted the surrender, and four of Russia's surviving big-gun battleships sailed into Japanese ports.

The decision was not, however, accepted by all Nebogatov's officers, and Captain Vasily Fersen of the cruiser *Izumrud* disobeyed orders to escape through the Japanese lines. Unable quite to reach Vladivostok, with fuel running out, *Izumrud* was run aground just inside Siberian territory. The battleship *Admiral Ushakov*, having become lost during the night, was unaware of the orders to surrender and was caught by the Japanese the next morning, outgunned and outnumbered. She fought back gallantly, with heavy casualties and reduced to a blazing wreck, until her captain, V.N. Miklouho-Maklay, ordered her to be scuttled. Like so many of her proud companions, she capsized, taking Captain Maklay with her, though 328 of her crew were rescued.

Thus perished the last of the capital ships of the First, Second and Third Russian Pacific Squadrons, and with it any hope of winning or – rather – of not losing the war. In this, history's most decisive of naval battles, Russia had lost all eight battleships which had set out under Rozhestvensky; twenty-one Russian vessels had been sunk, seven captured and a further six disarmed or interned. Nearly 5,000 Russian sailors had been killed, and almost 9,000 captured or interned, many of them wounded. Add to this ships lost at Port Arthur or in the Battle of the Yellow Sea. In consequence the Tsar had lost not just all three squadrons of his Pacific Fleet; to all intents and purposes, he had in fact virtually lost his entire navy. It would never recover from Tsushima. From being, at the beginning of 1904, the world's third strongest fleet, it now became a shaky sixth. And this great victory in the Straits of Tsushima had been achieved at the cost of just three Japanese torpedo boats, 117 dead and 583 wounded.

Because of the bravery they had shown, the survivors of the *Admiral Ushakov* were treated by their captors with special consideration. When the stubby Nebogatov flew his white flag, he was said to have resembled a bent old bearded dwarf; the defeated crews lined up on deck in dirty and ragged uniforms, 'like herds of tired grey sheep calmly awaiting their fate', in the words of one writer. Nebogatov too was received by the victors with samurai courtesy, and he and his officers were permitted to keep their swords. It was a tradition of Japanese chivalry, and humanity, that would die with Togo; certainly it would not be accorded to the defeated foe by the 1940s. The badly wounded Rozhestvensky, now a prisoner of war in a Japanese hospital, was treated with equal courtesy. Still lingering on the brink of consciousness, he remained unaware that Nebogatov had surrendered, and that his remaining ships were flying Japanese flags in the naval basin below. A Russian surgeon succeeded in removing the fragments of skull from his brain, and a few days later as he regained his senses the victor of Tsushima, Admiral Heihachiro Togo himself, came to visit him in hospital.

Togo comforted Rozhestvensky with kindly words. He apologized for the somewhat Spartan conditions in the hospital, and 'the absence of comforts due to such a distinguished patient'. There was no need, he assured the defeated Russian, 'to associate an honourable defeat with shame ... Defeat is a common fate of a soldier. There is nothing to be ashamed of in it. The only question is whether or not we have performed our duty.' Togo praised the courage of Rozhestvensky's men: they had fought 'most gallantly and I admire them all and you in particular. You performed your great task heroically until you were incapacitated. I pay you my highest respects.'

Togo himself seems to have been taken aback by the completeness of his own victory, reflecting in his memoirs how his battleships had taken 'years of labour to design and build, and yet they were only used for half an hour of decisive battle'. Though that might represent some diminution of the facts, that half-hour had certainly been *the* decisive half-hour – in fact, one of the most decisive in all naval history.

Accompanying the Japanese Commander-in-Chief at this remarkable bedside visit to the vanquished Russian Admiral was a young officer, a flag lieutenant called Isoroku Yamamoto. He had been wounded in the battle aboard the cruiser *Nisshin*, losing two fingers on his left hand, whether by enemy shellfire or by breech explosion of one of the ship's own guns was never quite clear. Nor does any record remain of what Yamamoto's thoughts may have been that day; but, given the fame that was to descend on him little more than a generation later, they can well be imagined. Here he was alongside the fallen commander of the navy of the biggest nation on earth now at the feet of this small, gentle-mannered Japanese. How had it come about? A tiny island nation defeating such a monstrous great power, both on land and at sea? Surely there was no limit to what such a nation, manifestly blessed by the gods like Japan, could go on to accomplish.

Rozhestvensky evidently responded with great dignity. In the only press interview he permitted, to a French reporter, he observed, 'During the first half-hour our men fought well.' But then they 'suddenly became demoralized by the terrifying effects of the Japanese fire, and all was then over ... I was literally enveloped in flames ...'

Rozhestvensky made no attempt at self-justification, nor offered any excuses, declining to respond to a savage attack on him in the Russian press by one of his own former officers, Captain Nicolas Klado. On 8 June the Tsar reassuringly telegraphed Rozhestvensky 'heartily' thanking him 'and all the members of your squadron who have loyally fulfilled your duty in battle to Russia and myself'. He wished the wounded Admiral 'a speedy recovery. May God console all of us.' But this was not how Rozhestvensky, or Nebogatov, would be treated on their repatriation home. While still a prisoner of war Nebogatov was dishonourably discharged by the Russian Admiralty. On his return to Russia, he and seventy-seven of his subordinate officers were arrested and taken before a court martial in December 1906.

On 28 August Rozhestvensky was deemed fit enough to leave hospital and begin the long voyage home. On the first leg of the journey, en route to Vladivostok, the Admiral had a foretaste of what might lie ahead for him at home when prisoners of war, being repatriated like him, rioted and broke into his cabin, demanding vodka and threatening 'the man who spilt our blood'. Back in St Petersburg, he was summoned before two courts of inquiry, where he took full blame for the defeat. He was honourably acquitted and retired on a generous pension. At subsequent hearings, however, he insisted on appearing, first as a witness, then alongside the accused. Nebogatov and three ships' captains, including the commander of the destroyer *Bedovy* to which Rozhestvensky had transferred his flag, were sentenced to death by firing squad on 25 December 1906. The sentences, however, were subsequently commuted to ten years in prison by order of Tsar Nicholas. Nebogatov was released from the Peter and Paul fortress in St Petersburg in May 1909 on the occasion of the Tsar's birthday. All the others served long terms of imprisonment.

Rozhestvensky lived another four years, in quiet retirement. There was a bizarre alarum in July 1908, when the Admiralty announced details of a requiem service to be held for him. It was perhaps a final bar in the hymn to the abysmal incompetence of the navy of the Tsar – the man who, with his councillors, really should have stood before the courts. The news was published far and wide in the European press; like Mark Twain on a similar occasion ('The report of my death was an exaggeration'), Rozhestvensky took some pleasure in retorting, 'You mustn't kill me off before my time.' He lived peaceably for another six months, mercifully spared the horrors of 1914, of which Tsushima and the whole Russo-Japanese War had been but a prelude

In the absence of radio, let alone television, news of the full extent of the catastrophe at Tsushima was slow to filter through to Russian centres of population. On 30 May 1905 a large, expectant crowd assembled on the quay at Vladivostok. The local press had led them to believe in a great victory; and rumours ran round relating the death of Admiral Togo and the destruction of his fleet. Then later there crept in three surviving Russian vessels, destroyers *Bravy* and *Grozny*, each of 350 tons only, and *Almaz*, described as a yacht converted into a light cruiser. They were all that was left of Rozhestvensky's proud armada. With them their crews brought horrifying tales of what had really happened: of blazing and shattered capital ships, turning turtle, of seas full of drowning Russian sailors, and a gravely wounded C-in-C taken into captivity.

When the full scale of the disaster reached European Russia, the streets burst forth once more into revolt, but this time with more ominous preparation than Bloody Sunday the previous winter. On 27 June the famous mutiny of the battleship *Potemkin* took place at Odessa – nominally over rotten meat, but greatly inflamed by the news of Tsushima. Seven officers, including the captain, were killed; *Potemkin* bombarded Odessa, and then sought asylum in Romania. Before it was quelled the mutiny had spread to other units in the Russian Black Sea

Fleet, now the only viable naval unit left to the Tsar. The standard of revolution was now truly raised, in what was to be a kind of dummy run for 1917, though the embers would – momentarily – appear to die down as Russia entered into a brief new era of remarkable, perhaps inexplicable, prosperity on the very eve of the Great War.

CHAPTER SIX

PEACE

After Tsushima, and coupled with Kuropatkin's defeat at Mukden, the time had clearly come to give peace a chance. The Russians had lost everything, but the Japanese also were almost at the end of their tether. Their armies in Manchuria were down to their last reserves, while Russian reinforcements still kept funnelling in down the Trans-Sib. At sea Togo had all but run out of ammunition, as well as stocks of good Welsh coal. The bores of his big guns were worn out and in need of replacement, which the Japanese arms industry could not provide. More dangerously, such had been the cost of fifteen months of all-out war that Japan's economy was tottering. Had it gone on much longer, the government would have had to give up and sue for peace on unfavourable terms. The country was simply exhausted, though none of this could be gleaned from the singularly uninformative and rigorously controlled Japanese press. In contrast, the immensity of the Russian landmass, and its vast population, could swallow its losses – at least superficially, and for a while. Even the meddlesome Kaiser was fearful that matters were getting out of hand.

A peacemaker was needed, a kind of honest broker, like Bismarck. Into the breech stepped the substantial figure of Theodore Roosevelt, twenty-sixth President of the United States who, at forty-two years old when he assumed office, was the youngest ever occupant of the White House. Roosevelt and his nation would not be thanked by the Japanese for their intervention.

Though a personality not prominently associated with works of peace on the international scene, 'Teddy' Roosevelt – 'Bull Moose', colonel of the Rough Riders who had captured Cuba's San Juan Hill during the Spanish–American War – threw himself into the process with his usual ebullience. Born a puny child, his early years dogged by chronic asthma, which forced him to sleep propped up in an armchair,

'TR' had turned himself, by sheer willpower as much as anything else, into the supreme man of action. Naturalist, explorer, big-game hunter, rancher, amateur boxer (which had recently cost him the sight of one eye), author and soldier, he was also a serious thinker. His book *The Naval War of 1812*, published at the age of twenty-four, established a professional reputation as a serious historian; and, a voracious reader, he thought deeply about history. TR also wrote numerous other books on hunting, the outdoors and current political issues, as well as frontier history. The inventor, and practitioner, of the expression 'Speak softly and carry a big stick',* Roosevelt once bellicosely remarked: 'I should welcome almost any war, for I think this country needs one.' He was the force behind the completion of the Panama Canal, and (in 1907) sent America's Great White Fleet on a world tour to demonstrate American power. He believed strongly that the doctrine of America's Manifest Destiny should now also be extended widely into the Pacific.

TR was undoubtedly one of the most remarkable, if not one of the greatest, men ever to occupy the White House. Yet as an international negotiator he was an unknown quantity. Inside the elaborate French Second-Empire-style buildings of the old State Department Building, with its black-and-white-tiled corridors (now the Eisenhower Executive Offices of the White House) he had a Secretary of State, the quiet and gentle John Hay. But Hay was quietly dying and happy to hand over control to the President. TR greeted this opportunity with characteristic enthusiasm, uniquely taking sole charge of US foreign policy.

For ten months Roosevelt had little doubt that Japan would win the war against the bullying Bear, an outcome he preferred. Following Togo's victory, somewhat undiplomatically he had congratulated his friend and fellow Harvardian Baron Kentaro Kaneko on 31 May 1905:† 'Every Japanese, but perhaps above all every Japanese naval man,

---

* Roosevelt first used the phrase in a speech at the Minnesota State Fair on 2 September 1901, twelve days before the assassination of President William McKinley, which thrust him into the presidency. Roosevelt liked to describe his style of foreign policy as 'the exercise of intelligent forethought and of decisive action sufficiently far in advance of any likely crisis'.
† Kaneko, the staunchly pro-American Minister of Justice, had been sent as special envoy from Japan to enlist American help in bringing the war to a speedy conclusion, and immediately made contact with his fellow Harvard alumnus Teddy Roosevelt. As he sailed from Japan he wrote in a poem: 'Bravely I head to my faraway former playground . . .' (Kaneko would be one of the few senior statesmen in Japan to speak out strongly against war with the United States as late as 1941; he died a few months after Pearl Harbor.)

must feel as if he was treading on air today.' Shortly after Roosevelt's inauguration in March 1905, Mukden had fallen with terrible losses on both sides, and with Marshal Oyama urging on his government the need for an early peace. At the same time Roosevelt began dropping subtle hints to the warring parties that the United States might be willing to offer 'helpful offices' in the quest for an end to the war. But any formal request that it do so would have to come from them. He kept his hand closely concealed. Britain and all the European powers, Roosevelt felt, had their own special agendas that were contingent on the outcome of the war. Simultaneously there was a looming crisis between France and the Kaiser over Morocco. TR then took off to hunt dozy black bears in the remotest corner of the Colorado Rockies, leaving in charge his close and trusted associate the Secretary for War, the portly William H. Taft. 'Camp Roosevelt' was cut off from the nearest telegraph office by thirty miles of snowdrifts and slush. There he awaited developments. Metternich could not have played it better.

Late on the evening of 25 April 1905, by which time Russia's Admiral Rozhestvensky was reaching the end of his remarkable 18,000-mile journey, and was but a month away from the *Götterdämmerung* at Tsushima, Roosevelt received a coded message from Taft. Quoting a message from the Japanese Foreign Minister, Baron Jutaro Komura, to his Ambassador in Washington, Kogoro Takahira, it contained a clear indication that Japan was now 'anxious to effect peace through you'. When he received it, the President had shot his third black bear (noting that it weighed about as much as the well-favoured Taft; but did he, one wonders, also have thoughts of the despotic Russian Bear?). Roosevelt was just recovering from a bad bout of recrudescent malaria. Snowed in at Camp Roosevelt he spent his convalescence reading. For relaxation, he turned to Pierre de La Gorce's *Histoire du Second Empire* (all seven volumes, which he had brought along with him to the Rockies), with his favourite hunt terrier, Skip, snuggling for warmth on his lap. Meanwhile the Russians were still sulking, the fierce Tsaritsa Alexandra vetoing any weakness being shown by her husband. Crossly TR wrote to Hay: 'The Tsar is a preposterous little creature ... unable to make war, and he is now unable to make peace.' In the forthcoming collision at sea, though Rozhestvensky was clearly superior in numbers, Roosevelt predicted with clarity of vision, 'my own belief is that

Japanese superiority in morale and training will more than offset this'.

On 6 May, the weather at last enabled the President, his dogs and his huntsmen, to come down from the Rockies. When news of Tsushima came in, even he was stunned by the completeness of Togo's victory. He loathed the Tsarist regime, but his sympathy for ordinary Russians and their culture made Russia much more congenial to him than Japan. What he could never understand about the Russian, however 'is the way he will lie when he knows perfectly well that you know he is lying' – surely a paradox which has perplexed negotiators dealing with Russia throughout the ages. The threat of revolution in Russia that followed Tsushima imparted to Roosevelt an extra sense of urgency. He pushed both his newly appointed Ambassador to St Petersburg (and another old Harvard friend), George von Lengerke Meyer, and the Russian Ambassador in Washington, Count de Cassini,* to apply more pressure on the Tsar, calling on Cassini to convey 'his frank opinion that the war was "absolutely hopeless for Russia"'.

It was the eve of the Tsaritsa's birthday, and therefore the Emperor of All the Russias was incommunicado. Nevertheless, Meyer persisted and went out to Tsarskoe Selo, where he read to the Tsar Roosevelt's grim forebodings of disaster, if peace could not speedily be concluded. Meyer could hear the cheerful sounds of Romanov children playing somewhere upstairs. Skilfully he had kept up Roosevelt's pretence that no prior initiative had come from Tokyo. Finally, and at last, Nicholas II acquiesced, with the proviso that it 'be absolutely secret as to my decision, should Japan decline . . .'

It was not until 10 June, by which time both belligerents (Japan being the first by two days) had accepted Roosevelt's formal 'invitation', that word was released to the world. The press was amazed, lauding Roosevelt's 'great tact, great foresight, and finesse'; the London *Morning Post* declared that 'as a diplomatist Mr. Roosevelt is now entitled to take high rank'. Far from waiting to be garlanded with laurels, however, the President had once again disappeared into the boondocks. This time it was to a dacha on the Rapidan in Virginia, scene of Civil War

---

* Marquis de Capuzzuchi di Bologna, Count de Cassini, was Russian of Italian lineage and born in Trieste, where his father was Russian Consul. When the Marquis went to Russia, he fulfilled a number of diplomatic missions for the Tsar. His grandson would be Oleg Cassini, the famous New York couturier.

fighting. There he fried eggs and steak for breakfast for himself and his entourage, working off the effects by axing down some trees. For ten days he kept, uncharacteristically, absolutely dumb. The correspondent of *The Times* of London complained that even the State Department didn't know what was going on. The British Ambassador, Sir Mortimer Durand, was one of the few whom TR was keeping in the picture, perhaps surprisingly considering that he rated Sir Mortimer's intelligence as being of 'about eight guinea-pig power'.* Britain nevertheless was one of the top players on the international scene. Durand faithfully passed on his information to the British Foreign Secretary, Lord Lansdowne, an astute statesman who had been instrumental in forging the Anglo-Japanese alliance of 1902, as well as the Entente Cordiale with France in 1904. The wheels of diplomacy started to turn, given extra impetus in Russia by the shocking news of the mutiny of the Black Sea battleship *Potemkin*.

Roosevelt's ailing Secretary of State, John Hay, died, leaving TR entirely on his own in the tricky world of international diplomacy. Finally the lock tumblers began to fall into place, with both combatants responding to Roosevelt's cajoling and bullying. The President wanted the negotiations to take place in the United States, under his aegis. But Washington DC, in summer, before the age of the air conditioner, was out of the question, so he chose the small New Hampshire town of Portsmouth.

To Portsmouth the Russians sent Sergey Witte, generally regarded as their ablest political leader and a staunch opponent of the war, who had been the Tsar's Minister of Finance. It was a curious choice, in that Witte was detested by both the Tsar and the Tsaritsa, but it proved to be a brilliant one for Russia. Another Russian of German origin, he was considered by the Court to be vulgar, cynical, arrogant, boastful and totally lacking in the modern-day quality of charisma. But on arrival in the United States he set out shamelessly to woo American public opinion, ostentatiously flattering Roosevelt.

Alongside the oppressive, self-confident bulk of Witte (he was almost six foot six, and wide in proportion – so wide in fact that he

* TR found the Ambassador a flabby walking companion, his inability to keep pace shinning up obstacles in Washington's Rock Creek Park a harbinger perhaps of Britain's declining powers.

could not easily fit into a New Hampshire bathtub), the Japanese representative Baron Komura cut an insignificant figure. With his droopy black moustache, he somehow appears in photographs as a defeated figure, while Ambassador Takahira, top-hat in hand, looks like a deferential tradesman, or a family retainer who had just been given the sack. Neither exactly conveyed the image of delegates from a victorious nation. But there were also extenuating reasons for the gloomy faces of the Japanese delegates: Takahira had just learned that, chronologically, the Japanese were recorded as having sued for peace two days ahead of the defeated enemy. This would signify a serious loss of face to report back to the Emperor.

Komura became increasingly glum as reports were arriving that the Russians were sending four fresh divisions to Manchuria; a winter campaign might have to be faced there. But, at home, all that the people could see, fed by a blinkered press, was the vision of Togo's Nelsonian victory at Tsushima. Where were its fruits?

The Russians agreed that Japan should regain embattled Port Arthur, but on lease only; they would recognize Japanese predominance in Korea, would withdraw from Manchuria and transfer to Japan the southern portions of the Manchurian feeder lines to the Trans-Siberian Railway. But they resolutely rejected Japanese demands for any financial indemnity ('not one kopeck', insisted the Tsar), or for the surrender of the northernmost island in the Japanese archipelago, the bleak territory of Sakhalin, with its close proximity to the Siberian coast. These were demands which Tokyo had regarded as paramount. At least twice it looked as if the negotiations were going to collapse, with Witte urging the Tsar to break them off. By the weekend of 25 August rumours ran round Portsmouth that the Russians were checking out of their hotel. That same weekend Roosevelt shocked his countrymen by taking off to dive to the floor of Long Island Sound, in a risky new-fangled submarine suitably named *Plunger*. It seemed symbolic of the state of affairs at Portsmouth; but TR refused to accept defeat. Twice he intervened with a personal appeal to the Tsar. He confided to his son Kermit at the time that 'The Japanese ask too much but the Russians are ten times worse ...'

At the eleventh hour, however, on Tuesday 29 August, the Portsmouth Conference ended. Witte placed a sheet of paper on the table with Russia's final offer. Japan could have half of Sakhalin, but no indemnity. Tokyo could perhaps have been offered better terms a week previously. Reluctantly but impassively, Komura accepted. The war was over, and a peace treaty would be formally signed on 5 September.

The Japanese delegates went home in a sombre and anxious mood. Witte was credited with having negotiated brilliantly, as Russia lost little in the final settlement. For his efforts, Witte was made a count.* Yet the *de facto* loss of the war would speed the beginning of the end of Imperial Russia. Mutiny and revolt were breaking out everywhere, fed by anger and resentment among the repatriated troops at the excessive bottlenecks on the Trans-Siberian Railway, such as were causing months, not just weeks, of delay on their way home. At one point mutinous troops and strikers actually controlled the railway, until a trainload of regular troops was sent out to restore order with the usual arrests, hangings and shootings. Historians subsequently wondered whether, had Russia decided to fight on, and had it won a semblance of victory in Manchuria, revolution in 1917 might yet have been staved off. By August 1905, against a Japan whose ground forces (and finances) were on the ropes, the Russians had assembled a new army already in Manchuria exceeding a million, and were in every way better prepared for action than they ever had been before.

If there was an overall winner, it was clearly President Roosevelt. From all sides came admiration for his cool and level-headed achievement in imposing peace on the two angry combatants. His friend the historian and journalist Henry Adams praised him as 'the best herder of Emperors since Napoleon'. Even the Tsar and Kaiser Wilhelm II applauded and thanked him. The Mikado was more enigmatically formal in his congratulations. The following year TR would, most justly, be awarded the Nobel Peace Prize, aged only forty-seven, and one of only three sitting Presidents to be so honoured;† he promptly gave the award money away to a charity – which he could ill afford to do. He could even permit himself to indulge in a modicum of self-

---

* Just before the outbreak of the First World War, Witte urged that Russia stay out of the conflict. His warnings went disregarded.

† In 2001, Roosevelt was posthumously awarded the Medal of Honor. He was the first and, to date, the only President of the United States to be awarded America's highest military honour, and the only person in history to receive both his nation's highest honour for military valour and the world's foremost prize for peace.

congratulation: 'It's a mighty good thing for Russia ... and a mighty good thing for Japan ... and a mighty good thing for *me* too!'

It would not however be enough to bring him back to the White House in 1912, at a time when the Western world could well have done with his peacemaking abilities.

TR seems to have sensed the dangers ahead. As the Portsmouth Conference had progressed, so his enthusiasm for Japan had waned. To his good friend Cecil Spring Rice, the British diplomatist whom he had wanted to see as ambassador in Washington in place of the mutton-headed Sir Mortimer Durand (which he became in due course), he wrote an extraordinarily perceptive and prescient letter:

> I am not sure that the Japanese people draw any distinctions between the Russians and other foreigners, including ourselves. I have no doubt that they include all white men as being people who, as a whole, they dislike, and whose past arrogance they resent; and doubtless they believe their own yellow civilisation to be better ... No one can foretell [Japan's] future attitude. We must, therefore, play our hand alone ... Germany and France for their own reasons are anxious to propitiate Russia, and of course care nothing whatever for our interests. England is inclined to be friendly to us and is inclined to support Japan against Russia, but she is pretty flabby and I am afraid to trust either the far sightedness or the tenacity of purpose of her statesmen; or indeed of her people.

Eight years earlier, addressing the US Navy War College, he had posed the hypothetical question: 'Japan makes demands on Hawaiian Islands. This country intervenes. What force will be necessary to uphold the intervention and how should it be employed?' He continued:

> In a dozen years the English, Americans and Germans, who now dread one another as rivals in the trade of the Pacific, will have each to dread the Japanese more than they do any other nation ... I believe that Japan will take its place as a great civilized power of a formidable type, and with motives and ways of thought which are not quite those of the powers of our own race. My own policy is perfectly simple, though I have not the slightest idea whether I can get my own country to follow it. I wish to see the United States treat the Japanese in a

spirit of all possible courtesy and generosity and justice ... If we show that we regard the Japanese as an inferior and alien race, and try to treat them as we have treated the Chinese; and if at the same time we fail to keep our navy at the highest point of efficiency and size – then we shall invite disaster.

As one historic consequence of Portsmouth, and of TR's intervention, henceforth the United States, having previously been no more than a bit-actor in the Pacific area, now became a major player. Critics would see it as the 'New American Imperialism'.

Only the victors, the Japanese delegates Komura and Takahira, left Portsmouth unhappy and fearful. Their fears were swiftly realized. At home there was angry and unprecedented reaction to the terms of the treaty. Once again, as ten years previously, many Japanese felt that they had been deprived of their rightful spoils, and by connivance between the Western powers. Such was the rigidity of Japanese censorship that, in February 1904, the Japanese had not even been informed of the outbreak of war until the evening of the following day.

Consequently, coming in on international wires, the news of the terms of the Portsmouth Treaty provoked a correspondingly violent reaction – in temperatures of 96°F (35°C). There was a mass anti-peace rally in Hibiya Park in Tokyo, and after some fiery speeches participants marched towards the Imperial Palace. Swords were drawn and the police overwhelmed. By the time order was restored the following night, seventeen people had died. Dozens of police stations had been burned down, together with many churches, newspaper offices and even trams. Over four hundred policemen and forty firemen and soldiers had been injured before martial law, and heavy rain, brought an end to the riots that were unprecedented in orderly Japan. The riots also led, a short while later, to the collapse of Taro Katsura's government on 7 January 1906. A new milestone had been established in Japan's relations with the US, and with the Western world as a whole. Nevertheless, two years later – through the door opened at Portsmouth – Japan annexed Korea, the dream of expansionist Hideyoshi all those centuries earlier.

Following the Portsmouth Treaty, aboard the ships of the Imperial

Japanese Navy in particular, there was angry grumbling at what was construed to be a diplomatic surrender. The shock of the riots was compounded a few days later by a tragic disaster which overtook Togo's valiant flagship *Mikasa*, three-and-a-half months after the guns had fallen silent at Tsushima. Anchored safely in Sasebo, she was blasted by an immense explosion which erupted in the after magazine. She sank in shallow water, together with 339 of her crew, nearly three times the fleet's total loss at Tsushima.* The exact cause of the explosion remains a mystery. In some respects it resembled that of the USS *Maine* in February 1898, which provided a catalyst for the Spanish–American War. There were immediate suspicions that the explosion on the *Mikasa* was an act of sabotage, in protest against the Portsmouth terms. Much more likely, however, was either crew carelessness or spontaneous combustion of decomposing nitrocellulose propellant.

Admiral Togo narrowly missed going down with his ship, having left the *Mikasa* only a few hours previously. Responding in kind to the chivalrousness with which he had been treated when lying wounded in hospital in Japan, Rozhestvensky sent Togo a telegram of condolence. For Japan it was a blessing that the disaster had not happened during the war; without Togo, the consequence for Japanese morale would have been at least as disastrous as the loss of Vice-Admiral Stepan Makarov had been for the Russians. From the hour of Tsushima, Togo had become the subject of hero-worship, amounting almost to semi-deification in Japan, where he would be lauded as 'the Nelson of the East'; for all his innate modesty, it was a title that delighted him. Honours were showered upon him, across the globe, including the Order of Merit awarded (in 1906) by King Edward VII. In Japan he collected such flowery decorations as the Collar of the Supreme Order of the Chrysanthemum, an honour held only by Emperor Hirohito and another royal prince, and the Order of the Golden Kite (1st class). Sparked by Japanese victories, in Calcutta a nationalist-minded poet, known as 'the Kipling of Bengal', composed these lines:

> Japan! Thy magnanimity like wild fire spread,
> The proudest European Powers thee now dread,

---

* Raised from the seabed the following year, *Mikasa* became a hallowed shrine, surviving the Second World War and now set in a magnificent park, adjacent to a statue of Togo.

Thou amazed all, all nations, thee the world adores,
Magnanimous Japan! thy praise like a torrent pours!

When he stepped down from command, very quietly as was his wont, Togo gave a pointed farewell address, larded with parallels to Nelson and Trafalgar. He ended with an admonitory glance to the future: 'The ancients well said: "Tighten your helmet strings in the hour of victory."'

The hero-admiral lived on into the 1930s, taking no part in politics except to register his objection to the discriminatory London Naval Treaty. Nevertheless, the myth of Japanese invincibility, which had grown up around him, would lie at the heart of the spiralling new militarism. On his death in 1934 at the age of eighty-six, Togo was accorded a state funeral with all honours. A seven-stanza poem of adoration on his death extolled him thus:

You are the treasure of Japan
The glory of the world
The embodiment of *bushido*
And the flower of the Far East.

Very different was the fate of Marshal Nogi, Togo's fellow victor in the ground conquest of Port Arthur and, later, Manchuria. He had been deeply shocked by the losses that troops under him had suffered in the prolonged assault on Port Arthur: some 56,000 dead, including his two sons. These weighed him down for the rest of his life. At the war's end he expressed the depth of his feeling in a poem:

As a leader of the Imperial Army, I took a million soldiers hostage.
The battle resulted in a mountain of dead bodies.
I am so ashamed of facing their old fathers.
A song of triumph? But how many men can return home?

After the Emperor had denied him permission to commit *seppuku* in atonement for his shame, Nogi spent the remainder of his life, and most of his personal fortune, on hospitals for wounded soldiers and on memorial monuments erected around the country to commemorate those killed during the Russo-Japanese War. On the day of Emperor Meiji's death in September 1912, Nogi committed ritual suicide. A moment before, his wife pierced her throat with a short sword, the traditional way of suicide for a woman of high birth. As a reminder of the old Japanese samurai tradition, Nogi's *seppuku* immediately created a sensation, and had a profound impact on contemporary writers. For the wider Japanese public, Nogi became a symbol of loyalty and sacrifice, and was sanctified as a 'war god', a *kami* – a mystical hero of a different order from Togo, but a mystical hero nevertheless.

In Japan, Togo's acceptance that he was 'the reincarnation of Horatio Nelson' was to become the root of fatal self-delusion as nationalism and militarism took hold in the 1920s and 1930s. A kind of mystical messianism regarded the low-loss victory of Tsushima 1905 as glorifying the 'new' Japan, where the national spirit, coupled with an illusion of invincibility at sea, encouraged leaders of both navy and army to contemplate expansion to the Asian mainland and the Pacific islands. Was there any foe divine Japan could not vanquish? It was to become a suicidally dangerous mythology, as lethal to Japan as Nogi's *seppuku* had been: a fateful display of hubris.

PART TWO

NOMONHAN, 1939

CHAPTER SEVEN

JAPAN GOES SOUR

After the laboriously concluded Treaty of Portsmouth, Imperial Japan launched itself into the new century laden with battle honours, on land as at sea, but also with a bitter sense of deprivation, of denial of its proper place in the sun, for which it had fought so hard. It had few real friends, but was brimming over with a hubris that would lead it to a fatal conclusion at Hiroshima four decades later. The *hara-kiris* of Marshal Nogi and his wife contained within them a dark omen. Already by the end of 1905 the world had become a much more dangerous place than it had been at the beginning of the previous year.

The peace which President Teddy Roosevelt had so triumphantly concluded at Portsmouth, New Hampshire, in 1905 had provoked bloody riots in Japan, with crowds chanting 'Don't stop the war!', revealing a bellicosity that might have shocked, or at least seemed alien to, Western observers. With TR the United States, revealing new interests in the Pacific, had now come forward as a potential fresh challenger to Imperial Japan. The way ahead was marked by a series of keynote treaties, and mutual 'understandings', over the next few years. In 1907, the so-called Gentlemen's Agreement was negotiated. The background was anti-Japanese discrimination in California, where a school board had ruled that children of Japanese descent would be sent to segregated schools. Through Roosevelt's interceding, Japan agreed to halt the flow of migrant workers to the US in exchange for the school board rescinding the order. Hence the immediate goal of the Gentlemen's Agreement was to reduce tensions between the two Pacific nations.

The Japanese government expressed, pointedly, its strong desire 'to preserve the image of the Japanese people in the eyes of the world'. But the agreement was never ratified by Congress. There followed a little-known but most significant treaty, the Root–Takahira Agreement, signed on 30 November 1908 between an outstanding US Secretary of State, Elihu Root (whom TR had appointed following the death of John Hay),* and Kogoro Takahira, the unhappy negotiator of the Portsmouth Treaty.

This agreement called for both nations to respect each other's territorial rights in the Pacific and the independence and territorial integrity of China. But although Root–Takahira discreetly marked an important milestone on the route of the United States to becoming a major player in East Asia, it did little to meaningfully curb Japanese expansion into China.

The greatest benefit Britain gained post-Tsushima undoubtedly stemmed from the digested lessons of the battle. The notes so assiduously made by Captain Willie Pakenham from his deckchair aboard the battleship *Asahi* arrived swiftly on the desk of the redoubtable First Sea Lord, Admiral of the Fleet 'Jackie' Fisher.

In a flash Fisher appreciated that Tsushima rendered the capital ships of every fleet in the world obsolete overnight. It was the monster twelve-inch (British-forged) guns that had sent the Russian fleet to the bottom of Tsushima Straits in a matter of minutes. Henceforth, thought Fisher, the fate of nations would rest on the all-big-gun battleship. It was fortunate for Britain that he had come to this conclusion before Admiral von Tirpitz and his boss Kaiser Wilhelm II. With exemplary speed Fisher ordered the construction of the world's first truly modern battleship. HMS *Dreadnought* was laid down on 2 October 1905, only four months after Tsushima, and was commissioned on 2 December 1906. It was an all-time record for warship construction, and a triumph for Britain's shipbuilding industry. An entirely new design, *Dreadnought* would remain in essence the role model for all capital ships until their extinction in 1945.

Following Tsushima, Tsarist Russia plummeted from being the third greatest naval power in the world to a poor sixth place; from being a first-rate force, it had come to be designated as only third-rate. By 1914 it had still not made good its stupendous losses of 1905, the nine battleships sunk during the war. The role of the Russian Black Sea Fleet in 1914–18 was to prove indeed a bad 'black' joke throughout the

* Like TR, Root would be awarded the Nobel Peace Prize.

war. It is a tragic story, which would eventually result in the deaths of many hundreds of thousands of British, Anzac, Turkish and Russian lives at Gallipoli in 1915. Was it really unavoidable?

Some historians do not regard alternative history, the 'what ifs', as altogether respectable. But I feel there are occasions when it is right and proper for the historian to postulate how consequences might have been transformed, had certain events taken a different course. For instance, what if of those great Russian battleships of Rozhestvensky – even half of them had not been sunk at Tsushima, some of them the most modern vessels then afloat? Might not even three or four of these powerful units, reinforcing the Russian Black Sea Fleet, have reversed the tide of events, persuading the shaky Turks not to enter the war on the German side? What an immense difference this could have made to the course of the war – those doughty fighters, the Turkish Army, not arrayed against us! As it was, by 1914 the Russian Navy had never recovered from Rozhestvensky's cataclysmic defeat. And by 1918 Turkey would have lost its entire empire.

Again, consider the influence of those Russian reverses of 1904–5 upon the rulers of Germany. Ironically, though he had supported Russia, the defeated nation, Kaiser Wilhelm II had been one of the principal beneficiaries of the Russo-Japanese War. Without firing a shot, he had witnessed the destruction of the fleet of one of his most immediate potential enemies in Europe, and the humiliation of its army in defeat in far-off Manchuria, at the hands of a small nation which he had once denigrated as 'little yellow monkeys'. He was a vain and foolish man given to faulty speculation, but on the strength of such a lamentably poor showing, would it not be worth taking a risk in Europe, to launch a knock-out blow against the French enemy in the west while the Russian behemoth was still floundering in its own incompetence and the mud of eastern Europe? How much better would Moltke's and Tirpitz's sturdy Teutons perform against the vaunted 'Russian steamroller', now shown to be so profoundly flawed?

Finally, suppose that the reverses in the Far East, the humiliating fall of Port Arthur, had not taken place. Bloody January, the Revolution of 1905, would most probably have been avoided in European Russia. And then, without that dummy run, might not the world-shaking cataclysm of October 1917 also not have occurred? Supposing, despite the loss of its fleet and the devastating defeat of Kuropatkin's army at Mukden, Russia had – as some of its leaders recommended – still fought on, against a Japan then so close to exhaustion itself, as described earlier? Might not some last-minute national triumph of arms in distant Manchuria have muffled the drums of revolt in St Petersburg, forestalling the events of 1917? Or at least have postponed them until Germany was decisively defeated, and not just through a fragile armistice in the west? How might the course of history not have been affected by one, or all, of these 'what ifs'?

Of all the belligerent nations in the First World War, none came out of it better than Japan. In 1914, the deal with its long-standing ally, Britain, was that it was to be rewarded with all of the German possessions in the Pacific. Loyally it helped the Royal Navy clear German raiders from the area, and sent an efficient flotilla of destroyers to protect convoys in the Mediterranean. Both functions materially helped Britain achieve its number-one role of defeating the German Navy in the Atlantic and North Sea. At the war's end Japan was indeed given Germany's island colonies in the Pacific – the Mariana, Caroline and Marshall Islands – as well as its strategic treaty port on the coast of Tsingtao. (There the Japanese Navy conducted, portentously, the world's first naval-launched air raids, from a seaplane-carrier.) In 1915 Japan exploited its position to impose its far-reaching Twenty-One Demands on China; it was a warning of which way nationalist thoughts might turn in the post-war world. These Demands were immediately opposed by an outraged America. Britain, engaged in a life-and-death struggle in Flanders, could do little more than register a bleat of protest.

In 1918, following the Bolshevik Revolution in Russia, Japan and the United States sent forces to Siberia, to bolster the armies of the White Movement leader Admiral Alexander Kolchak against the Bolshevik Red Army. Landing at Vladivostok, the Imperial Japanese Army initially planned to send more than 70,000 troops to occupy Siberia as far west as Lake Baikal. Once more Japan met with strong opposition from the United States; and its troops were the last to be withdrawn, with considerable reluctance. There were dual motives in Tokyo for lingering: firstly, there were still vivid memories of the cost of achieving victory over Kuropatkin in Manchuria in 1905; secondly, here on this critical frontier of Imperial Japan was now a new potential foe which, having just murdered the Tsar and his whole family, was the declared enemy of all imperialism. It was a frontier which the Japanese Army in particular would watch with extreme nervousness over the coming decades.

The Great War, however, had cost Japan, for all its strategically valuable acquisitions, just a couple of hundred dead – by far the lowest casualty list of any combatant, representing 0.2 per cent of the forces deployed.* The wartime boom boosted Japan's shaky economy enormously, transforming it from a debtor to a creditor nation. Exports quadrupled between 1913 and 1918. Large combines such as Mitsubishi rose to the top. The war and the acquisition of German territories on the coast of China would give Japan greatly advanced leverage there in years to come. Most significant, however, 1919 saw its representative Saionji Kinmochi sitting alongside the Big Four (Lloyd George, Orlando, Wilson, Clemenceau) at the Versailles Peace Conference. Japan gained a permanent seat on the Council of the League of Nations, a place at the top table. Despite that relatively small role in the First World War, it had emerged as a great power; nevertheless, the Western powers, its fellow victors, had rejected Japan's bid for a racial equality clause in the subsequent Treaty of Versailles. This would sting, as would continuing racial prejudice in the United States against Japanese immigration to California. (Back in December 1910 Teddy Roosevelt had made the prevailing American standpoint abundantly clear in a letter to his Secretary for War William H. Taft: 'Our vital interest is to keep the Japanese out of our country . . . The vital interest of the Japanese, on the other hand, is in Manchuria and Korea . . . our interests in Manchuria are really unimportant, and not such that the American people would be content to run the slightest risk of collision about them . . .')

Meanwhile, tiny as their populations were, those islands in Micronesia would swiftly feel the boot of Japanese occupation: they 'afforded a living to Japanese shopkeepers, restaurateurs, and brothel proprietors', wrote one historian, but 'None of this was as important as their potential strategic value . . .' Above all they would provide vital pieces

---

* By comparison, Britain had suffered nearly 1 million dead, the USA 117,000, and Russia and Germany each somewhere in the neighbourhood of 2 million.

in the race to build the vast empire of 1942. Occupation of these minute specks of coral in the Pacific also gave the Japanese Navy a rationale for vastly expanding its budget, to double that of the army's. Thus, as the 'peace era' of the 1920s began, it would gain significant political influence over national affairs, and would intensify its rivalry with the army, a development fraught with danger for the rest of the world. At the same time the imagined threat of Soviet Russia in Manchuria (it was no more than imagined because in fact Lenin, and later Stalin, had their hands full coping with the implementation of the Soviet system at home) would give the army an excuse to thrust its needs constantly into the foreground.

The then provisional President of China, President Yuan Shikai, foretold with clarity: 'Japan is going to take advantage of this war to gain control of China.' As it proved, Japan would exploit the opportunity of the Great War while the European powers were too busy to stop her, to impose her Twenty-One Demands on China. These demands included an insistence on Japan's railway and mining claims and access to harbours, bays and islands along the Chinese coast. In Barbara Tuchman's phrase, they made 'incursions into Chinese sovereignty and territory which were to twist the history of the twentieth century'. Yuan Shikai, in a weak position internally as his power was challenged by other local warlords, and unsupported abroad by the distracted Allied powers, was unable to risk conflict with Japan. So he accepted appeasement, a tactic followed by his successors, and agreed to an abbreviated document, the Thirteen Demands. These formed the basis of a treaty that was signed by both parties on 25 May 1915. Thus abbreviated, the treaty gave Japan few advantages that it did not already possess. On the other hand, the United States reacted strongly to Japan's rejection of the Open Door Policy which had promoted equal trading rights in China for all nations. Japan's closest ally at that time, Great Britain also expressed concern over what was perceived as Japan's overbearing, bullying approach to diplomacy, and the British Foreign Office in particular was unhappy with Japanese attempts to establish what would effectively be a Japanese protectorate over all of China. With rare prescience, the Foreign Office noted in 1921: 'Japan stands little chance of survival unless she can obtain control over the resources of China . . .'

In China, the overall political impact of Japan's actions created much public ill-will towards Tokyo, resulting in a significant upsurge in nationalism. A large-scale boycott of Japanese goods would be just one consequence.

Japan's wartime boom dissipated swiftly, leading to rapid inflation. In August 1918, rice riots caused by this inflation erupted in towns and cities throughout Japan. They demonstrated just how fragile in essence the Japanese economy remained. In 1919, in Korea there was an unexpected rebellion; it was crushed, but at least 7,000 protesters were massacred, many of them students. This was so shocking that even the Japanese government acknowledged that something had gone badly wrong.

Nevertheless, as across all the warring countries jubilant in the new peace, in the early 1920s Japan experienced moments of exhilaration and liberalism. Down Tokyo's Europeanized centre, the Ginza, long-haired young men in bell-bottom trousers, coloured shirts and floppy ties were to be seen strolling 'with young women in bobbed hairdos'. There were the 'Marx Boys', the 'Mobos' ('modern boys') and 'Mogas' ('modern girls'), the latter two often found tripping down the Ginza, hand in hand. Post-war Tokyo was marked by the trappings of 'a skittish, sometimes nihilistic hedonism that brings Weimar Berlin to mind', observed historian Ian Buruma; 'on the whole, then, it was a good time to be young'. By stern old-fashioned Meiji standards this mood was very daring; the elders tut-tutted, but it prevailed, at least for a while. To Japanese historians this was the era of *ero, guro, nansensu* – or 'eroticism, grotesquerie and nonsense'.

It was a time of lovers' suicide pacts, but it was also when the first women's university was established in Tokyo; there were moves towards universal suffrage, and women's rights in general. A wealthy Anglophile who emulated upper-class Britain, Takaaki Kato, Prime Minister in the mid-1920s who headed perhaps the most democratic regime in inter-war Japan, managed to pass a law giving the vote to all men over twenty-five with a steady income. Yet only a week later a conservative Peace Preservation Law made it illegal to participate in any form of organized opposition to the *kokutai*, or national polity.* In

---

* *Kokutai*, a difficult term to translate, was a semi-mystical Japanese concept which had something in common with Rousseau's philosophy of the General Will.

practice this meant that communists or radical socialists could face up to ten years in jail. So much for political freedom.

Forms of government in Japan in the 1920s and 1930s may seem strange, if not incomprehensible, to Western minds. At the top of the pyramid, of course, was the Emperor, the Mikado, claiming divine descent. But was he a constitutional ruler, like the sovereign of Great Britain; or was he an autocrat unique in his own right? On the death of the great Meiji Emperor in 1912, followed by a wave of ritual suicides, had come the Emperor Taisho. Of a weak physique, he had died fourteen years later, in 1926. However, it was during his reign, known as the Taisho Democracy, that political power moved modestly from the oligarchy of ageing statesmen, the *genro*, to the Diet and democratic parties. But this brief bout of liberalism faded on the death of Taisho. His successor, the twenty-five-year-old Hirohito, 124th in the direct lineage of Mikados, was academic by inclination, interested in natural science and marine biology. To stiffen him up he had regular tutorial sessions from the venerable Admiral Togo, victor of Tsushima, who remained an influential figure in navy politics until his death. Under the Japanese constitution, the Emperor could act only on the advice of his ministers and the Chiefs of Staff of the navy and army. The ministers of the armed forces did not, however, have direct access to the Emperor; the admirals and generals did. He was so hedged in by protocol that, rather like the Oracle at Delphi, it was often not clear what the Emperor's actual wishes were. Dangerously, the military and naval commanders with their direct routes of access could progressively interpret these as they found most convenient.

As the 1920s progressed, in common with Europe and America, Japan was hit by the world depression. For small farmers, life became grim to the point of starvation. The indigenous silk industry was savagely hit by tough US tariffs. The population had risen from 44 million to 56 million by 1920. Land hunger was acute; and the road to immigration in America was barred. In 1923 Tokyo and Yokohama were devastated by the Great Earthquake. Perhaps 100,000 died. In the hysteria that followed, Koreans, communists and anarchists were blamed for this natural phenomenon and attacked by mobs – and even by the police; mass killings took place. Yet within four years the two cities had been rebuilt, not least through generous aid from the United

States. Nevertheless, out of the ashes arose a new kind of nationalism/ imperialism. The ashes were fanned by the results of the Washington Naval Conference of 1922, the first disarmament conference ever to be held, but one invested with all the trimmings of old-style Western imperialism. Its aim was manifestly to impose a check upon Japanese naval expansion, much to America's advantage. There emerged the 5:5:3 equation – meaning, in simplest terms, that the US and Britain would each be allowed to build five new capital ships, but Japan only three.

In the eyes of many Japanese this was no fair way to treat a wartime ally. Meanwhile the Anglo-Japanese alliance of 1902, which had proved so profitable to both sides and was due for renewal this same year, was allowed to expire. Britain now cast in its lot with the other Anglo-Saxon superpower, America – a switch that Washington strategists saw as a way of ending British influence over Japan. Perhaps history would see this as an unfortunate development, insofar as it left Japan feeling, once again, dangerously isolated and bruised. Henceforth Britain's role as chief exporter to Japan of heavy machinery, and weaponry, dwindled. General Giichi Tanaka, who, of staunch samurai stock, had served as an aide to Kodama in the 1905 war and would later become a nationalist prime minister, castigated the Washington Conference as 'an attempt to oppress the non-Anglo-Saxon races, especially the coloured races, by the two English-speaking countries, Britain and the United States'.

In 1920, California, followed by fifteen other states, passed tough alien laws, and two years later the United States Supreme Court ruled Japanese nationals ineligible for US citizenship. Ambassador Masanao Hanihara warned the US Congress not to exclude Japanese in the proposed Immigration Act of 1924, because there would be 'grave consequences'. Senator Henry Cabot Lodge called this a 'veiled threat', and the bill passed easily, causing considerable offence in Japan.

All this marked the rise of serious anti-Anglo-Saxon sentiments in Japan, coinciding with a period of political turbulence. In November 1921 Prime Minister Hara was murdered by a young right-winger, starting what would become a pattern in Japanese political life. In December an anarchist fired a shot at the future Emperor Hirohito, but missed and was swiftly executed.

The confused and turbulent 1920s moved into the dangerous 1930s, the period that Japanese historians call the 'dark valley'. In 1930 the London Naval Conference allowed Japan to have 69.75 per cent of what Britain and America were allowed on heavy cruisers and 100 per cent of their allowance on submarines. A Captain Isoroku Yamamoto, he who, as a young flag lieutenant, had accompanied Admiral Togo to the bedside of the defeated Russian admiral after Tsushima, and now champion of the Japanese Navy's budding aircraft-carrier arm, forcefully ensured that there would be no limitations on naval aircraft; Japan alone of the naval powers already had four experimental aircraft carriers. But after Prime Minister Hamaguchi had managed to limit the navy budget to 374 million yen, he was severely criticized by the nationalists, and in November 1930 was shot and wounded near the same spot in the Tokyo railway station where Hara had been killed. Despite several major surgical operations, Hamaguchi died the following August. Sinister right-wing, nationalist secret societies, such as the Cherry Blossom Society (Sakurakai), the One Evening Society (Issekikai, formed in 1929) and the Black Dragons, began to proliferate. Under the inspiration of a fanatic called Ikki Kita, regarded as the founder of Japanese fascism, a grouping of politically dissatisfied young army officers got together to form a secret society with the objective of launching a *coup d'état* at some suitable future date, which would combine the power of the Emperor with that of the armed forces.

The curious thing about these conspiratorial Japanese factions, though they could indeed be loosely termed fascist, was that, in contrast to European experience, they never grew to comprise any mass organization such as Hitler or Mussolini would have at their disposal. 'What is more,' noted the historian W.G. Beasley, '... their avowed function was not to seize power but to destroy it. Out of chaos, they believed, would come in some mysterious way a better Japan.'

In all this, a central and vaguely sinister role was played by the 'Shinto myth', defined as a mystical bond, unlike anything to be found elsewhere in the world. In May 1932, the seventy-seven-year-old Prime Minister, Japan's twenty-ninth, Tsuyoshi Inukai, was gunned down by one of these gangs, comprised of eleven navy fanatics, in his own house. The trial that followed led merely to light sentences, which weakened not only the rule of law, but also, in the long term, the young

Japanese democracy. Inukai's death effectively marked the end of civilian political control until after the Second World War. Of the fourteen prime ministers who governed Japan between 1932 and 1945, only four were civilians. Yet, as this violent decade of economic stress unravelled, Japanese politics would be seen to be run not by respectable political parties, but by cabals of courtiers, military *caciques* and bureaucrats, whose decisions, Ian Buruma has written, 'were often forced on them by fanatical subordinates'.

But it was abroad, in the inhospitable territories of northern Korea and southern Manchuria, and the leased areas around Port Arthur, won during the 1905 war and designated 'Kwantung', where the real roots of power resided. Here sat Japan's Kwantung Army. Nominally its original role was to guard the railway line and fixtures of the South Manchuria Line, which terminated in Mukden (or Shenyang today),* against local banditry. It was, however, gradually to grow into the most powerful unit of the whole Imperial Japanese Army and became a law unto itself. Its command was the most prestigious in the officer corps. As it developed, the Kwantung Army became not unlike those self-contained and self-ruling legions of ancient Rome, deployed to hold the marches of empire in its furthest corners, keeping the barbarians at bay, but also capable of overthrowing the home rulers themselves. The harsh remoteness of the bleak Manchurian steppes had its influence on those posted out there. It was an ideal breeding ground for the perversion of the old principles of samurai and *bushido* with which Japanese militarism of the 1930s now clad itself. The troops, mostly of peasant origin and led by officers of the poorer middle class, were subjected to brutal discipline. They in turn would achieve levels of power and authority beyond their reach in the homeland. Senior officers and NCOs would have served under heroes like Kodama and Nogi in 1905. Accordingly they imposed on their subordinates exaggerated notions of invincibility, while burnishing the legend of the old hero Admiral Togo.

The Kwantung Army was pushed in two directions: one motivation

---

* Once a pioneer frontier town, Mukden/Shenyang now boasts an urban population of nearly 6 million, of whom 91 per cent are imported Han Chinese, far outnumbering the native Manchus (who once ruled Imperial China). Shenyang is now much the biggest industrial city in northern China.

was fear of the Russians to the west, now resurgent under Soviet rule and eager to requite the humiliations of the past; the second was a terrible racial contempt for the Chinese to the south. It was a contempt, deep ingrained, that far exceeded any perceived slights by Anglo-Saxons towards the Japanese, indeed even exceeding that of Nazis for the Slavs; within only a few years it would overflow in the shape of monstrous genocidal brutality and cruelty. Invisible to the West, the Kwantung Army was itself divided into two powerful factions, calling themselves the Kodo-ha (or 'Imperial Way School') and the Tosei-ha (or 'Control School'). Both were equally expansionist, and ultra-nationalist. The noisier of the two, containing many young officers who favoured a regime-change by *coup d'état*, was the Koda-ha which was obsessed with thoughts of war against the Soviet Union in Siberia. A first step in that direction would be the occupation of all Manchuria. In contrast, the Tosei-ha plotters thought it prudent to stay on friendly relations with the Russians, but make China the main objective of expansion, once a base in Manchuria had been secured. Thus both factions of the Kwantung Army were committed to an early occupation of all Manchuria, and to a programme of aggression on the Asian mainland.

In September 1931 Seishiro Itagaki, the Kwantung Army's Chief of Intelligence, and Colonel Kanji Ishiwara carried out a carefully plotted fake attack in Mukden. They blew up a railway line and blamed it upon Chinese 'terrorists'. The tracks were in fact only slightly damaged, with trains passing over them soon after the explosion. But the 'Mukden Incident' was sufficient to provide a pretext for the well-prepared Kwantung Army to move in and occupy, within a matter of hours, all the key points across this large territory.

Tokyo was not entirely surprised; rumours of a coup had been rife for some time, and the Minister of War despatched a major-general to Kwantung GHQ with orders to forestall the coup. But, illustrative of how much support the activists there had at home, the General concerned went in leisurely fashion by train to Mukden, where he allowed himself to be regaled in a geisha-house by one of the plotters. By the time his letter had been delivered, on 19 September, the coup had been carried out. In violation of orders from Tokyo, the Kwantung Army C-in-C, General Shigeru Honjo, ordered his forces to expedite operations all along the South Manchurian Railway. His troops captured virtually every city along its 730-mile length in a matter of days. Thus the whole of the vast, rich province of Manchuria – covering more than the total land area of France and Germany combined – was occupied with lightning speed, and now became Japan's puppet state of Manchukuo. Industrialists and land-poor peasants alike poured in. It also offered a vital springboard for an assault on either China or Russian Siberia. Both were in the minds of the Kwantung plotters. With great foresight, the Kwantung Army replaced the Russian wide-gauge railway line with its own narrow gauge. This meant that, in the event of broader conflict, and any Soviet invasion of Manchukuo, the Russians would be unable to supply their forces there from the Trans-Sib, while the Kwantung Army would have the reverse advantage.

Manchuria was the first, the precursor, of all the expansionist land-grabs of the future Axis powers. Given its immense size, its acquisition certainly promised the space and the basic resources that Japan claimed it needed. Could the voracious appetites of Japan's industries and the land-hunger of a soaring population be satisfied only by conquest and expansion? (One cannot help comparing the 65 million of the 1930s, when Japan already had access to the overseas territories of Taiwan and Korea, with a prosperous modern Japan, shorn of all its possessions outside the home islands, yet with a population almost twice as large.) The coup in Manchuria shocked the well-meaning Mikado, his weak eyes immersed in the study of marine molluscs and bent on keeping out of everyday politics; he had not been consulted, though the hotheads of Kwantung claimed to have acted in his name. The Kwantung Army had committed an act of gross insubordination, but – in the face of success – Tokyo proved powerless to counter events.

Outrage swept the outside world, particularly the United States. Nobody, however, was in a position to do anything. The nominal landlords of Manchuria, Generalissimo Chiang Kai-shek's nationalist Kuomintang, who had ruled in Peking since 1928, were, as usual, in disarray at home; only adjacent Soviet Russia could have moved, but Stalin was likewise far too preoccupied with his own problems at home. From Geneva, the League of Nations protested. Japan declared this to be an unacceptable rebuke, and flounced out of the League in 1933, complaining that it was being victimized by the rest of the world.

Its delegate, Yosuke Matsuoka, made a strange speech in which he compared Japan to Jesus Christ. A month later Hitler would come to power in Germany.

So Japan's Kwantung Army got away with a massive territorial acquisition, plotted by a few army colonels. It was an encouragement to Japanese nationalism for the future, though it meant that Japan now was isolated as never before, a dangerous situation which the Meiji Restoration had sought so diligently to avoid. During its fourteen years of occupation under Japanese Army control, Manchukuo rated as one of the most brutally run regions in the world, with the greatest suffering meted out to its despised Chinese inhabitants.

On 26 February 1936, Tokyo endured its heaviest snowfall in thirty years. Early that morning young officers of the Koda-ha faction launched a coup with over a thousand men attempting to take over the centre of Tokyo. Old, respected public figures were murdered. The leaders, none above the rank of captain, claimed that they were merely performing their duty as loyal subjects of the Emperor. This was *gekokujo*, an inversion of the normal order, with the lowly ruling over their lords. But Hirohito did not see it that way. It was mutiny, and the mild-mannered Mikado, laying aside his microscope, now stamped his foot, ordering the rebels to be crushed. Martial law was imposed. The rebels gave up, and thirteen of them were executed, including Ikki Kita. Temporarily the Koda-ha faction lost its sway; but, paradoxically, the political power of the army was strengthened, as well as that of the Tosei-ha, the hotheads bursting to move on China. Two weeks later, Hitler marched into the Rhineland; and at the end of the year Japan signed a pact with Germany, thus aligning itself with Hitler against the Soviet Union. The paths of aggression were mapped out.

On 7 July 1937, in the far south-west of Manchukuo, menacingly close to Peking, a Japanese private, Shimura Kikujiro, relieved himself beside the Marco Polo Bridge, then strolled off into the so-called demilitarized zone. The soldier was not away for very long, but since he was presumed to be missing on roll call, his commander insisted on combing the area for him. Private Kikujiro was later found unharmed. Meanwhile, however, there had developed a full-scale 'incident', which was about as trumped up as the Mukden Incident of 1931. There was an exchange of fire; then, from 9 July onwards, Japanese and Chinese

violations of the ceasefire began to increase, and a build-up of reinforcements on both sides escalated, with four divisions of Chinese
troops moved to the border, and three Japanese. In charge of the
Japanese troops was Kanji Ishiwara, now a general of the Kwantung
Army. In Tokyo Prime Minister Fumimaro Konoe's government made
statements threatening to step up Japan's mobilization, an even more
aggressive move than the Kwantung Army could have hoped for.
Meanwhile in command of the Chinese forces was the new nationalist
leader Generalissimo Chiang Kai-shek. Though debilitated through
having to fight a war on two fronts – they were also locked in a struggle with the communist forces of Mao Tse-tung – and though poorly
armed, Chiang's forces resisted the Japanese incursions with greater
vigour than had been expected. Efforts to defuse the escalating conflict
failed, largely thanks to the hard-line militarists within the Japanese
General Staff. After launching a bloody attack on the Japanese lines
on 27 July, Chiang's forces were defeated and forced to retreat. The
Japanese then moved in to pacify areas surrounding Peking. Chiang's
access to the city seemed threatened, and negotiations failed.

Then, on 9 August 1937, a Japanese naval officer was shot in Shanghai. The war proper now began, a war that Japan would never be able
to bring to a conclusion, with consequences that would shortly expand
into world conflict. In December 1937 Japanese forces, their strength
swiftly increased to 200,000 men, seized Peking, Shanghai and
Chiang's provisional capital, Nanking. There followed the Nanking
Massacre, in which an estimated 250,000 to 300,000 Chinese – men,
women and children – were slaughtered in one of the most shocking
atrocities ever recorded. There was no trace here of the old-style samurai chivalry, as had been shown the defeated Russians in 1905. In its
place was reflected the years of vicious indoctrination, in which Japanese soldiers had been told that the Chinese were an inferior race, the
Japanese divine. In the years succeeding the Rape of Nanking could be
seen the hand of hubris, the victors of 1905, followed by Manchuria,
followed by Nanking, persuading themselves that they could now with
equanimity take on the Soviet colossus as well as China; and what else
besides?

Meanwhile, what was the rest of the world thinking as Japanese
militarism rampaged, first across Manchuria, then into northern

China? When, in 1933, Yosuke Matsuoka, sleek and sinister, all in black, had stalked out of the League of Nations, the delegates, representing almost every nation on earth, sat stunned. 'We are not coming back,' declared Matsuoka as he left the chamber.* But in response to the Japanese incursions the League did nothing, its members declaring that they had neither the power nor the will. Britain and France were still licking their wounds from 1914–18, as was even the United States, tardy and modest though its contribution to that conflict had been. Soviet Russia, the one country that might have acted, was paralysed – as it had been in 1931 – by purges and confusion at home. That first act of aggression by Japan would of course present Hitler with a perfect blueprint for the *Anschluss* with Austria in 1938, and then the uncontested annexation of the Czech Sudetenland. If Neville Chamberlain could write off the dismembering of Czechoslovakia as 'a quarrel in a faraway country between people of whom we know nothing', the violation of distant Manchuria would surely be even less troubling to Britain or America.

As for Japan and the Japanese themselves, the British view of their former allies showed a mix of supercilious derision, little short of racial contempt, and only moderate alarm. The pre-war American view was probably little different. In Britain in the 1930s Japan was known for its gimcrack, cheap exports such as lacquered paper parasols that would last an afternoon. Books of the era reveal a steady increase in derisive anti-Japanese sentiment in the US, not to mention all the anti-Japanese movies of the 1930s. They (the Japs) had such bad, astigmatic eyes, it was claimed, that they couldn't possibly fly sophisticated planes. Aboard the battle cruiser *Repulse*, shortly before she was sunk by Japanese dive bombers, senior officers were heard to observe that 'those Japs are bloody fools . . . can't fly . . . they can't see at night, and they're not well trained . . .' As late as 1939, one American wrote, 'The Japanese as a race have defects of the tubes of the inner ear, just as they are generally myopic. This gives them a defective sense of balance

---

* Matsuoka was Minister of Foreign Affairs up to the early days of the Second World War, and was a fervent supporter of an attack on Siberia. He later admitted, however, that 'Entering into the Tripartite Pact [with Germany and Italy] was the mistake of my life. Even now I still keenly feel it. Even my death won't take away this feeling.' He died in obscurity, in an Allied prison in 1946, while awaiting trial on war crimes charges.

... the one physical sense in which an aviator is not permitted to be deficient.'

Hence the belief that the Japanese would simply never dare provoke a war with the United States. When the first Zero fighter attacked, senior Allied officers could not believe that the Japanese could independently design such an aircraft. In the Philippines, nine hours after Pearl Harbor, General MacArthur insisted that the pilots could not have been Japanese but must have been white mercenaries. One distinguished *New York Times* journalist, Otto Tolischus, would proclaim that the 'Japanese mind works in a more elemental way ... as a woman's is supposed to do'. Even an erudite curator from the Smithsonian Museum in Washington could inform President Franklin D. Roosevelt, encouragingly, that 'Japanese skulls are some two thousand years less developed than ours ...'

This supercilious attitude of 1930s Anglo-Saxons reminds one all too vividly of the contempt in which the Russians held the Japanese back in 1904. Understandably, it stoked up more resentment and hatred in Japan. Smugly, the British, distracted by Hitler's rampages in Europe, allowed their forces to sit without undue concern behind the giant coastal guns of Singapore, which would be a match even for the super 18.1-inch guns of the battleship *Yamato* (alas, they were pointing the wrong way: the Japs would come by land, from behind, not by sea). America, with its more immediate Pacific interests, had harboured a much more critical view of Japan for some time, but had avoided taking any action. Then, on 12 December 1937, Japanese planes strafed, bombed and sank a US river gunboat, the humble flat-bottomed *Panay*, anchored on the Yangtse River. Three men were killed, and forty-three sailors and five civilians wounded. Two newsreel cameramen aboard were able to film the attack. Survivors were later taken aboard a British gunboat, HMS *Ladybird*, which had herself been fired on earlier the same day. Eventually the Japanese apologized, and paid America a handsome indemnity of $2,214,007.36. They claimed that their pilots had been unable to see the (very clearly painted) markings on the ship. US Navy cryptographers, however, had intercepted radio traffic which showed that the attacking planes were acting under orders and that there had been no mistake. The following month an American diplomat, John M. Allison, the Consul at the Embassy in Nanking, was struck in the face by a Japanese soldier. For a moment it looked as if America might be on the verge of war with Japan. However, deeply isolationist at the time, with a large majority of its people determined to avoid any foreign entanglements whatsoever, and its forces at a low point, it turned the other cheek. Nevertheless, the two incidents turned US public opinion strongly against the Japanese.

CHAPTER EIGHT

ZHUKOV, SORGE, TSUJI

All through the 1930s the bellicose Kwantung Army was leading Japan further and further towards adopting its own aggressive stance. In 1939, a small border incident in Mongolia might seem to have little bearing on the colossal onslaught that would engulf Stalin's Soviet Russia just two years later. But military adventures seldom happen in a vacuum; one leads to another, or they are otherwise interconnected, whether by events or by personalities. The Battle of Nomonhan, or Khalkhin Gol, as the Russians and their Mongolian allies called it, though it was fought thousands of miles away from Moscow, came to be laden with significance for the defence of the city which, in the autumn and winter of 1941, would prove to be one of the most decisive engagements in the whole of the Second World War.

Nomonhan would throw up two figures who would play a leading role in Hitler's defeat before Moscow, his first on land and an early turning point in the whole war. One was Georgy Zhukov, the un- known junior general later recognized as the most successful Allied commander of the whole war. At Nomonhan he would first try out the double-envelopment strategy which was to destroy the German Sixth Army at Stalingrad in 1942. The second important figure was Dr Richard Sorge, Russia's ace spy in Tokyo, whose intelligence reports would enable Stalin to take gigantic risks in the struggle for Moscow. An earth-shaking change of strategy would emerge from Japan's hu- miliation on the field of Nomonhan: it would give up its ambitions in Soviet Siberia and instead 'go south' in quest of plunder and raw materials, to the oil-rich East Indies, the Philippines, Singapore – and Pearl Harbor.

On 1 June 1939, as war clouds were building up over Europe, the forty-three-year-old middle-ranking Russian general Georgy Zhukov arrived in Moscow (restored as the Soviet capital in 1918). Responding to an urgent summons to the Kremlin, he had set forth with considerable trepidation from his post in Minsk, where he was a mere deputy to the C-in-C of Byelorussia. Was he going to be charged with being an 'enemy of the people' and end up in the Lubyanka prison, followed by speedy execution with a bullet in the back of the head? Stalin's Great Purge, in which many of Zhukov's generation of Soviet generals had met a grisly and generally unwarranted death, was just completing its terrible run. The dead included three marshals of the Soviet Union, headed by Mikhail Tukhachevsky (reckoned to have been one of the most outstanding military brains of his time), thirteen of Russia's fifteen army commanders, more than half the corps, divisional and brigade commanders, the commanders-in-chief of the navy and air force, and many other leaders of both these services. The numbers ran into thousands, if not hundreds of thousands. Exactly why the purges took place, no one can be quite sure even today; was it simply the Georgian tyrant's fear of an army coup against his brutal and incompetent rule? Suffice to say that, as late as 1939, on the brink of a general world war, no senior officer in Stalin's Russia could feel safe.

What could be held against Tukhachevsky was that he came from the impoverished nobility. In this respect, Zhukov was unassailable: his proletarian antecedents were impeccable. He was born into a poverty-stricken peasant family in Kaluga a hundred miles south-west of Moscow, and everything about him indicated his peasant stock. In his teens, he had been sent to Moscow as an apprentice to a cobbler. During the purges Zhukov had attempted to keep his nose clean and avoid all involvement. With the bull neck, barrel chest, large hands and somewhat coarse features of a Russian *muzhik*, he would become renowned for his ruthlessness, his unhesitating expenditure of lives and his merciless punishment of failure.

Nevertheless, the summons – without explanation – to report to the People's Commissar for Defence, Kliment Voroshilov, in Moscow without delay would have filled him with anxiety. An old party hack, later described by those who knew him as a 'bag of shit', the Ukrainian Voroshilov would be responsible for repeated military disasters, yet was regarded by Stalin as a safe pair of hands. Notably he had been his hatchet-man during the purges, personally signing at least 185 execution lists.

Zhukov's concern was heightened when he reached Voroshilov's antechamber and was told by the aide to go in. 'I'll see to it that all essentials are packed for you for the long journey,' the aide added ominously.

'What long journey?'

'Go and see the People's Commissar. He'll tell you all about it.'

After a routine enquiry about his health, Voroshilov informed Zhukov: 'Japanese troops have made a surprise attack and crossed into friendly Mongolia which the Soviet government is committed to defend ...' Showing Zhukov a map of the invasion area, Voroshilov continued: 'I think they've started a big military gamble. At any rate, it's only the beginning ... Could you fly there right away and if need be assume command of the troops?'

Zhukov assured him: 'I am ready this minute.'

'Good. The plane will be waiting at the Central Airfield at 1600 hours ... A small group of military experts will be flying with you. Goodbye now, and all the best.'

Zhukov departed for his new appointment with a mixture of relief, evidently, that his 'long journey' was not going to take him to the dungeons of the Lubyanka and enthusiasm for the task ahead, which, he wrote in his memoirs, he approached with 'a feeling of joy'. Twice in his lifetime Russia had been humiliated by the Japanese in its Far Eastern province: once in 1905, and again during the Russian Civil War of the 1920s when they had occupied eastern Siberia and had left only with the greatest reluctance in 1925 – the last of the intervention forces to leave. It was clearly time that these combative orientals were disciplined. Given the threat from Hitler in the west, Zhukov appreciated that a limited operation to shut down provocations from Japan's puppet state of Manchukuo, and secure the Soviet back-door in the Far East, assumed a very high priority.

A limited operation it did indeed seem to be. Once again the Kwantung Army had slipped its leash. To a tidy, rational Western mind its motivation might, to this day, have seemed irrational, if not inexplicable. The raw material wealth of eastern Siberia was largely unexploited. There was oil in the northern part of Sakhalin Island, which Japan coveted, but nothing compared to that which was to be found in the islands of the East Indies to the south. The hotter heads of Kwantung hoped that maybe one day Bolshevik Russia in the east, a deeply flawed power, could be rolled back as far as Lake Baikal. Otherwise there was a deeply ingrained fear that the boundless commitment which Japan had taken on in China was menaced as long as its flank with Soviet Russia (which was then arming Chiang's Kuomintang forces) was insecure. So Soviet power in the area had to be neutralized: or perhaps taught a brisk lesson: a preventive strike, on a modest scale?

As we shall see in the next chapter, in late May, the Japanese had mounted an offensive in the disputed zone east of the Khalkhin Gol River, on the eastern border of Mongolia. Today the attack still seems politically questionable and militarily inept, and not with hindsight alone. East of Lake Baikal in Siberia, after all, the Soviets were believed to have between twenty and thirty infantry divisions. The Japanese forces seemed quite inadequate to the task. Yet it would be hard to think of a frontier that was riper for an 'incident'. On either side there were forces which hated, distrusted and despised each other. Only a generation previously vicious wounds had been inflicted, at Port Arthur and Mukden. Since its *coup de main* in 1931, Japan had acquired a new frontier over 1,800 miles long between the new puppet-state of Manchukuo and its neighbours, the Soviet Union and Stalin's first satellite, the People's Republic of Mongolia. Running through barren, sparsely populated land, much of it was poorly demarcated in that originally the frontier lines had been internal divisions within the Manchu empire. Since the Russian Civil War there had been hundreds of border incidents, lesser or greater; one of these had come about when the Amur River had shifted its course. From Russia's point of view, its tenuous lifeline between Vladivostok and the west was greatly at risk; at one point the frontier of Manchukuo came within only two-and-a-half miles of a key bridge on the Trans-Sib Railway.

Yet most of the incidents were initiated from the Japanese side. There was a congeries of right-wing politicians in Tokyo, linked to activists within the Imperial Japanese Army – notably the Kwantung Army, with a Major Masanobu Tsuji much to the fore – who believed that the empire had certain inalienable rights in the Siberian hinterland that lay behind Manchukuo. Their memories reached back to the glorious triumph of Mukden in 1905 (without considering that it had been a very close-run thing, its heavy casualty list making it a pyrrhic victory indeed). They recalled how more recently, during the anarchy of the Russian Civil War, some 70,000 Japanese troops had been the last to quit Siberian territory, shooed out by the United States. There were those who thought that all Siberia from Lake Baikal to Vladivostok, with its great empty spaces and largely untapped mineral wealth, should come under Japanese dominion. To them it was the Soviet empire, so rickety in appearance, that was Japan's natural enemy in the 1930s, its Marxist ideology fundamentally hostile to Imperial Japan. Fuelling the smouldering tensions in Soviet–Japanese relations had come Japan's signing up to the Anti-Comintern Pact with Nazi Germany in November 1936.

In the summer of 1938 the most serious of the border incidents occurred over some disputed heights at Changkufeng, on the Tumen River that bounded Manchukuo to the east. From the Soviet point of view, Changkufeng was perilously close to Vladivostok. The Japanese incursion seems to have been triggered by the defection of a Soviet general, Genrikh Lyushkov, who had commanded all NKVD forces, the dreaded secret police, in the Soviet Far East. He was said to have provided the Japanese with important intelligence both on the poor state of Soviet Far Eastern forces and on the continuing purges of senior army officers. It was a major intelligence coup for Japan, yet from it their analysts allowed themselves to draw exaggerated conclusions about the damage the purges had done to the Soviet forces facing them. The Changkufeng Incident escalated, with Moscow mobilizing the Pacific Fleet. The Japanese forces suffered a humiliating local defeat and, after ten days of bloody fighting, were pushed off Soviet-claimed territory. A ceasefire was negotiated, but not before the Russians had suffered 800 casualties, while the Japanese had lost approximately twice that number. The Russian commander, General Vasily Blyukher, was blamed for the excessive Soviet casualties and executed. Both sides withdrew, bloodied and with hackles raised.

Inferiority in manpower, in weaponry and in generalship would all contribute towards the Kwantung Army's coming failure at Nomonhan. Yet perhaps as telling as any of these was one factor which worked, undetected and unseen, to defeat Japanese arms: poor intelligence. As Alvin D. Coox puts it in his impressive study: 'no one expected the

Russians to become heavily involved in the Nomonhan fighting', and 'It is undeniable that Japanese underestimation of the Red Army aggravated the shortage of hard facts.'

Even if the Kwantung Army had been of the very first order, nothing could stand up against the one ace in the pack held by the Kremlin. Whereas most of the British and American successes in the domain of intelligence in the Second World War came from intercepting signals (sigint), the Soviets held the advantage in human intelligence (humint), in material supplied by operators such as the Cambridge spies Burgess, Maclean and Philby. But in terms of sheer value, none could approach the status of Moscow's man in Tokyo, Dr Richard Sorge.

Born of a German father and Russian mother in 1895, Sorge was badly wounded on the Western Front in 1916 and invalided out of the German Army, decorated with the Iron Cross. While convalescent, he described himself as 'plunged into an intense confusion of the soul' and joined the German Communist Party. In the 1920s he served an apprenticeship in Moscow, where he was recruited into the GRU (military intelligence). He then moved to Shanghai, working as the editor of a German news service and for the respectable *Frankfurter Zeitung* newspaper. There he set up an intelligence ring, in which one of his agents was Max Clausen, also a German Communist. In those early days Sorge seems to have done remarkably little to cover up his communist sympathies. Then, in 1933, the year Hitler came to power, his GRU controllers ordered him to Tokyo, to set up an important spy ring. He operated under the codename of Ramsay and was joined by Clausen. But he first went via Berlin, where he managed to weave his way into the Nazi ranks and read much Nazi propaganda. Inclined to be a heavy drinker (which was to contribute to his eventual downfall), Sorge claimed that he attended so many beer halls with his new acquaintances in Berlin that he gave up drinking lest alcohol lead to indiscretion.

The network he created included, as radio operator, Max Clausen, and various other Comintern agents, including Max Clausen's wife Anna who served as a courier. Hotsumi Ozaki, another Sorge recruit, became a member of Prime Minister Fumimaro Konoe's inner circle and would acquire much valuable intelligence from Konoe, which

Sorge promptly despatched to Moscow.* The GRU appears to have attached top importance to the establishment of Sorge's network.

Meanwhile Sorge achieved a close friendship with Major-General Eugen Ott, a military attaché who in April 1938 became the German Ambassador in Tokyo and who confided in him as a devoted Nazi (Sorge had conspicuously joined the Tokyo branch of the Nazi Party in 1934). Ott seems to have told Sorge everything he, or Moscow, wanted to know. The intelligence was promptly sent to Moscow on unbreakable one-time pads. As Sorge was to admit in his later confession (extracted under torture), his principal assignment in the 1930s was 'to observe most closely Japan's policy towards the Soviet Union following the Manchurian Incident, and at the same time to study very carefully the question of whether or not Japan was planning to attack the Soviet Union'. Sorge remained faithful to his creed: 'to free the world from capitalist imperialism and militarism, and . . . make wars impossible in the future. All difficulties, shortages and mistakes in the Soviet Union were only regrettable transitional phenomena.'

Though he seems to have left numerous traces of his past communist life, to none of his German friends in Japan did Sorge 'ever betray by the slightest hint, or slip of the tongue, that he had first-hand knowledge of the Soviet Union'. He visited Manchuria, and by 1935 he and fellow spy Yotoku Miyagi were able to prepare an elaborate diagrammatic chart showing the leadership, alliances and enmities of the rival factions in the Japanese Army. Thus he was uniquely qualified to interpret the insurrection that hit Tokyo in February 1936. As Miyagi correctly deduced, 'it would be a turning point, leading to a drastic redirection of Japanese politics, with the army becoming the motive power in political life'. That, as we have seen, is precisely what happened.

Sorge warned Moscow of the likelihood of Japan's adventure in China, and in June 1938 the German Embassy made him privy to information acquired from the interrogation of the defecting Soviet General, Lyushkov. A hundred per cent loyal to Stalin, Sorge was profoundly shocked by what Lyushkov had revealed of the debility of the Soviet armed forces in the aftermath of the Great Purge. What particularly shook him was the temptation that such material could

* When the Sorge ring was broken up in 1944, Ozaki achieved the rare distinction of being the only Japanese national to be executed for treason in the Second World War.

spark in the mind of Hitler as the Soviet Union's number-one potential enemy. As he remarked later: 'One consequence of Lyushkov's report was a danger of joint Japanese–German military action against the Soviet Union.' It was, observed his biographers F.W. Deakin and G.R. Storry, '... Sorge's main task to contribute towards the avoidance of such a disaster.'

It is not clear whether in 1939 Sorge tipped off Moscow about the impending Japanese attack at Nomonhan; there appears to have been a temporary breach in communications, possibly because Sorge's GRU controller was himself caught up in the purges. What is known, however, is that Sorge was able to assure Moscow that the Nomonhan Incident would not be allowed, by either the Japanese government or the army, to escalate 'into real war'. He was recorded as expounding to Ott during the battle that 'If the Japanese Army wanted to drive the Red Army from its present positions, then 400–500 tanks would be required; and this was beyond Japan's industrial capacity. Germany ought to study the whole Nomonhan Incident more deeply and should reject the old idea that the Red Army was incapable of putting up serious resistance.'

History would shortly reveal that, disastrously, Hitler chose to give credence to Lyushkov's report. As it was, Sorge's report about the limitations of Japan's objectives, and its military capacity, would prove of immeasurable value to Stalin in the formulation of his tightrope strategy in the summer of 1939. It would also have prescribed to him the size of Zhukov's forces that would be required to smash the Kwantung Army deployed at Nomonhan.

In April 1939, eight months after Changkufeng, at Kwantung Army HQ Major Masanobu Tsuji promulgated a fiery Order 1488. In it were contained 'principles' for dealing with any future such frontier clashes. These instructed that 'if the enemy crosses the frontiers ... annihilate him without delay ...' To accomplish this, it would be permissible therefore 'to enter Soviet territory, or to trap or lure Soviet troops into Manchukuoan territory ... In such an event, however, never abandon friendly dead or wounded ... In the event of an armed clash, fight until victory is won regardless of relative strengths or of the location of the boundaries.'

If 'the enemy' were 'to violate the borders', the Order continued, Japanese units 'must challenge him courageously ... without concerning themselves about the consequences, which will be the responsibility of higher headquarters'. It all indicated that the Japanese High Command, swallowing its own agitprop that the Soviet Army in the Far East was but a paper tiger, had refused to learn anything from Changkufeng: for instance that the Soviet Army in Siberia was tougher, was better equipped in tanks and (especially) artillery and had been significantly reinforced. The Japanese intelligence staffs would revise none of their low assessments of Soviet military power in the Far East. 'If we do not seize an opportunity such as this to hit the Russians and thus show the power of the Imperial army, then the Soviet–Manchukuo border will hereafter be dominated by Soviet forces, and that will only leave roots for trouble in the future.'

Major Tsuji can be taken as an avatar of Japanese aggression in Kwantung and afterwards. Like the villain of some Victorian melodrama, he would pop up everywhere in the Pacific war zone where there was trouble, spreading the doctrine of Japanese racial superiority and the supreme honour of suicidal resistance. Born at the beginning of the century, Tsuji was thus brought up in that generation of Japanese steeped in the legends of heroism of the 1904–5 war, that pyrrhic victory on land, for whom the self-immolating Marshal Nogi was the ultimate hero.

Tsuji published various writings that were read by a vast public in Japan. They were hymns of self-praise, but even if only 25 per cent were trustworthy they still reveal a phenomenal man of war, utterly fearless (and wounded many times), with a transcending genius for military planning, and an irresistible ability to put his ideas across to senior commanders.

At Kwantung Army GHQ, Tsuji's slot was simply that of Senior Operations Staff Officer, but his powers ranged much further. He was present at the Rape of Nanking (over which his writings draw a discreet veil). And almost single-handedly he seems to have prepared the brilliant operational plan by which the Japanese Twenty-Fifth Army infiltrated on bicycles down through the jungles of Malaya, ultimately to capture Singapore from the rear, forcing humiliating surrender upon a British army of 130,000 men in February 1942.

Nicknamed the Wolf, or the God of Operations, he was also responsible for training a force in the jungles of Taiwan and southern China, which he led from the vanguard. After Malaya, Tsuji appears in the Philippines; then he turns up in Guadalcanal during 1942–3, planning – and leading – two final attempts by the hard-pressed Japanese defenders to dislodge the US Marines. From there he went as special emissary to the Emperor to urge evacuation.

After that, Tsuji reappeared in Burma in the latter stages of the war. In every theatre where he set foot, there emerged charges of brutality and war crimes: the massacre of Chinese civilians in Singapore, the executions of US prisoners of war during the Bataan Death March and of government officials in the Philippines, and numerous killings in China. None, however, was more shocking than that with which he was charged in Burma. As the war historian Max Hastings writes, he was reported there to have dined on the liver of a shot-down American pilot, damning as cowards his comrades who refused to share it with him: 'The more we eat, the brighter will burn the fire of our hatred for the enemy.'

With the ending of the war in August 1945, Tsuji's career continued to be almost equally unorthodox. Though placed high on the Allied wanted list of Japanese war criminals, and regarded as the most notorious of these to evade trial after the war, he managed somehow to escape by going into hiding in Thailand. Unconfirmed accounts had it that he was helped through collaboration with the CIA, who were then working with the rump of Chiang Kai-shek's regime in southern China. Once a moratorium on the war trials had been pronounced, Tsuji returned to Japan, where his memoirs* became best-sellers and brought him renown. He was elected as a Member of the Diet; then, in 1961, he set off on his travels again, this time to war-torn Laos. There he disappeared, presumed caught up and killed in the civil war. At his home town of Kaga a memorial statue, dressed in a formal tailcoat, stands to honour his memory. Sometimes one may wonder what kind of people would want to commemorate a man like Masanobu Tsuji.

The basic military ethos of apostles of *gekokujo* like Tsuji, which would propel Japanese forces all the way through the Pacific War, was

---

* Notably his blood-and-thunder account of the Fall of Singapore, *Japan's Greatest Victory, Britain's Worst Defeat* (trans. Margaret E. Lake, New York, 1997).

Admiral Togo leading the action at the Battle of Tsushima in his flagship *Mikasa*.

Admiral Togo visiting the defeated Admiral Rozhestvensky in hospital after the Battle of Tsushima, 1905.

Marshal Georgy Zhukov presenting the Soviet Order of Victory to Field Marshal Bernard Law Montgomery, 5 June 1945.

Two Wehrmacht soldiers on guard west of Moscow in December 1941.

Opposite page, clockwise from top left

Georgy Zhukov *(centre)* among the Soviet generals at Nomonhan.

A Soviet postage stamp featuring a portrait of Richard Sorge, 1965.

Soviet soldiers inspecting a captured Japanese tankette – a Type 95 Ha-Go – at Nomonhan.

The God of Operations: Colonel Masanobu Tsuji.

A hastily assembled force of Moscow women gouge a huge
tank trap to halt the Panzers.

The road-oriented Wehrmacht force of 1941 was not prepared for the terrible conditions
of unpaved Russian roads, and their transport became stuck in the *rasputitsa*.

Left to right Admiral Raymond Spruance, who was appointed to lead the carrier attack on the Japanese at Midway and Admiral Isoroku Yamamoto, Commander-in-Chief of the *Kido Butai*.

The flight deck of USS *Yorktown* shortly after the first Japanese bombing attack of 4 June at the Battle of Midway. The dense smoke is coming from a hit on the ship's funnel, but the radar and guns can be seen still on alert.

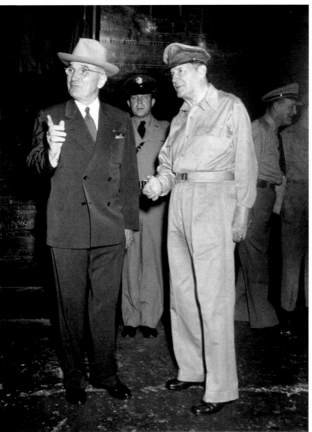

Above British soldiers surrendering to a Japanese patrol following the capture of Singapore in February 1942.

Left President Harry S. Truman *(left)* and General Douglas MacArthur at Wake Island, October 1950.

(left to right) General Henri Navarre, Colonel Christian de Castries and General Rene Cogny reviewing the honour guard during inspection of the camp at Dien Bien Phu, February 1954. Two of the men can be seen limping on canes due to war wounds.

Viet Minh soldiers assaulting French positions in the Dien Bien Phu battlefield, April 1954. It is worth noting that this photograph – among others taken by the Vietnamese – is likely to be a reconstruction, taken a few hours after the actual event.

Rejoicing Viet Minh troops on a victory parade through Hanoi, October 1954.

simply stated. It was a repetition of Georges Danton's famous war-cry from the French Revolutionary Wars – 'de l'audace, encore de l'audace, toujours de l'audace' – and, coupled with that, the notion of 'no surrender'. Of the heroes of 1905, if it was to Admiral Togo that Tsuji and his apostles looked for the touchstone of daring, it was even more to Marshal Nogi that they turned for lessons of self-sacrifice. This would be repeatedly evoked in the 1930s as representing the soul of Divine Japan, the Will of the Emperor. Delving back into samurai glories of past centuries, the *philosophes* of the military brotherhood controlling the Kwantung Army latched on to the principle that death in battle was the noblest of all achievements, whereas to surrender a post, or be taken prisoner, was the worst imaginable disgrace. There wasn't even a word in the current military lexicon for retreat, fall-back or withdrawal; instead commanders would speak of 'moving in a different direction'. Unheard of was that manoeuvre popular in the British Army, 'falling back to prepared positions', let alone, as experienced in the American forces' worst moments in Korea in 1950, the 'Bug-Out', or disorderly flight.

From Tsuji at Kwantung Army HQ would come regular enjoinders that, in the event of conflicting orders, the recipient was always to obey that which was most aggressive. Young officers were constantly inculcated with the notion that, in battle, moral and spiritual strength would win out over material factors, a tenet deeply rooted in the 1905 war. Here was a philosophy which would bring Japan some astonishing and cheap victories during the early, aggressive stages of the Pacific War but would ultimately lead to utter ruin through its belief that spiritual values could eventually win over the material weight of the most potent economy the world had ever seen. And, more immediately, it would lead to a similarly decisive defeat – though it was visible more locally – in the forthcoming Nomonhan Incident.

Ever since the Changkufeng Incident, Tsuji and the Kwantung hotheads had been spoiling for a fight, unhappy with the alleged timidity of higher headquarters and displeased with the doves in their midst. The Kwantung Army as a whole was resentful of the vacillation and interference of the General Staff in Tokyo.

Meanwhile, unnoted in Hsinking, the capital of Manchukuo, a particularly bellicose speech was delivered by Marshal Voroshilov marking October Revolution Day in Red Square on 7 November 1938. Referring to the recent fighting at Changkufeng, he warned that if another such border violation occurred, the Red Army would not confine itself merely to repelling the incursion: 'it is more convenient and easier for us to crush the enemy in his own territory'. In a report to Moscow, General Grigory Shtern, commanding all Soviet forces in the Far East, warned that, although Changkufeng was only an episode, 'it was a real operation of modern war for which the Japanese troops had undergone special training and the Imperial Staff had carried out detailed reconnaissance over many months'. Moscow was beginning to take these small-time operations in its distant Far East with extreme seriousness.

Thus was the scene set for the next 'incident', at Nomonhan.

CHAPTER NINE

THE INCIDENT

The Battle of Nomonhan took place diagonally at the opposite end of Manchukuo to Changkufeng. There the furthest eastern parts of the People's Republic of Mongolia (Stalin's first satellite) and Inner Mongolia (nominally Chinese) together formed a salient, shaped rather like a pig's snout, biting a chunk out of western Manchukuo. It was a miserably harsh, semi-arid area of mostly flat, sometimes gently undulating, sandy plains and grassland studded with occasional short scrub pines and low shrubs. The climate was extreme; in May the days could be hot, with freezing nights. In July and August, the daytime temperature regularly rose above 100°F (38°C), but the nights remained bitter. Mosquitoes and enormous horseflies swarmed in the summer, making netting imperative. There was little rainfall, but in the summer, especially in August, dense fogs often rose at dawn. It was hard to see what strategic value the area might have to either side. But to Tsuji and his fellow planners it composed a vital flank wherewith to pursue the stalemated war with China, and equally a flank on which the Russian Bear, if untamed, could thwart Japanese intentions.

The frontier in question was actually one of the few stretches where there could be, or should have been, a clear demarcation: along the meandering Halha (or, in Russian, Khalkhin Gol), a modest river starting in the Greater Hsingan mountain range in southern Manchuria (Manchukuo) and flowing to the north-west to empty into Lake Buyr Nuur. At Nomonhan it was a meagre fifty yards wide and roughly six feet deep, flowing over a sandy riverbed.

This was the border claimed, reasonably enough, by the Japanese for their new puppet-state of Manchukuo. The Russians, however, on behalf of their Mongol clients, had drawn a shorter, arbitrary line some ten miles further east, through the small village of Nomonhan. This claim was based on the fact that, from time immemorial, and

133

unchecked through the Qing dynasty, Mongolian nomads had habitually taken their shaggy little ponies across the Halha to graze on
the marginally less wretched pasture there. Then, one day in spring
1939, the ponies came across accompanied by armed Mongol cavalry
troopers. Shots were fired by Manchukuo frontier guards. On 4 May
a further party of more than fifty Mongolian horsemen was observed
setting up positions close to Nomonhan. A firefight ensued that lasted
for ten hours and gave rise to several casualties. The situation began to
escalate rapidly, with each side giving very different accounts of who
was responsible.

Although at the time twenty-seven out of Japan's thirty-seven divisions were committed to the war in China, as a token of how seriously
conflict with Russia was taken a whole division, the 23rd, was now
despatched to the desolate front at Nomonhan. The 23rd was a new,
formation, a 'triangular' division based on three regiments only. Its
troops had come from training in sub-tropical Kyushu Island, and it
was said to be 'near the end of the queue' for equipment. It was therefore assigned to what was originally believed to be a quiet backwater.
The division was short on machine guns, and particularly deficient
in anti-tank weapons; but was enemy armour likely to appear on the
plains of western Manchuria? The 23rd was commanded by a rather
gentlemanly commander of the old school, the fifty-two-year-old
Lieutenant-General Michitaro Komatsubara. Considered to be one of
the Imperial Army's leading Russian experts, Komatsubara had served
two tours as a Military Attaché in the Soviet Union. He was solidly
built, wore eyeglasses and sported a small moustache. Meticulous in
his habits, he kept detailed diaries, wrote long letters and composed
poems; but he had had no combat experience. Though he had an air
of gentleness about him, he was described as also exuding 'a sense of
gloom'. In common with all in his command, Komatsubara was steeped
in the gospel according to Masanobu Tsuji, Senior Operations Staff
Officer at Kwantung Army GHQ, now promoted lieutenant-colonel.
But, given that Nomonhan was such a remote and unimportant location, not one of the Kwantung Army headquarters officers knew where
it was; 23rd Division staff had difficulty in locating it themselves.

Komatsubara's 23rd Division, entirely reliant on the Kwantung
Army for information, says Alvin Coox, 'knew nothing about enemy

forces behind the river line'. Later staff officers at Hsinking none-theless admitted that the Japanese strength would still have been insufficient to annihilate hostile forces in the Halha region, 'since those forces proved to be far larger than had been anticipated at the time'. They knew that the nearest Soviet railhead from which remote Nomonhan could be reinforced was at Borzya, some 400 miles away, and was itself on a single-track spur of the Trans-Sib Railway lead-ing from Chita and Lake Baikal. In contrast the 23rd Division could be swiftly supplied, or reinforced, over Manchukuo's well-developed network of railways, with a railhead at Handagai just fifty miles dis-tant. Little was known about the Soviets' strength in hand, or their potential. But did that matter? Were they not the same torpid Russian enemy, a backward race, that Nogi and the parent generation to Tsuji and Komatsubara had drubbed so decisively just three decades earlier, and were now cowed by a generation of communist muddle, brutality and mindless purges?

So some time in mid-May 1939, a troop of forty Mongolian cavalry crossed the Halha River and established a camp on a dusty knoll at Nomonhan – thus well inside what the Japanese regarded as being home territory. A Manchukuoan cavalry unit was despatched to see them off. There was an exchange of fire, resulting in casualties. Each side reported the incident to its senior formation. The Battle, or War, of Nomonhan, had begun. General Komatsubara, mindful of Tsuji's Order 1488, reacted strongly, sending forward a whole battalion of his reconnaissance regiment under Lieutenant-Colonel Yaozo Azuma, some 220 cavalrymen supported by one so-called tankette,* to de-stroy the intruders and 'punish' the Soviet aggressors. An even more powerful force, consisting of 800 infantrymen of Colonel Takemitsu Yamagata's 64th Regiment, accompanied by an artillery unit, was sent in to back up Azuma, and would strike from the north boldly down the Halha. The aim was to encircle the Soviet forces that entered the dis-puted territory between Nomonhan and the Halha, and 'destroy them'. Accordingly, Azuma thrust down the east bank of the Halha, near the confluence of the small Holsten stream which ran into the Halha from the east. He would turn and form an anvil on which Yamagata,

---

* The Japanese tankette was a feeble toy, carrying one machine gun and with armour so thin that an ordinary small-arms round could penetrate it.

swinging westwards from Nomonhan, could crush the enemy with a hammer blow. That was the plan, and – on paper – it looked like a powerful riposte against a small force of largely Mongolian horsemen.

Overhead the ubiquitous Tsuji had taken to the air to watch the unfolding action from a light aircraft. Landing, he pointed proudly to a bullet-hole in the fuselage. But he had seen nothing to suggest to him that the enemy was being reinforced. He certainly could not have known that, in Moscow, merely from reading newspaper accounts that were based on Manchukuoan press releases, the Soviet High Command had become alarmed and had ordered General Nikolai Feklenko to send his 57th Army Corps, currently stationed in the Mongolian capital, Ulaanbaatar, towards the Nomonhan battle zone. Unaware of any pending crisis, the unhappy Feklenko was caught out, away on a hunting trip. Knowing, however, what failure under the Soviet regime could signify, he returned to base at once and promptly despatched a scratch force towards the battlefield. It included heavy artillery, tanks and armoured cars, which Komatsubara's forces did not have, and against which they lacked any sensible protection.

On the ground Komatsubara's attack had swiftly run into trouble. His was a complex plan* which required careful co-ordination, but radio communication between Azuma and Yamagata's units broke down immediately as a result of 'chronic equipment failures'. By 28 May, Azuma found himself caught in a trap, relentlessly bombarded by Soviet 122mm heavy guns, and harried by tanks – and unaware that Yamagata had become bogged down. Without effective anti-tank weapons, Azuma's men improvised with suicidal tactics. Infantrymen equipped with fuel-filled bottles and a short fuse (what would later become known as Molotov cocktails) would clamber atop enemy tanks, lever open the hatch and throw their bomb inside. The fuel would ignite murderously inside the tank, but the odds were that the heroic assailant would not survive, either engulfed in the tank's flames or else shot down by machine-gun fire from the accompanying Soviet tanks. They were well named 'human bullet' (*nikuhaku*) anti-tank teams. Azuma's force, writes Coox, was soon in grave trouble, 'short of water, lacking time to eat or to tend to their horses since the preceding

---

* The dangerous Japanese penchant for excessively complex plans would be seen again, this time at a more decisive level, at the Battle of Midway in 1942 (see Part Four).

night, pounded by artillery, low on ammunition, and plagued by sand-storms that clogged their weapons'.

Particularly grievous was the state of the horses, caught out in the open by Russian shellfire. Azuma's staff urged him to try to break out of the enemy ring while there was still time. But no, his instructions (as drafted by Tsuji) were to resist to the end, while holding fast to the river junction they had been ordered to secure. In the early hours of 29 May, Azuma's men drove off a Russian grenade-throwing attack, storming out of their shallow trenches 'like fierce lions and tigers'. But casualties were high, with both of Azuma's company command-ers killed. Exposed in the bitter cold of the Manchurian nights, his men (from sub-tropical Kyushu Island) suffered badly, only to be faced with the searing heat of a waterless day. By the afternoon of the 29th the Russians were closing in for the kill. Calling on the last nineteen survivors around him to join in a *banzai* charge, Azuma leaped out of his trench, and was cut down immediately by Soviet machine-gun fire. Virtually the whole of his 200-man force was wiped out. Meanwhile Colonel Yamagata's main force had fared little better, suffering some 25 per cent casualties. (Yamagata himself survived, only to commit suicide in battle three months later.) According to some Japanese accounts, before the end of the affray, Tsuji turned up at Yamagata's command post, an unwelcome arrival, to berate the Colonel for not relieving Azuma, and ordering him to go out and personally bury the bodies of Azuma's men.

Despite this expensive reversal to Japanese arms, costing some 2,000 casualties, from Kwantung GHQ Tsuji's office mystically proclaimed 'one victory and one defeat'. Implicit in this 'victory' was the heroic death in battle of Lieutenant-Colonel Azuma. After it, according to Japanese official history, 'remorse ate at the heart of General Komat-subara'. There was even a suggestion made by the Kwantung Army commander, General Kenkichi Ueda, that, if a fresh division were sent in to redeem this failure Komatsubara should follow the example of Marshal Nogi and commit *seppuku*. Nevertheless at Hsinking a new offensive plan would soon be in preparation under the aegis of Tsuji. Meanwhile, there had been a fact-finding visit from Tokyo by Tsuji's counterpart Colonel Masazumi Inada, Chief of the Operations Sec-tion at the Army General Staff (AGS). His first question had been

'Where's Nomonhan?', then he had returned to base with the usual limp recommendation when confronted by the *gekokujo* movers and shakers at Hsinking: leave matters in the capable hands of the Kwantung Army. And this even though he himself had come away with a 'gnawing suspicion' that Hsinking did not fully comprehend the seriousness of the international situation, or the reasoning that underlay the General Staff's caution. To lend additional weight to this caution, on 31 May, Stalin's new Foreign Affairs Commissar, Vyacheslav Molotov, addressing the Supreme Soviet, gave warning that 'by virtue of our treaty with Mongolia, we shall defend its frontiers as energetically as our own . . . patience has its limits'.

It was the following day that General Zhukov was summoned to the Kremlin by Voroshilov and prepared for his 'long journey'. Five days later he would arrive at 57th Corps headquarters in eastern Mongolia at Tamsag, 100 miles behind the front on the Halha River.

At this point timings become all-important, in relation to the much bigger game that was about to be played out at the other end of the world, in Europe. On 15 March 1939, Hitler marched into Prague, thereby occupying the rump of Czechoslovakia, in direct breach of the Munich agreement with Neville Chamberlain. With the destruction of Czechoslovakia went any hopes that still existed for the maintenance of peace in Europe. Clearly Poland would be next on Hitler's list. On 22 May, as Komatsubara was launching his first attack against the Soviets in Mongolia, Italy and Germany entered into a Pact of Steel. Signed by Hitler and Mussolini, it pledged each party to support the other in case of war. Even Chamberlain now prepared for war.

All through that menacing summer of 1939, Britain and France scrambled desperately, if not indecorously, to form counter-alliances in eastern Europe. Stalin was not impressed by the feeble support they could offer. Not surprisingly, given their history, the Poles would not permit Russian troops to enter their territory. Unlike most west European leaders the Kremlin had studied, and taken seriously, Hitler's rantings in *Mein Kampf*. Poland, Stalin recognized, would only be a bridge to Hitler's main ambition, the subjugation of Soviet Russia. The situation in Europe was a keg of gunpowder; and meanwhile Russia's back door in the Far East was being hammered on by an aggressive and expansionist Japan. Though theirs was the bite of a flea compared with what Hitler could do in the west, the Japanese would, as a matter of urgency, have to be crushed ruthlessly before Stalin could feel safe to pursue any diplomatic manoeuvres in Europe, and certainly before they might be tempted to join the Pact of Steel. In no way could the USSR face a war on two fronts, in two continents. Stalin was contemplating a non-aggression treaty with Germany which in August would come to be realized in the Molotov–Ribbentrop Pact. Thus it came to pass that a great deal would depend on this little 'border incident' in the faraway wastes of Mongolia: all of this invisible to the players in Europe at the time.

Oblivious to all this, and to the state of the Soviet forces in Mongolia, the Kwantung Army pursued its plans as if in a vacuum. Its intelligence remained abysmal. By way of avenging the destruction of the Azuma–Yamagata column, on 27 June a devastating air raid was launched on the forward Soviet air bases of Tamsag Bulak and Bain Tumen deep in Mongolian territory. Newly arrived Russian planes were just forming up there. One hundred and twenty Japanese planes took part, an unprecedented number for that time. Needlesss to say, the bombers were accompanied by the ubiquitous Tsuji, whose hand was to be seen in the planning of the raid. Exultant, he counted twenty-five enemy planes destroyed, and nearly a hundred more shot down by Japanese fighters as they struggled to take off.

As with so many events in this war, the raid was carried out entirely on the initiative of the Kwantung Army. Deceitfully it was launched only hours before orders forbidding any such aerial activity arrived from the AGS in Tokyo. When he heard of this latest escalation in the war, the Emperor was furious and prohibited any further air attacks into Mongolia. Colonel Inada, generally regarded as a friend of the Kwantung clique, telephoned to excoriate his opposite number at Hsinking as a 'damned idiot', accusing him of indiscipline and bad judgement. But Tsuji and the disciples of *gekokujo* turned a blind eye, telling themselves that they were, as always, executing the real wishes of the Emperor, surrounded as he was by weak-kneed and corrupt advisers. An incensed Tsuji took the opportunity to demand autonomy for the Kwantung Army in 'trivial' border matters. He later wrote that 'tremendous combat results were achieved by carrying out dangerous operations at the risk of our lives. It is perfectly clear that we were carrying out an act of retaliation. What kind of General Staff ignores the psychology of the front lines and tramples on their feelings?'

He characterized the conflict between the Kwantung Army and the Tokyo General Staff as typical of the antagonism between combat officers and 'desk jockeys'. But this embracing of downright insubordination even towards the Emperor seemed to indicate a militarist regime that was running off the rails.

Seen purely as a tactical achievement, however, the Tamsag Bulak raid was a tremendous coup for the Japanese, gaining for them mastery of the air over the battlefield which they never lost. What a tragedy it was for the Western world that the defenders of Pearl Harbor, Malaya and the Philippines two years later could not have known of the skill with which the Japanese Air Force could attack a ground target. Many US and British lives might have been saved, not to mention great warships like *Repulse* and *Prince of Wales*. As an immediate consequence, in Moscow Voroshilov's rage transcended that of the Mikado. The heads of the Soviet airmen held responsible would roll. The deputy commander of the Mongolian Army was denounced as a Japanese agent and saboteur and shot. Meanwhile, as a priority the newly arrived Zhukov would be sent every reinforcement he called for – and, as would prove to be his wont in the Second World War, he called for a lot.

It was thus in a somewhat charged atmosphere that Tsuji and the staff at Hsinking planned their grandiose July offensive, their considerable self-confidence greatly boosted by the recent aerial success. With the usual deficiency of hard intelligence, that self-confidence replaced ignorance of the realities of the battlefield. All across the Japanese lines there was, however, 'ample evidence of the transcendent importance of fighting spirit'.

Kwantung aerial reconnaissance had spotted large formations of Soviet road transport heading westwards from the front, and deduced that this indicated an enemy withdrawal. They were, however, quite wrong. What they saw were in fact empty vehicles returning from the front-line formations having delivered their heavy cargoes of fuel, ammunition and food under cover of night. It was a massive shuttle system, organized by Zhukov's predecessor, General Shtern, a phenomenal achievement of the rickety Soviet system whereby more than

4,200 vehicles trucked in some 55,000 tons of material from the distant railhead at Borzya, over 400 miles of rough, dusty tracks. By comparison the Kwantung Army could muster only 800 vehicles. This supply feat would completely deceive the Japanese as they prepared to attack. At the same time Japanese intelligence chose to disregard reports of a large number of enemy tanks moving up.

Since the Azuma disaster, for which he felt a deep sense of personal responsibility, Komatsubara had been committed to a period of what the Japanese call 'self-reflection'. Nevertheless, as Coox points out, 'almost none of the lessons from the fighting in May had been mastered by the time the next stage of the Nomonhan Incident broke out'. In broad terms, Komatsubara's offensive at the beginning of July would be a more ambitious variant of the Azuma–Yamagata plan. It would comprise a bold pincer movement in which the main weight of the 23rd Division, reinforced by a regiment from the 7th Division, would cross the Halha and, sweeping deep into Mongolian territory, take the Soviet defences from the rear. Simultaneously the enemy would be attacked frontally by a powerful strike force, commanded by Lieutenant-General Masaomi Yasuoka and containing the Japanese Army's only operational tank brigade. The principal objective would be the so-called Fui Heights, which in fact were no more than a 'raised pancake' about a mile to one-and-a-half miles across and no more than forty or fifty feet higher than the surrounding country. But, close to the confluence of the Holsten and the Halha, it was considered to be a commanding position in the forthcoming battle. The whole attacking force would total 15,000 men, 120 pieces of artillery, 70 tanks and 180 aircraft. It certainly seemed a powerful body with which to correct a small boundary dispute.

On the night of 2/3 July, while Zhukov was still lining up his forces for a massive riposte, the Japanese achieved a brilliant tactical success. A battalion of the 71st Infantry Regiment rowed silently across the Halha River on a moonless night and made an unopposed landing on the west bank opposite the Fui Heights. Tsuji went along on the operation, which he had planned himself: the objective, to trap and destroy the enemy forces at the river junction. Conditions for the advancing Japanese troops were appalling: with little transport they were forced to slog across sand baking under the fierce sun at over 100°F (38°C), fifteen hours a day, carrying eighty-pound packs. At night they froze on the shelterless steppe, tormented by the swarming mosquitoes. Soon there was an acute shortage of water. Men of one unit launched a crazed charge to capture a Russian machine gun, simply so that they could drink its cooling water; others tried to assuage their thirst by licking the blood of their wounds. The plight of the horses was particularly pitiful. No lessons seem to have been learned since the disastrous Azuma operation in May.

Gradually Tsuji's operation began to peter out. The daring raid across the river had managed to establish only one bridge, and this was so rickety as to make passage by tanks and heavy equipment impossible. So the Japanese infantry who had established the bridgehead found themselves without armoured support. Russian artillery fire, inflicting heavy losses on the crews, effectively destroyed the Japanese bridging equipment. General Komatsubara, in a state of misery, decided to withdraw his tenuous bridgehead across the Halha. While the new offensive was still in the planning stage, back at Hsinking GHQ, General Inada had remarked sadly that if he were Komatsubara 'he would kill himself'. The moment was approaching when the unfortunate Komatsubara would feel somewhat the same.

Meanwhile, on the other side of the lines, at his Mongolian HQ Zhukov was taking over. Furious at the success of the Japanese air raid on Tamsag Bulak, his rage had been compounded by the fact that the Japanese crossing of the Halha had caught him on the back foot, before he had been able to assemble his sledgehammer blow. Had it been backed up by greater force, Zhukov recognized late in the day, the move could have led to a wedge threatening his whole forward position. Knowing of the fate of Mongolian deputy commander Luvsandonoi, who was denounced as a saboteur and shot, Zhukov might well have felt an uneasy twitch in the hair at the back of his bull neck. Meanwhile, he had damned his predecessor, Nikolai Feklenko, for being 'badly organized, and [having] poor intelligence'. The disorganization of the May battle, reported Zhukov, was the result of 'poor tactics, ill-conceived battle management, and a failure to calculate and anticipate enemy manoeuvres'. On arrival he had asked Feklenko tartly whether operations could be directed seventy-five miles behind the front, and it had soon become clear to him that the 57th Corps headquarters knew little about the situation on the battle front.[*]

Without hesitation Zhukov now threw in piecemeal the whole of his newly arrived 11th Tank Brigade and elements of a Mongolian cavalry division. On his first sight of the Nomonhan battlefield he had recognized what that mastermind of armoured warfare, the fallen Tukhachevsky, would have seen: that the open, sandy wilderness was ideal for armoured warfare on a large scale. By July the Russian tanks had been much improved; they had external netting to deflect the Japanese Molotov cocktails, and hatches that could no longer be prised open. The Japanese *nikuhaku*, the human bullets, did indeed become suicide weapons. As of Nomonhan, Japan could field somewhere over a thousand tanks, but most were poorly armoured, inadequately armed and designed for an infantry-support role. This emphasis left the Imperial Japanese Army without a tank capable of taking on other tanks, a deficiency which made itself felt in the Nomonhan campaign.[†] Russians dubbed the IJA's tanks and tankettes 'cute little toys', whereas a Japanese infantryman gazing through binoculars found it 'embarrassing to say', but 'the Japanese tank-gun barrels looked like a little boy's penis, just protruding, whereas the Russian barrels were really long. "No contest!" I thought . . .'

By contrast, the Russians by 1939 already fielded an excellent anti-tank gun, the 45mm, which could slice through Japanese armour of a mere 15–17mm thickness, at ranges of up to 1,500 yards. They had improved their main battle tank, the BT-7, by 1939 standards one of the most mobile in the field, capable of a fast 40mph (it could also run on wheels on roads, by shedding tracks, which was unusual, but of little use in Mongolia where there were no roads). Its revolutionary suspension had been stolen from an American designer J. Walter Christie, and would subsequently be used by the Russians in their T-34, the

---

[*] Perhaps surprisingly, Feklenko lived on to become an army commander in the disastrous 1941 battles in the Ukraine, surviving the Second World War altogether.

[†] With the priority of steel, constantly in short supply, being granted to the navy, the Japanese Army was never able to rectify the shortcomings of its tanks. The warning of Nomonhan was slow to be recognized. After 1941, and with the entry of the United States into the conflict, priorities shifted to providing the weapons of naval warfare and defending the empire from the advancing Americans. Thus the tanks that Allied forces in the Pacific faced were primarily designs of the 1930s, such as the Type 97 medium and Type 95 light tanks, which had been Japan's mainstay at Nomonhan.

most successful tank of the Second World War.* At only 14.5 tons, the BT-7's light armour was sufficient to stand up to Japanese anti-tank weapons, and its 45mm gun could knock out any of the 'toy' Japanese tanks that came within range. Nevertheless, one heroic Japanese battalion commander, Major Adachi, was watched by his men as he mounted a BT-7, with his sword drawn, only to be cut down by tracer from another tank.

In the torrid heat of a Mongolian July, General Komatsubara was slowly losing the initiative, his offensive across the Halha being ground to a halt by Zukhov's improvised counter-attacks. There now took place the first major tank-versus-tank battle in the history of war. It was hugely costly to both sides. The Japanese attacked with the whole of two tank regiments, which in fact comprised almost all the armour of the Kwantung Army. Kwantung Army standing regulations forbade the abandonment of a tank under fire, even if the machine were knocked out. Crewmen were ordered 'to share the fate of their tank, saving their last bullet to commit suicide'. But many Japanese infantrymen in the July battles claimed that they never saw a friendly tank in action. 'Retreat and surrender were not merely dishonourable, they were literally impermissible. In some cases they could be capital offenses punishable by death,' comments historian Stuart D. Goldman. It was a throwback to Japanese samurai concepts of martial honour. To add to the problems of the Japanese tank crews, the Russians also deployed a cunning 'secret weapon': rolls of high-tensile piano wire which became entangled in the tracks of the lightweight tanks, bringing them to a standstill to be picked off by Russian guns. Nevertheless, the tank battle was also costly to the Russians. In the counter-attacks, Commander Yakovlev of the 11th Armoured Brigade, who personally led from the front, was reported as having died a 'glorious death'. He was subsequently made a Hero of the Soviet Union, while the tank in which he died still stands as a monument on the battlefield today.

The most damage was wreaked by Zhukov's heavy artillery, superior

---

* Instead of adopting the native Christie suspension, which gave tanks greater speed, mobility and a lower silhouette, in the Second World War American tank designers, in their Grant and Sherman main battle tanks, went in for modified tractor suspension. The tanks were cheaper to produce – but they were not cheap when it came to the lives of crews. British tankers nicknamed the Sherman 'the Ronson': 'one flick and it lights.'

in both range and calibre. Early on in the battle, a heavy Soviet shell landed squarely on Komatsubara's 23rd Division HQ, killing his Chief of Staff, Colonel Ouchi, and inflicting terrible carnage among the tethered horses. It shook morale badly, even affecting Tsuji, who was in the HQ at the time. Japanese 120mm guns, with their feeble maximum range of 5,500 yards, could hit back only if deployed close to enemy lines, thus exposing them to deadly counter-battery fire. In contrast to the Japanese who had expended two-thirds of their ammunition in the first two days of the offensive, the Russians – despite their immense supply problems across Mongolia – seemed to have an inexhaustible stockpile. To some Japanese officers, writes Goldman, the battlefield 'seemed like one vast Soviet firing range'.

By the end of the second searing week of July, Komatsubara had lost his hard-won bridgehead across the Halha, though he maintained a tenuous foothold just east of it, provocatively still in territory claimed by the Soviets. The Holsten pincer attack had failed, yet the Japanese command remained typically upbeat. Kwantung Army commander General Ueda sent Komatsubara a telegram congratulating him and praising 'decisive combat results'. Komatsubara relayed the commendation to his subordinate commanders. Once more this was wishful thinking. Overall Japanese casualties had now risen to 15,500, forty-five planes, all their tanks and much of their artillery.

Soviet losses too had been heavy, with more than 5,000 casualties by the end of July, but Zhukov now had a ready supply of fresh reinforcements flowing in across the Trans-Sib. In contrast, Komatsubara had virtually nil reserves coming to support his battle-worn and greatly diminished units. All air attacks on Mongolian bases were now strictly forbidden by Tokyo – a serious handicap. The fault lay squarely with the Kwantung Army; since its commanders had lied so brazenly about the scale of the Nomonhan 'border incident' in the first place, back in May, they could not now call upon Tokyo for fresh reserves.

Thus, as Komatsubara's July offensive ended, he stood with some 70,000 fatigued and under-equipped troops facing a high-grade force of 100,000 under Zhukov – with do-or-die orders from Stalin to win at whatever cost, and swiftly. By August, Zhukov could call on 200 aircraft, 800 armoured vehicles, 45,000 men in three rifle divisions and 200 heavy guns.

The hand of a ruthless commander had made itself felt the moment Zhukov arrived at his front-line HQ. To Moscow he stigmatized his hapless predecessor, General Feklenko, as 'an enemy of the people'. Bulletins were posted warning his troops that, if they failed to carry out orders, they would be brought before military tribunals and severely punished. 'I call upon you', urged Zhukov, 'to show courage, manliness, audacity, braveness and heroism. Death to despicable cowards and traitors.'

On 13 July he issued a decree announcing that two soldiers had been shot for cowardice. Six days later 57th Corps was reorganized into the 1st Army Group and given operational independence, an arrangement designed to ensure that Zhukov could act without interference, except for instructions coming directly from the General Staff in Moscow. The command picture was completed on 31 July when Zhukov was formally promoted from Komdiv (divisional commander) to Komkor (corps commander) – the equivalent of a four-star general in a Western army. It was a meteoric ascent for a young and relatively untried general. But Zhukov knew that his neck would be on the block in the event of failure, or even of partial success. What he did not know were the motives in high-level European realpolitik that lay behind Stalin's priorities. Zhukov was there, not merely to punish a minor border incursion, but to inflict major damage on an enemy power such as Tokyo would not forget.

By their very nature the Soviets were expert in the art of *maskirovka*, or deception. The Kwantung Army, with its weakness in intelligence work, lent itself as the ideal partner. Accordingly, a handbook called *What the Soviet Soldier Must Know in Defence* was distributed to Zhukov's units and deliberately leaked to the Japanese. Russian troops were observed to be digging in vigorously on the centre of the line, across the Halha and opposite Nomonhan, apparently building defensive works – *maskirovka*! All this was precisely the kind of information Tsuji and the apostles of hubris at Hsinking found most readily digestible. It must mean, they deduced, that the July fighting had in fact battered the Russians into some kind of submission. But, thanks notably to Sorge's precise intelligence, Zhukov had very different intentions. On 20 August, he first struck at the centre of the Japanese line, from behind the defensive works that his troops had been so laboriously, and visibly, digging. Japanese intelligence at once concluded that this was the focal point of a new Soviet effort. Obligingly Komatsubara sent forces to hit back at this part of the line. Soon he was committed, locked in a bitter fight from which it became harder and harder to disengage.

Then Zhukov pounced, attacking from both wings of the battlefield, with massive armour backed strongly by aircraft, in a double-envelopment manoeuvre. The defenders had been reinforced by elements of General Kunisaki's 7th Division, but these were paltry compared with the forces Zhukov had in hand. The flanks of the unsuspecting Japanese were held by Manchurian troops, poorly equipped and ill trained, in effect at best half-hearted colonial forces.*

The Japanese order of battle, strengths and locations were clearly itemized for Zhukov by Sorge's intelligence. On the southern flank Zhukov's deputy commander, Major-General M.I. Potapov, with his armour sliced through these inferior Manchukuoan forces, caught quite unprepared, and struck brutally into Komatsubara's unprotected rear areas. A similar blow smashed through the Manchukuoan formations that were supposedly protecting the northern flank. Heavy artillery barrages and aerial bombardment of unprecedented violence rained down on the defenders. Japanese resistance was impeded by the ban imposed by Tokyo on any further air strikes on Mongolian territory.

At Nomonhan there would be three phases: first, the brutal frontal attack to pin down the Japanese forward defence line, along the eastern slopes of the Halha; secondly, the penetration of both flanks, with the attackers wreaking havoc among Japanese artillery batteries and command centres; and, finally, the wider envelopment thrusts aimed at Nomonhan itself and the total destruction of an army unable (indeed, forbidden) to escape.

There were two factors that principally dictated the force of Zhukov's attack. As the Japanese troops shivered in their lightweight uniforms and poorly protected shelters, cold winds at night heralded the end of the campaigning season with the onset of winter. But much

---

* Comparisons would be made three years later, at Stalingrad, with the unfortunate Romanians left holding the vital German flanks where Zhukov, once again, would strike with decisive force.

more pressing was Stalin's urgent need to have a clear-cut victory in the east as he concluded his immensely risky manoeuvring with the arch-enemy, Hitler, in the west. Starting on 20 August, the assault had to be clinched within the week.

Zhukov's 'softening-up' preparations on 20 August hit the Japanese positions like a cyclone. His heavy artillery pounded the flimsily built shelters without let-up for as long as ten hours, with an apparently bottomless supply of shells. Of course Komatsubara's men had received no warning from Tsuji's staff. By midday units were experiencing great difficulty in obtaining supplies of ammunition, food and water. On the southern flank, Potapov, smashing through the Manchukuoan units holding it, bent back the line some ten miles. The Manchukuoans fled. Far to the north, the two Mongolian cavalry regiments supported by Soviet armour easily routed the opposing Manchukuoan cavalry flanking the key Fui Heights. In the Japanese cavalry that faced them, 80 per cent of the horses were killed that first day; the rest stampeded or were injured. 'Although the sight was grisly, the horse soldiers were relieved to a certain extent because there was neither water for the animals nor time to attend to them,' writes Coox. The commander of a Reconnaissance Regiment, Lieutenant-Colonel Ioki, had no water of his own but depended entirely on the division trucks to haul in supplies daily. Now the vehicles could not get through. Against such an emergency, the Japanese had dug ten wells, around fifteen feet deep, but from them only a trickle of water could be drawn with mess tins. Every well had been smashed by the bombardments. 'The men used towels to wipe up night dew and then chewed on the cloth to wet their parched throats.' The Russians now moved up guns of every calibre, including 152mm, and blasted the strongpoints at short range, firing over open sights. Flamethrowers burned out bunkers and dug-outs, followed by infantry who moved in with grenades and bayonets. At the Fui Heights, a desperate charge was attempted by the 1st Company of Major Ikuta's 1st Battalion (26th Infantry Regiment), but was abandoned after losing sixty-five of its eighty-five men. One badly wounded soldier wrote despondently: 'To be killed is all that remains.'

The attackers seemed to know the location and the fighting value of every single Japanese and Manchukuoan unit. How did they know? Where could the crucial information possibly have come from? Who

would have thought that the source was a fun-loving German journalist living high on the hog in Tokyo itself? It was not until 0900 on
21 August that Kwantung Army HQ learned officially from the 23rd
Division about the attacks that had been launched more than twenty-
four hours earlier.

By the end of the 21st, the inner prongs of the Soviet envelopment
were gradually constricting the enemy, on the wings in particular. A
Japanese staff officer reported that the 23rd Division's defences had
already been 'split widely'. The following day, 22 August, when the unfortunate General Komatsubara called upon a regimental commander
(Colonel Sumi of the 26th Infantry Regiment) to mount a counter-
attack, Sumi responded in a manner seldom heard in a Japanese Army
unit: 'No, sir, it can't be done. My unit is a regiment in name only. I
have only about two companies and a battalion commander with me.'
Later Sumi explained that 'I felt that Komatsubara's plan was suitable
for a "picnic" not combat.' But he replied to the General: 'I am thinking
of fighting and dying where I am located. Please let me do so.'

By the end of 23 August Potapov's armour had broken the whole
IJA defensive structure. Accounts by the outgunned and outmanoeu-
vred Japanese defenders caught up in the merciless fighting make
poignant reading. One of Ioki's reconnaissance companies, for instance, was reduced to four or five men. The walking wounded were
ordered to accompany their comrades, but those who felt that they
could not make it were given hand grenades, with the implication that
they should kill themselves rather than be taken prisoner. A sickening
incident took place when Russian tanks of the 9th Armoured Brigade,
breaking through deeply behind the enemy lines, overran a Japanese
field hospital (though the Japanese claimed that it was liberally covered with Red Crosses), crushing the wounded on their litters.

On the 24th Tsuji happened to be present at the command post of
Major-General Morita commanding 14th Brigade of the newly arrived 7th Division. There Soviet armour had overrun a quartermaster
dump, destroying valuable food supplies. 'Barrels of pickled apricots
were breached, drenching the soil with red juice that looked like blood,'
in plain sight of the hungry defenders. Sitting down to eat that night,
Tsuji and Morita were surprised by an enemy air attack; dowsing the
candle, they jumped into an anti-aircraft trench. If hostile aircraft could

attack by night as well as day, Tsuji feared that would mean that the Russians had regained 'aerial supremacy'. At that moment, a subaltern burst in and shouted that the Fui strongpoint had fallen, together with every officer and man. Tsuji reacted furiously, berating the wretched man: 'What do you mean by "annihilated"? You are alive, aren't you?'

When Japanese counter-attacks did take place, and not until the fifth day of the Soviet onslaught, preparations were made on the spur of the moment, and planning and execution were generally slipshod. Tsuji flew back to Hsinking to report on the situation at the front. There he encountered disbelief, almost amounting to paralysis, as the HQ staff took on board the full extent of the disaster unfolding at Nomonhan. From the well-marked map taken from a dead Soviet officer, Tsuji was able to tell them that the numbers of Soviet forces attacking apparently exceeded the Intelligence Section's previous estimates by a factor of two, and exceeded Japanese strength by a factor of four or five. On his way back to the front, his plane was shot down. Indestructible as ever, however, he managed to make his way to Major-General Kobayashi's command post on foot, which would place him closer to the fighting than even he had anticipated. There one of Kobayashi's units (he commanded Komatsubara's main infantry resources) had charged into the enemy positions and been almost annihilated by Soviet tanks. Casualties were becoming insupportable for the Japanese. Frequently there were cases of a mere corporal becoming an acting company commander, with a first lieutenant taking over a whole battalion.

The list of senior officers killed or wounded by 25 August made sombre reading: Colonel Sakai's 72nd Regiment alone had lost 323 killed (including thirty-one officers), and 377 wounded (twenty-one officers, including Colonel Sakai himself). Kobayashi himself had been hit in the thigh by a tank-shell fragment and fell to the ground, bleeding profusely. The troops ahead of him broke under fire. Fleeing 'like a tidal wave', they never noticed or else ignored the fallen General, whom they trampled with their boots until his wound became gory and filthy.

Equally hard hit by long-range Russian 152mm guns were the Japanese artillery. Exasperated by the non-stop shelling, a commander of a heavy artillery regiment, Lieutenant-Colonel Someya, decided to commit suicide after two of his battery commanders had been killed. Having destroyed his heavy guns, Someya made a valedictory speech exhorting his men to die 'like beautifully falling cherry blossoms'. Then he killed himself.

Komatsubara's men more or less gave up their counter-attacks after 26 August. Soviet infantry of the southern and northern forces had further shrunk the envelopment trap by that day. Japanese bastions were falling in ever more rapid succession, and reinforcements were halted by the Soviet Air Force, as escape routes to the east were severed. More and more senior commanders were killed, several by their own swords. Still fanatical resistance continued in pockets. 'We will be annihilated,' said a young second lieutenant. 'But we are Japanese soldiers' was regimental HQ's automatic response. Accounts of suicidal bayonet charges, in keeping with Kwantung indoctrination, proliferated. One regimental commander shot his wounded men with a revolver, at their own request, 'sending them to heaven'.

By the 28th, the Soviet net was closing in on Komatsubara's divisional command post, now reduced to no more than 'an open, conical dip hardly more than 150 metres in diameter and three metres in depth'. Tsuji, on his fifth volunteered visit to divisional HQ, found the situation almost untenable, the General helpless. He later wrote, 'it was like a living hell' as he listened to the moaning of the wounded. For the sake of honour, Tsuji urged that the divisional commander should be saved. But Komatsubara decided not to try to break out. Meanwhile in a nearby bunker that housed the commander of the 71st Regiment, Lieutenant-Colonel Higashi, the Colonel was pleading with the severely wounded to 'please kill themselves bravely when the enemy approached to close quarters'. That evening Higashi's men saw him leap out of the trench, brandishing his sword and shouting defiantly as he charged a Soviet position: 'I am Lieutenant-Colonel Higashi, forty-nine years old!' He was instantly cut down, his intestines ripped open. Yet his mind remained lucid, and he lay in the dug-out continuing to give orders, telling his orderly to report to Komatsubara that he had conducted 'an unskilful operation but I could not do better'.

By now, Komatsubara's HQ was experiencing a hell of its own. When a shower of hand grenades were thrown in at point-blank range, his Chief of Staff Colonel Okamoto had his knee torn to shreds. Under intense fire, surgeons successfully amputated his shattered leg with only a local anaesthetic. 'Okamoto uttered no sound during or after the operation.' Although Okamoto had lost a lot of blood and said he felt cold, he never complained. Instead, locking his hands behind his head, he was reported to have gazed at the sky, remarking, 'My, but the stars are really beautiful tonight.'* Such was the innate stoicism of Japanese soldiers of the period.

By 27 August Zhukov felt confident enough to issue a decree to the 1st Army Group announcing that the Japanese forces on Mongolian territory at Khalkhin Gol had been surrounded and destroyed. What remained was the mopping up of isolated groups of a thoroughly beaten force. Nomonhan was reoccupied, but Zhukov adhered strictly to his orders from Stalin not to occupy an inch of territory beyond the claimed ante-bellum border. This had been a battle only to destroy a military threat. Repeatedly the words appear in Red Army orders: 'We must teach them a lesson.' The result: a total defeat for the Japanese, though this would never be accepted by Tsuji and the Kwantung Army. For neither side was it a cheap lesson. Long afterwards, vultures as big as a man were observed hovering over the grisly field of battle. Casualty estimates differ widely. The Japanese officially reported 8,440 killed and 8,766 wounded, while the Soviets initially admitted 9,284 total casualties. It is likely that these figures published at the time were reduced for propaganda purposes. Some sources claim that the Japanese suffered 45,000 or more soldiers killed, compared with Soviet casualties of at least 17,000. In recent years, with the gradual opening of the Soviet archives in the 1990s, a more accurate assessment of Soviet casualties has emerged, citing 7,974 killed and 15,251 wounded; later, in a 2001 publication, the Soviet losses are given as 9,703 killed and missing. Given that Zhukov was never one to blanche at heavy losses, it seems that the combined Soviet and Mongolian casualties were considerably higher than admitted. On both sides many died in hospital from disease.

Japanese casualties were particularly appalling in relation to the number of participants. Of the 15,975 officers and men of Komatsubara's

---

* Remarkably, Okamoto survived but was murdered mysteriously in a hospital bed the following year.

23rd Division, 30 per cent were killed in action; 34 per cent wounded, 4 per cent missing and another 8 per cent reported as sick – a staggering loss ratio of 76 per cent.

There were also some 3,000 Japanese prisoners of war taken. The figure may seem suspect, given the prevailing Japanese ethos. Mention has already been made of the spirit of 'no surrender' imbued in the troops by Tsuji and other fanatics of the Kwantung Army. The precept ran that a soldier taken prisoner disgraced his Emperor and his family and was 'to be despised and shunned as a coward'. The harsh regime of *bushido* pursued returning Japanese POWs even well after the war. Captivity was a matter of eternal shame which had to be concealed from everybody, including parents and kin. Post-war returnees were subjected to rigorous courts martial, followed, if they were lucky enough to escape execution or lengthy prison sentences, by 'spiritual education' during which the subject was forbidden to have any contact with the outside world – certainly not his own family. It was hardly surprising that many opted to remain and face an even more uncertain future in Stalin's Soviet Russia.*

Though the Battle of Nomonhan was effectively won by the end of August, sporadic fighting continued into September as the Kwantung Army continued to believe in some kind of miracle. Finally an armistice was concluded on 16 September. From different motives both Tokyo and Moscow were deeply reticent: Japan out of the shame of defeat, Stalin through the complex workings of his deeply suspicious mind, fearful of any factor that might upset his tortuous current dealings with Hitler. In the *New York Times* of 4 October, its well-informed correspondent Hugh Byas reported that the scale of Japanese losses 'had not been expected'. His report was headed: 'TOKYO ADMITS DEFEAT BY SOVIET; CALLS MONGOL BATTLE "DISASTROUS"'.

This was not however the spin events would receive at Hsinking. Nomonhan had been a setback, yes, but nothing more. Now the hotheads there, and in Tokyo, were already at work on new plans. Next it would be the turn of the navy. For years Nomonhan would remain the unknown war, and not just because it had been eclipsed immediately

---

* There would be a curious inversion of this in 1945 when many thousands of Soviet POWs liberated by the Western Allies after the collapse of Nazi Germany opted to remain in the West and had to be repatriated by force.

by the more momentous event of the Second World War breaking out in Europe just as the fighting on the bleak steppes of Mongolia came to an end. Unlike the war of 1905, there were no naval or military observers present, such as the meticulous Captain Pakenham RN, and certainly no war correspondents.

As the battle came to an end at Nomonhan, on 28 August Zhukov started a letter to his wife which he completed three days later:

> Hello, My Darling Wife
> Greetings and all my affectionate kisses to you . . . Since 20.8. I have been conducting a continuous battle. Today the destruction of the Japanese Samurai will be completed . . .
> Today I received the report that I had been awarded the title of Hero of the Soviet Union. Obviously you will know about this already. Such praise by the government, the party, and Voroshilov obliges me to try even harder to fulfil my duty to the Motherland.
> Affectionately and lovingly all my kisses to you
> Until we meet again soon,
> Zhorzh.

In terms of public awards and citations most of the laurels for the victory were heaped upon General Grigory Shtern,* Zhukov's predecessor and nominal superior. But within the conclaves of the Kremlin, where it really mattered, Zhukov was the man of the hour, the rising star. He had won a brilliant victory, the Red Army's first since the Civil War, exacting a suitable revenge for Russia's humiliating defeat in the 1904–5 Russo-Japanese War. From Nomonhan, like Napoleon after the battles of Arcole and Rivoli, the ruthless young General emerged with more than just a reputation. He had gained invaluable command experience in battle. At Nomonhan he had employed the techniques that later would become his hallmarks: the ability, like Napoleon, to 'see only one thing' and then concentrate all on a *point d'appui* of weakness. Proved adept in the art of *maskirovka*, he also displayed great patience in building up superior strength and then striking with devastating force at his enemy's most vulnerable point, co-ordinating massed

---

* Shtern was arrested in June 1941 during a new purge of the Red Army, possibly with anti-Semitic undertones, and was executed four months later. Following Stalin's death his reputation was posthumously rehabilitated.

artillery, armour and motorized infantry with tactical air support – and with no qualms about accepting casualties when necessary. His superb deployment of the double envelopment would stand him well in front of Moscow in 1941, and again at Stalingrad the following year. There his tactics would be a carbon copy of Nomonhan. It could be said that, if Waterloo had been won on the playing-fields of Eton, then Stalingrad was won on the bleak steppes of Mongolia.

In Tokyo, failure at Nomonhan brought down the government, leading Japan a further stretch down the road to the military, fascist government of General Hideki Tojo – and to the Pacific War. Little more than modest strictures were meted out to the personnel of Kwantung Army HQ for involving the country in so foolish and disastrous a war. Writing in 1950, only months after receiving amnesty for alleged war crimes, Masanobu Tsuji, newly promoted colonel, offered the following explanation, which was neither an apology nor an excuse: '. . . I have to admit that we at KwAHQ could have acted more wisely, if we and those at AGS had kept cool heads.'

The major consequence that defeat at Nomonhan had for Japanese strategy was to cancel once and for all any contemplation of the 'go north' policy, a decision which would be promptly, and most usefully, relayed to Moscow by Richard Sorge. The Japanese war party, still bent on expansionism and the acquisition of raw material, now directed their energies to 'go south': the attack on Pearl Harbor, Singapore and the Philippines. Even if they had learned nothing from Nomonhan, strategically, what they had picked up there by way of battle-craft undoubtedly helped the IJA in its initial successes in the subsequent Pacific War. Despite his disastrous interventions at Nomonhan, the hand of Tsuji would be seen often in campaigns like Malaya, where he played a leading role in devising the tactics of infiltration that would shatter the British defences. Those early triumphs would also cause the Western Allies to overvalue the IJA, which they might not have done had they been able to observe the Kwantung Army's reverses in the summer of 1939 at Nomonhan.

For Moscow the timing of the victory at Nomonhan had immeasurable significance. By 31 August, Zhukov's forces had completed the third phase of their offensive, and essentially won the undeclared war at Nomonhan. Next day, on 1 September, the Germans invaded

Poland. The Second World War had begun. Stalin had played his hand with consummate skill. Realizing in the summer of 1939 that he would get nothing out of any defensive alliance with France and Britain to stave off Germany, and full of suspicion (not unreasonably) that their intentions were to get Germany and Russia committed in war against each other, he performed the most amazing volte-face of the age. He entered into a non-aggression pact with Hitler. The timing was critical. Stalin knew that Hitler intended to move on Poland in early September. Yet he could not afford to take any strategic risk in Europe so long as he had a belligerent Japan gnawing away at his backside in the Far East. On 18–19 August Hitler was applying maximum pressure on Stalin to receive his Foreign Minister Joachim von Ribbentrop in Moscow without delay. Only on the 20th was Zhukov ready to launch his sledgehammer attack at Nomonhan. On 23 August, Ribbentrop arrived in Moscow to conclude the agreement that would seal Poland's fate and unleash war in Europe, the Molotov–Ribbentrop Pact. That was the very day, the first day, that Zhukov could report to Moscow, bullishly, that he was about to complete the total destruction of Japanese forces at Nomonhan. With some glee Ribbentrop passed on to Hiroshi Oshima, the Japanese Ambassador in Moscow, the news that the Russians had assured him that they had won a great victory at Nomonhan. Oshima retorted that that could not be true, for an IJA staff officer who had passed through the Nomonhan area one or two weeks earlier had reported to him that the situation was 'very favourable' to the Japanese.

Nevertheless with his diplomatic finessing Stalin was still facing huge risks. Although he knew through Sorge that the Japanese Army was not prepared for all-out war with the USSR, on past form he could not be absolutely certain that Kwantung would act rationally, or obey the instructions from Tokyo. What would have been the consequences if Zhukov had failed? With a still menacing Japan barking at his rear, Stalin would hardly have risked marching into eastern Poland. Consequently, in launching Barbarossa in June 1941, Hitler would have started a crucial couple of hundred miles further down the road towards Moscow. Moreover, when he reached Moscow, the invaluable reinforcements from Siberia which turned the tide in its defence would not have been available. They would still have been locked up in the defence of the Soviet Far East, against Japan.

Stalin's handling of armistice negotiations with the defeated Japanese was masterly. Aware of the importance of 'face' in Tokyo, he ensured that the victorious Russians would demand no reparations and make no territorial claims. Zhukov's forces would not move one inch beyond the border at Nomonhan. It was sufficient that, badly mauled, the Kwantung Army had 'learned a lesson' and would not again commit aggression against its Soviet, or Mongolian, neighbours. Memories of Kuropatkin's disastrous campaign in Manchuria were still kept alive in the Kremlin. Here, too, was perhaps a precedent that General MacArthur could well have studied before his triumphant rush to the Yalu River in 1950.

The consequences of Stalin's brutal play of realpolitik with Hitler in August 1939 are etched in history. Once again unhappy Poland would be subjected to another division. As the Wehrmacht smashed in the western doors of Poland, the Russians would move in to occupy its eastern provinces. That was the secret deal as agreed in Moscow: Stalin would occupy the three Baltic states. He would launch a dismal war against Finland, all with the objective of gaining a defensive belt for Soviet Russia against its new ally, Nazi Germany. But it would also bring the Red Army face to face with Hitler's Wehrmacht, with no buffer state of Poland between them any longer.

Perhaps, in the realms of 'what if?', it might have saved a great deal of pain and loss on all sides if the details of the Battle of Nomonhan had been more widely known at the time. Had Hitler, for instance, been able to take on board the full potential of the Red Army as evinced by Zhukov's performance, he might have been warier of launching Barbarossa in the summer of 1941. Then again, awareness of the Japanese capacity for fanatical suicidal bravery at Nomonhan, as well as the Tojo regime's dedication to aggressive war, might have helped the US in its conduct of the Pacific War. It might even have persuaded Roosevelt to place Pearl Harbor on something more of an urgent war footing. But these were lessons that, unseen, could never be learned.

PART THREE

MOSCOW, 1941

CHAPTER TEN

GENERAL SUMMER

In the course of 1941, hubris would lead Hitler into committing in quick succession the three greatest mistakes of his career, mistakes of historic and fatal proportions. First was Operation Barbarossa itself, the decision to invade the vast landmass of Russia; second was his tardy commitment to an all-out attack to capture Moscow – as his predecessor Napoleon had done a century-and-a-half earlier; third, and the most ruinous of all, was his declaration of war on the US on 11 December, a mere week after his offensive on Moscow had finally ground to a halt. These were red-letter decisions of terrifying consequence.

It was, however, well before the first Panzers rumbled into Soviet space that Hitler's genius for war began to let him down, replaced by the hubris that would eventually destroy him and the Third Reich. His strategic planning was grossly flawed. In the first place the Barbarossa timetable had been disrupted by a quite unnecessary sideshow when he moved to crush Yugoslavia and clear the British out of Greece. That meant that, instead of starting his campaign in May, as soon as the quagmires of the spring *rasputitsa* (the twice-yearly mud season) had dried out, and the short campaigning season had begun, Hitler delayed until the last week in June. By a curious coincidence of history, he and Napoleon in 1812 set off within a day of each other. Napoleon delayed for the much more valid reason that he had to wait until the grasses of the steppe had grown sufficiently to fodder his horses. As it happened, it was not 'General Winter' that defeated both Napoleon and Hitler, but 'General Summer'. In the short but intense summer heat of 1812, the horses of Napoleon's cavalry, as vital to his operations as the Panzers were to Hitler, perished from thirst and fatigue; while Hitler's Panzers would arrive before Moscow worn out and disabled, *hors de combat* from the dust of summer before the first snows even fell.

On the eve of Barbarossa, there was a fundamental disagreement between Hitler and his top generals over strategic priorities. The Führer's instructions were 'Leningrad first, the Donetsk Basin [the great industrial area in the eastern Ukraine] second, Moscow third'. He had no doubts that his invincible Wehrmacht could march on all three objectives at once. To him, Moscow was of 'no great importance'; instead he saw victory achieved through destruction of the Red Army west of the capital. In the first crucial weeks and months of the campaign Hitler would have his way. Initially, as in France, the campaign went superbly well. On the very first morning, Stalin's unprepared air force lost over 1,200 aircraft, most of them on the ground, lined up wing tip to wing tip (many of them newly delivered).*

Hitler had been encouraged by the humiliation inflicted by the Finns on Soviet forces in the Winter War of 1939–40 – a war triggered by Stalin's desire for a defensive buffer. Employing the crude, post-1918 tactics of infantry attacks unco-ordinated with armour, such as Zhukov had discarded at Nomonhan, the Red Army in Finland suffered horrendous casualties at the hands of a small but doughty nation. According to Nikita Khrushchev, who was then head of the Communist Party in Ukraine, the Soviet leaders had believed that 'All we had to do was to raise our voice a little bit, and the Finns would obey. If that didn't work, we could fire one shot and the Finns would put up their hands and surrender.' It was an illusion that was swiftly shattered when the Finns fought back with a skill the Russians could not match. Despite the assurances of Kliment 'bag of shit' Voroshilov, in command of the campaign, that 'All is well, all is in order, all is ready,' in 105 days of savage fighting the Soviets suffered 200,000 casualties, including 50,000 dead, out of a total of 460,000 men. Over 3,350 artillery pieces and about 3,000 tanks, a hundred times as many as the Finns had, supported by 1,300 aircraft, were deployed on the Karelian Isthmus alone. It was a miserable war for the Soviet soldier, ill equipped by comparison with his adversaries. As historian William R. Trotter has written, he 'had no choice. If he refused to fight, he would be shot. If he tried to sneak through the forest, he would freeze to death. And

---

* In fact, Soviet losses were probably far higher: according to a post-war Russian historian, Viktor Kulikov, some 3,922 Soviet aircraft were destroyed over the first three days, 2,000 of them on that first day.

surrender was no option for him; Soviet propaganda had told him how the Finns would torture prisoners to death.'

The following June brought Hitler's stunning Blitzkrieg in France: the most powerful army in the west destroyed in six weeks at a cost in German lives not much higher than Zhukov's losses at that one small confrontation in Mongolia. Stalin was astounded and appalled, almost taking the French defeat as a personal affront. To Khrushchev he exclaimed: 'How could they allow Hitler to defeat them, to crush them?' It upset all his calculations, which were predicated on a repeat of the costly and long-drawn-out trench-war stalemate of 1914–18, leaving Germany so debilitated that it would be years before it could risk unleashing a war on the Soviet Union.

On 2 June 1940, as the French Army was disintegrating and Churchill was pulling the British Expeditionary Force out of Dunkirk, Zhukov had his first meeting with Stalin. One can assume that Stalin was content to see the victor of Nomonhan back in western Russia. Three days later Zhukov, still in his early forties, was promoted to the rank of full general.

There was one far from negligible reason why the Russians would be so badly handicapped in the first days of the war. When Soviet forces had moved into the buffer zone of eastern Poland in 1939, Stalin had given priority to the grisly myrmidons of Lavrenty Beria's NKVD. Among a host of brutal arrests and executions of Poles was included the massacre of some 20,000 Polish Army officers at Katyn, in one of the worst atrocities of the war. It was hardly surprising that as a consequence the Soviet Army was treated as an enemy force imposed upon a resentful and hostile population, rather than as an ally come to protect them from German invasion.

Especially grave was Stalin's own refusal to recognize the imminence of catastrophe. From the early months of 1941, warnings of Hitler's intentions came in by the score. They came from trusted Soviet agents like Anthony Blunt in London and Sorge in Tokyo; from Churchill, and from Roosevelt. The warlord immured with his yes-men in the Kremlin refused to believe any of them. On 5 March 1941, among many such warnings, Sorge sent to Moscow a microfilm of German documents indicating a German attack in mid-June. It received an icy comment: 'We doubt the veracity of your information.' His report was then banished to the limbo of 'on file'. For whatever reason, Stalin seems personally to have become disenchanted with his ace spy, and was reported as having damned him, just before Barbarossa, as 'this bastard who's set up factories and brothels in Japan and even deigned to report the date of the German attack as 22 June. Are you suggesting I should believe him too?'

Under mounting pressure in Tokyo, Sorge was infuriated by the Kremlin's disregard for his information. 'Why didn't Stalin react?' he asked, baffled. It strained his nerves at an increasingly difficult time, as the Japanese secret police were closing in on him. He took to drinking ever more heavily.

As late as 15 June, when Zhukov and Marshal Semyon Timoshenko (who had replaced Voroshilov as Commissar for Defence) came to him begging for reinforcements on the frontier, Stalin waved aside their fears, declaring, 'We have a non-aggression pact with Germany. Germany is up to her ears with the war in the west and I am certain that Hitler will not risk creating a second front by attacking the Soviet Union. Hitler is not such an idiot and understands that the Soviet Union is not Poland, nor France and not even England.'

Three days later, on 18 June, the two generals tried once again to persuade Stalin and the Politburo to put the army on full alert. The meeting lasted for three hours. Stalin became increasingly irritable, always a warning sign. He accused Zhukov of warmongering and 'became so abusive that Zhukov fell silent'. Stalin repeated: 'But you have to understand that Germany on her own will never fight Russia. You must understand this.'

Egged on by the murderous toady Beria, Stalin managed to persuade himself that all this intelligence was simply a plant, designed to set the Germans on the Russians. He would trust Hitler rather than Church-ill, persuaded that, on past form, the Western democracies were more deeply committed ideologically to the destruction of the Soviet state than was Nazi Germany. In short, he refused to believe that a greater villain than Joseph Vissarionovich Stalin could possibly exist. On the evening of 18 June, a German deserter came over with irrefutable intelligence on the date of Barbarossa. He was shot for his pains. All those last days Soviet forward troops could hear the sound of the German Panzer mechanics tuning their tank engines. Yet, right to the very end, to the fateful 22 June – and even beyond – Stalin would continue to insist that no provocation should be offered to the Germans. At the very last moment Stalin decided to call up 800,000 reservists – a process to be completed by 10 July. It never was; it was too late.

By 10 July, the Panzers were well inside the Soviet Union. Attacking all along the longest continuous front ever known, which stretched for 1,800 miles from the Baltic to the Black Sea, the most fearsome attacking force in the history of war swept eastwards. It totalled 3.8 million men (including some 500,000 from Hitler's eastern European allies such as Romania and Hungary), with 4,300 tanks, 4,389 aircraft and 7,200 artillery pieces supported by 600,000 motor vehicles and 750,000 horses.

The land force comprised 148 German divisions, of which nineteen were Panzer and twelve motorized infantry. They were faced (on paper) by some 5.5 million Soviet men under arms, but just under 3 million that could be counted as front-line troops, with around 20,000 tanks (many of questionable battleworthiness) and 35,000 aircraft – though only 11,000 were actually serviceable on 22 June. The German phalanx was led by battle-hardened commanders such as Heinz Guderian, progenitor of the *Panzerkorps*, who had romped through France the previous summer and more recently had crushed Yugoslavia. Their self-confidence was high, and they regarded their forces as more or less invincible and the foe contemptuously as 'a colossus with feet of clay'. They estimated that it would take six to eight weeks to destroy the Soviet Union. Nevertheless, only a genius or a madman could have attempted such an invasion; in a short space of time Hitler would prove to be more of one than the other.

General Dimitry Pavlov, commander of the key Western Front, was enjoying an evening at the Minsk Officers' Club, together with his Chief of Staff Vladimir Klimovskikh and the district deputy commander Lieutenant-General V.I. Boldin. A popular comedy, *The Wedding at Malinovka*, was playing to a full house. The evening pleasures were interrupted by Colonel Blokhin, head of intelligence in the Western Special Military District, who reported to Pavlov that 'the frontier was in a state of alarm'. Despite the warnings, not a single order had so far been issued to either the Red Army or the navy.

On hearing the news of the attack, Zhukov rang Stalin early in the morning, to be told by an aide, 'Comrade Stalin is sleeping.'

'Wake him up immediately. The Germans are bombing our cities.'

Three minutes later Stalin was on the telephone. Zhukov reported the situation, and was answered by silence. 'Did you understand what I said?' Zhukov asked. Still there was silence.

Stalin still couldn't believe what he was hearing. Then, when told of the destruction of his air force, he remarked, 'That's a monstrous crime, those guilty of it should pay with their heads.'

Beria was ordered to investigate. Molotov wrung his hands and exclaimed, 'What have we done to deserve this?'

If anybody should have 'paid with his head' for the initial Soviet disasters it should surely have been Stalin himself. In a democracy, he would without doubt have fallen, but such was the regime of terror he had created around himself that he was untouchable. For several days he retreated into his shell in his dacha, leaving Molotov to broadcast the terrible news to the people of the Soviet Union.

> Citizens and Citizenesses of the Soviet Union! Today, at four o'clock in the morning, without addressing any grievances to the Soviet Union, without declaration of war, German forces fell on our country, attacked our frontiers in many places and bombed our cities . . . an act of treachery unprecedented in the history of civilized nations . . . The Red Army and the whole nation will wage a victorious Patriotic War for our beloved country, for honour, for liberty . . . Our cause is just. The enemy will be beaten. Victory will be ours . . .

Later that same morning in Berlin, Hitler proclaimed: 'Before three months have passed, we shall witness a collapse of Russia, the like of which has never been seen in history.' The omnipotent Red Tsar, regarded as the unshakeable 'man of steel', seemed quite unable to focus. After a while Stalin emerged from this semi-paralysis, shaken but able to resume his vice-like control as before. It might well be said that, with Stalin in those parlous days, the war was all but lost; yet without him it almost certainly would have been.

Only on 3 July would Stalin broadcast to the nation. That same day, Colonel-General Franz Halder, Hitler's Chief of Staff of the Army, noted in his diary that it was 'probably no understatement to say that the Russian campaign has been won in the space of two weeks'. Certainly the Panzers, having swiftly broken through the feeble, ill-organized crust of the Soviet border forces, had been slicing their way into Russia at a speed that made the previous year's French campaign look almost pedestrian. In May 1940, they had swept through to the Channel, 200 miles in ten breathtaking days; in the first days of Barbarossa they would frequently achieve the same advance in a couple of days. A German veteran of the campaign, Axel von dem Bussche, who as a young captain in an elite infantry regiment fought his way to the outskirts of Leningrad and then wintered in Tsar Paul's Palace of Pavlovsk, told me many years ago how that first summer he 'never saw a dead German, nor a T-34 tank'.

Within twenty-four hours of the beginning of Barbarossa, the Germans had rent a great hole eighty miles wide in the Soviet defences. By 29 June, after one week's fighting, Minsk, the capital of Byelorussia, one-third of the way to Moscow, had been taken; by 10 July the Soviet Western Front alone had lost 4,799 tanks, 9,477 guns, 1,777 combat aircraft and 341,000 soldiers. In less than three weeks Field Marshal Fedor von Bock's Army Group Centre had advanced nearly 400 miles along the road to Moscow. Two hundred out of 340 military supply dumps fell into German hands in the first month. Writes Rodric Braithwaite, 'Russian soldiers surrendered, in huge numbers, in formed units, without firing a shot.' On 16 July, Smolensk, on Napoleon's route to Moscow, and little more than 200 miles distant from the capital, fell; while the beginning of August brought the Panzers to the gates of Leningrad in the north. Kiev, capital of the Ukraine on the great River Dnieper, was reached, bypassed and encircled by 16 September. Against the advice of his generals, Stalin ordered that Kiev be held, regardless of cost: another disastrous decision. A savage ten-day battle ensued in which the Soviets lost the staggering total of 450,000 men and nearly 4,000 artillery pieces from forty-three divisions engaged. Kiev fell, nevertheless.

The Panzer thrusts deep into Russia would surround and cut off immense bodies of ill-trained and poorly equipped Soviet troops. The technique was known as *Kesselschlacht*, or 'cauldron'. Once the cauldron was sealed, the German infantry would move in to mop up. Unimaginable numbers of prisoners were taken. Over 400,000 were taken on the frontiers, another 600,000 at Kiev: altogether a total of over 3 million by the end of 1941. After Kiev, the Red Army defenders no longer outnumbered the Germans, and there were no more immediately available trained reserves. To defend Moscow, Stalin could field only 800,000 men in eighty-three divisions, but no more than twenty-five divisions were fully effective.

The fate of the huge numbers of Russian POWs, who were not granted protection stipulated under the Geneva Conventions, was appalling. Fewer than 40 per cent survived, and many of them, on their return home, were condemned to the Gulag camps for having surrendered. It was Nazi policy to starve the prisoners to death as part of the strategy set out in Reichsmarschall Hermann Göring's infamous 'Green Folder' whereby the entire urban population of Russia was to be 'reduced', to generate an agricultural surplus to feed Germany and to create the promised *Lebensraum* or living space for German émigrés. Close on the heels of the invading army followed Heinrich Himmler's murderous *Einsatz* squads, who with equal efficiency rounded up Jews, Gypsies and commissars to be despatched in mass executions. It was all part of Hitler's ideological strategy against a whole people whom he considered to be *Untermenschen*, and who were to be totally eradicated, rather than simply defeated in battle.

Here was one more fundamental error which would lead to Germany's undoing. In many areas of the western Soviet Union, and especially the occupied Baltic states, on 22 June the invaders were welcomed as bringing freedom from Stalinist oppression. In the Ukraine particularly, where millions had starved under the communist 'planning' of the 1920s and 1930s, the Wehrmacht was greeted with the traditional offerings of 'salt and bread'. But views soon changed as news of the excesses of the *Einsatzgruppen* and the fate of the POWs crept out. Red Army units caught up in a *Kesselschlacht* now fought on to the death, or joined up to form partisan bands that wreaked terrible havoc behind the German lines. What opportunities Hitler threw away with his policy of brutality would be shown later in the formation of a whole army of Soviet renegades led by a general, Andrey Vlasov, who had fought heroically until taken prisoner in July 1941.

Through August and into September the massive Wehrmacht onslaught ground on through the relentlessly scorching plains, where there was seldom any cover for man or beast. Yet it was also grinding down the attackers. The demands made on men, horses and machinery were gigantic, and unprecedented. Russian counter-attacks were ceaseless, and there were repeated strikes far to the rear by increasingly well-organized groups of Soviet partisans. Hitler's war machine, after all, was an instrument designed for short, sharp Blitzkriegs, not for a prolonged offensive over thousands of miles of hostile enemy territory. Commanders at the front were now aware that the machine was running down, just as the Russian dust destroyed bearings and tracks on the Mark IV and Mark III tanks that had waltzed across France the previous year. Their concerns were relayed back to the High Command in Germany. Colonel-General Franz Halder, the dapper Chief of Staff of the Army Command, had recorded in his diary on 3 July that the campaign was already won, but by the beginning of August he had changed his tune and was admitting more solemnly:

> we have underestimated the Russian colossus . . . [Soviet divisions] are not armed and equipped according to our standards, and their tactical leadership is often poor. But there they are, and if we smash a dozen of them the Russians simply put up another dozen. The time factor favours them, as they are near their own resources, while we are moving farther and farther away from ours. And so our troops sprawled over an immense front line, without any depth, are subjected to the incessant attacks of the enemy.

The German rate of advance fell from twenty miles per day to five miles. None of these gloomy, almost defeatist thoughts would be allowed to trickle through to the Führer, guarded as he was by toadies like the 'lackey' General Wilhelm Keitel of the Armed Forces Supreme Command. Allegedly treasonable reports, such as that 'some Panzer Divisions have only ten tanks left', would not reach him.

But the reality was that, by September, none of Hitler's three ambitious objectives in Barbarossa had been achieved. Leningrad had been reached but not captured – after a brutal and bloody intervention by Zhukov, sent in by a desperate Stalin. So Hitler had to resort to siege warfare in an attempt to starve the great city to death.* Meanwhile icy

---

* An estimated 900,000 civilians died during the 900-day siege, but Hitler never entered the city.

blasts of wind blowing off Lake Ladoga to the north-east were already bringing intimations that the dread Russian winter was not far away.

At the other end of the colossal front, Hitler had captured half the Ukraine, including the capital, Kiev. But the rich eastern half, with industrial plums like Kharkov and the Donetsk Basin, remained out of his grasp. In the crucial centre, the road to Moscow lay barred. It would in fact take Hitler nearly three months longer to reach its outskirts than it had taken Napoleon. For despite their deserved reputation for lightning armoured warfare, the Germans were almost as dependent as Napoleon on horses, and on the stamina of their men on the march. It turned out to be their greatest weakness.

At the end of August, the Soviet High Command, the Stavka, ordered Zhukov to command the 24th Army in a spoiling offensive at Yelnya, fifty miles south-east of Smolensk, to pinch out a German salient which was threatening the capital from the south-east. Under the threat of encirclement the Germans started retreating, and on 6 September Yelnya was retaken. It was the most substantial reverse that the Wehrmacht had suffered up to that date and the first successful Soviet offensive operation since Barbarossa began. As Rodric Braithwaite stresses, Yelnya reinforced Zhukov's reputation with Stalin as a ruthless commander, 'the right man for a rough affair, in Molotov's phrase'.

It was, however, a typical Zhukov battle, fought without regard to casualties – a pyrrhic victory for the Red Army. With overall losses estimated at 31,853, it seriously drained the forces left to cover Moscow after all the disasters of the summer, resulting in another huge *Kesselschlacht* trapping a further half-million men. Meanwhile, however, another factor had emerged that would tilt the war in favour of the defenders: the T-34 main battle tank, which now began to make its appearance in mass formations on the battlefield.

Developed only the previous year from the light BT-26 tanks Zhukov had deployed at Nomonhan, the new T-34 was unquestionably not just a battle-winner but a war-winner, and would generally be regarded by all sides as the best all-round tank of the Second World War. After many upgrades and improvements, its basic design would go all the way through to 1945 and beyond, when it would appear in the Korean War and even in various conflicts in the Middle East. Based on the Christie suspension, which gave it excellent cross-country performance though weighing thirty tons, it could move at over 30mph. A low profile of eight feet made it an elusive target. Carrying a high-velocity 76.2mm gun, it was the most powerful anti-tank weapon on the field. No German tank of 1941–2 vintage could stand up to it, while the T-34's thick sloping armour made it hard to knock out. The T-34 ran on tracks substantially wider than its German rivals, which meant that it could operate on snow, ice and the mud of the autumn *rasputitsa* where Guderian's Panzers failed. It was a fundamentally simple, indeed crude, design, allowing it to be produced in large quantities. If the early T-34s had a flaw it was their very simplicity: only the unit commander's tank carried a radio; and the cramped turret had room for only two, so the commander had to double up as gun-loader – an almost impossible duplication of tasks.

Having trained in spacious Sherman tanks during the Second World War, I can vouchsafe that no Western tankers would have put up with the crudeness and angular discomfort of the T-34. Nevertheless, facing the Barbarossa onslaught with only handfuls of T-34s at the outset, by the end of 1941 Stalin could field nearly 3,000 – to the shock and distress of the attacking Germans.

At last disturbed by these factors, together with the waning of the brief campaigning season in Russia, Hitler began to change his mind. Working on him most forcefully had been Field Marshal Fedor von Bock, commander of the key Army Group Centre, the general closest to Hitler's Nazi ideology. A leader who lectured his soldiers about the honour of dying for the German Fatherland and nicknamed 'Der Sterber' (literally 'the Killer'), Bock had led Army Group B during the French campaign in 1940. Along with almost all the German front-line commanders in Operation Barbarossa, he had constantly, and vehemently, urged Hitler to concentrate on an all-out drive towards Moscow. Besides the psychological importance of capturing the enemy's capital, they had pointed out that Moscow was a major centre of arms production and the centre of the Soviet communications and transportation system. Also, intelligence reports indicated that the bulk of the Red Army was deployed around Moscow for an all-out defence of the capital. Thus a co-ordinated offensive towards Moscow could force the Soviet Army into a final, decisive confrontation. Hitler, however, had remained immovable, ordering his Panzer specialist, Guderian, to send Army Group Centre's tanks to the north and south, temporarily halting the drive to Moscow.

Accordingly, on 9 September, Bock was instructed to prepare an operational order for an all-out drive to capture Moscow. Under the codename Operation Typhoon, the assault on Moscow it was to begin no later than 30 September. Bock's Army Group Centre would be re-inforced and replenished with men and vehicles. It would be composed of three infantry armies (the Second, Fourth and Ninth) and three tank armies, representing the cream of the most powerful remaining elements of the Wehrmacht forces in Russia.

On 16 September Bock issued his operational directive for Operation Typhoon. The three Panzer armies were to spearhead the attack. The Third (under Hermann Hoth), which had been withdrawn from the drive on Leningrad, would lead in the north. The Fourth (under Field Marshal Günther von Kluge) would lead the drive in the centre; and Guderian's Second Panzer Army would thrust up from the south after its victory in the Ukraine. Hitler considered that besieged and starving Leningrad could be allowed to wither on the vine, while in the Ukraine he would halt any move to thrust further east, into the rich area of Donetsk or towards the Caucasus. That could be deferred, if necessary, to spring 1942, once Moscow was in German hands. His strategy was to carry out another irresistible *Kesselschlacht* to send out-flanking forces to the north and south of Moscow, then close in to cut the city off from the rear. But did he now have the wherewithal? Front-line commanders like Bock and Guderian thought not, but kept their doubts to themselves. No one knew better than Guderian, who had nursed the Panzer weapon from infancy, just how exhausted his ar-moured spearheads were. And what about the dreaded Russian winter, which was now just around the corner?

Bock had assembled over a million men: three armies, three Panzer armies, and seventy-eight divisions, with 1,000 tanks and 14,000 guns, backed by 600 planes, representing the best, the most elite, that remained to the Wehrmacht. Despite heavy losses over the past three-and-a-half months of non-stop combat, this was still a more formidable force than that which had smashed French defences the previous year. Facing them, organized into three fronts, were some 1,250,000 Soviet soldiers, 3,232 tanks, 7,600 guns and 936 aircraft (of which probably only 500 were still operational). Many of these troops would soon be battered and exhausted from their struggle to avoid annihilation in the impending Bryansk and Vyazma *Kesselschlacht*.

Starting on 2 October, the first blows of Operation Typhoon struck home with devastating power. Moving up from the south to concentrate on Moscow, Guderian's Second Panzer Army conjoined with Kluge's Fourth to trap yet another large Soviet force in two vast pincer movements between the centres of Vyazma and Bryansk (some 150 miles west of Moscow and 220 miles south-west respectively) in order to open the road to Stalin's capital. A total of five Soviet armies found themselves encircled in the Bryansk–Vyazma *Kesselschlacht*. Moscow's first line of defence had been shattered. By 10 October the Germans had captured another 673,000 Soviet prisoners. A quarter of a million Soviet soldiers had been killed or wounded in these two battles, in addition to the hundreds of thousands captured. Once again, Stalin was unable to believe what was happening. The air force commander who delivered this latest piece of bad news was arrested and handed over to the NKVD.

Stalin now had only 90,000 men and 150 tanks upon which he could draw for the defence of the capital. For the Panzers the road to Moscow must at last have seemed open – weather permitting. But, once again, it would prove to be late – very late – in the campaigning season.

As if the summer had not been draining enough, the weather now turned against the invaders with a vengeance. At first the autumn rains brought relief by damping down the fearsome dust of the summer. Then, as they strengthened, they brought with them the curse of the autumn *rasputitsa*, the bottomless sticky mud that turned the Russian roads, the majority unpaved, into unnegotiable quagmires. A road-oriented force like the 1941 Wehrmacht was not prepared for these conditions. The Panzers with their narrow tracks sank out of sight. The 600,000 large western European horses that the Germans used for essential supply and artillery movement also floundered, while the smaller, tougher indigenous Cossack ponies of the Red Army were much better suited to the conditions. Photographs of that campaign show a Wehrmacht staff car being dragged through the *rasputitsa* quagmire by twenty infantrymen, or transport horses sunk up to their bellies in the glutinous mud.

If life was harsh for the invading soldiery, it was incomparably worse for the civilians caught up in this most savage and merciless of conflicts. Imbued with Hitler's doctrine calling for a war of extermination against *Untermenschen*, the invaders showed little compunction about turning inhabitants out of their homes to face death by starvation or cold, or tearing down their primitive dwellings to provide firewood. Meanwhile the Russian civilians themselves faced draconian edicts requiring them to fulfil the policy of 'scorched earth' so that nothing should be left standing that might benefit the occupiers. It was a leaf taken out of the book of their ancestors of 1812, followed to the letter. As the Wehrmacht pushed ever further east, it drove before it an ever-increasing tide of homeless refugees who had lost everything and had nowhere to go. That sublime chronicler of the misery of the war in Russia, Vasily Grossman, wrote at the time of the Vyazma–Bryansk debacle:

> I thought that I'd already seen a retreat, but I had never seen anything like this before, nor even imagined it. It was a Biblical Exodus! The vehicles were travelling in eight lines, engines screaming hysterically as dozens of lorries tried to get themselves out of the mud. People were driving huge flocks of sheep and cows over the fields, further off horse-drawn carts creaked along, thousands of carts, covered with coloured sackcloth, plywood, tin, carrying refugees from the Ukraine, still further ahead there were crowds of pedestrians with sacks, bundles, suitcases. It was not a stream, not a river, it was the slow movement of a flowing ocean, hundreds of yards wide from side to side. There were the black and white heads of children looking out from the covered carts, the Biblical beards of Jewish elders, the headscarves of peasant women, older men in Ukrainian caps, black-haired girls and women. And what calmness there was in the eyes, what wise grief, what a sense of Fate, of universal catastrophe!

Profoundly moved, Grossman added: 'If we are to be victorious in this terrible, brutal war, it will be because deep in our nation we have people with these great hearts and souls, people who spare themselves nothing, like these old women, the mothers of these sons, who in their great simplicity "lay down their lives for their friends", as simply, as generously, as that poverty-stricken old woman of Tula, who gave us her food, her light, her firewood, her salt. They are like the righteous of the Bible. They illuminate all our people with a miraculous light. They are a handful, but they will be victorious.' The fear that drove on this human tide was fanned by proliferating reports of the atrocities being committed by the Germans on Soviet territory, including the murder of 30,000 Jews in the Ukraine. These had included Grossman's mother.

Grossman was to be proved right about the Russian spirit. But the Russian weather had further torments in store for the invaders. After dust and then mud would come snow.

CHAPTER ELEVEN

GENERAL WINTER

On 5 October 1941, at his Leningrad GHQ, Zhukov received orders from Stalin to return to Moscow at once and stabilize the front.

'Can you get on a plane and come to Moscow.'

'I request to fly at dawn.'

'We await you in Moscow.'

'I'll be there.'

'All the best,' Stalin said.

Stalin decreed that the wreckage of the Reserve and Western Fronts be combined into a single Western Front under Zhukov. It was on this front that the main weight of the German assault on Moscow would fall. It was not difficult for Zhukov to deduce at once that the situation at the front was dire, more dangerous than any time since 22 June. On 3 October, Guderian, plunging deeply northwards in brilliantly sunny weather, had taken the important centre of Oryol, supposedly over a hundred miles behind the Russian front line. Thrusting on to Tula, he opened a southern flank directly menacing Moscow. The following day, the 4th, was the day that Stalin lost all contact with General Ivan Konev's shattered Western Front; he threatened to have Konev shot, and probably would have done but for a strong intervention from Zhukov. There was now a twelve-mile hole in the Moscow defences. On the 5th Soviet planes reported a long column of Panzers heading down the Ukhnovo highway, only sixty miles from Moscow. Passed was the famous battlefield of Borodino that had helped guard the route to Moscow in 1812. The following day the first snows fell. On the 8th Zhukov, by now back in the capital, warned the Stavka that the roads to Moscow now lay virtually undefended, and that the available reserves were 'encircled'.

It would be hard to think of a commander better suited to take over the defence of Moscow at this desperate time than Georgy Zhukov. Only forty-four years old, almost everything he had touched seemed to bring success: after Nomonhan, having escaped from any blame for the Finnish debacle, he had appeared as eleventh-hour rescuer of Leningrad in the late summer of 1941; his counter-stroke at Yelnya in August–September, which had inflicted one of the first and heaviest reverses on the Germans, had delayed the German advance on Moscow for several crucial weeks. He was unafraid of heavy losses; on the contrary, he would go down in history as a butcher. Nor was he afraid of Stalin: those close to the scene were often stunned to see Zhukov fearlessly answering back, standing up to the Red Tsar. Surprisingly, 'Stalin seemed to accept it as normal,' noted one corps commander. Time and again Zhukov would lash out at Stalin's call for costly and uninspired 'frontal attacks', time-wasting ventures which would rob his offensives of their momentum. His most serious criticism was the overall lack of mobile formations.

Zhukov, writes his biographer Geoffrey Roberts, came across 'as a general willing to execute the orders of his superiors without demur and who expected the same of those serving under him'. His style of command was to seize the initiative, by personal reconnaissance and bold offensive action, followed by 'the skilful coordination of ground and air assets, and acceptance of heavy casualties if the situation demanded it'. If the situation presented itself, he was keen to repeat the tactics that had succeeded so well against the Japanese at Khalkhin Gol, but on a much larger scale: namely, to pin down the enemy main forces in the centre 'while powerful mobile forces attacked on the flanks, creating openings and encirclements that could be exploited by strong reserves'. But this would have to wait until the balance of forces was more favourable, at Stalingrad late the following year.

On taking over at a moment when morale was at rock bottom, Zhukov had issued to all his forces on the Leningrad front his Order 0064 of 17 September 1941 decreeing that 'all commanders, political officers [commissars], and rank and file who leave the line of defence without prior written instruction of the Front or Military Council are to be shot on sight'. He could well assume in his new command that, if Moscow were lost, he would lose his head too. By late October

Zhukov's forces had succeeded in halting the German attack at least temporarily, and he felt able to declare: 'I will wear him [the enemy] out and then beat him.'

On 17 October, the Stockholm correspondent of the London *Daily Telegraph*, covering the Moscow front, reported a serious worsening of the situation. That the steely Soviet censors would permit transmission of news that the Germans 'had at one point penetrated the line and reached the outer line of defences' only sixty miles west of the city, and that 'both sides sustained heavy losses', indicated that things were going badly indeed. The key bastion of Mozhaisk, the Borodino of 1812, had fallen, and a surge of panic swept through the city. Successive waves of refugees brought more tales of the Wehrmacht's brutality and its apparently irresistible impetus.

To keep up pressure on the embattled Muscovites, the Luftwaffe took to round-the-clock terror bombing of civilian areas. Although much damage and many casualties ensued, the raids could never reach the intensity of the Blitz on London the previous winter. Operating at extreme range from home bases, Göring's elite force was handicapped by lack of munitions, as well as inadequate repair facilities. And the Luftwaffe over Moscow found itself flying into flak even fiercer than that which had protected the much larger area of London. Its limitations showed up the weakness in the whole strategy of attempting to subjugate so vast a country with the means that had overpowered France in six short weeks.

That first panic at the beginning of October sparked looting and random killings. The dread scent of collapse even infiltrated into the inner recesses of the Kremlin. A 'sinister snow' of black flakes from the ashes of documents being burned there drifted across the city. On 19 October Beria told Molotov, 'We should abandon Moscow. Otherwise they will wring our necks like chickens.' There must have been many thousands of Russians who would have been eager to do the wringing, if only they could reach Beria's own murderous neck. There were rumours, which still persist, that in early October Stalin put out feelers, via Bulgarian intermediaries, for an armistice. Orders were sent out from the Kremlin (which were inevitably picked up by the shaky citizens of Moscow) to evacuate the government to Kuybyshev, a city on the Volga 500 miles to the east. At the same time measures were set in motion to ship by the score whole factories eastwards to the Urals. It was a staggering undertaking, given the prevailing shortages of transport and manpower. Requiring forty carriages and thirty-five goods wagons alone, the entire Bolshoi Theatre and its artists were transported to Kuybyshev.

Travelling with the Bolshoi was the thirty-five-year-old composer Dmitry Shostakovich. He recalled scenes of panicky chaos, as travellers trampled on one another in the slushy snow to get aboard trains at the Kazansky Station. His family struggled through the mob carrying in their hands a sewing machine and a child's potty. The journey took seven long days and nights, but when they reached Kuibyshev conditions were as comfortless as they had been on the train, the family packed into one room with fourteen other people, all sleeping on the floor. Working on a new symphony, he had developed writer's block: 'As soon as I got on that train something snapped inside me ... I can't compose just now, knowing how many people are losing their lives.' But when later he heard of the German defeat in front of Moscow, 'he finished the symphony in a burst of exuberant energy in less than two weeks'. It was to become the renowned Seventh, or Leningrad, Symphony.

Another train, complete with a special refrigeration plant and shock-absorbers, was employed in shipping out Lenin's grisly mummy from its resting place in Red Square; this seemed a curious priority for a city on the brink of defeat, and with no rolling-stock to spare. On the other hand many of the innumerable arms and heavy manufacturing plants in Moscow were shipped east, lock, stock and barrel, including the factory producing the key T-34, which – with extraordinary speed – was soon turning out this prize piece of fighting equipment from a new site safely in the depths of Siberia.

In his moving book, *Moscow 1941*, Rodric Braithwaite graphically describes the remarkable exodus. One of those evacuated was a student at Moscow University, who later became a world-famous nuclear scientist, Nobel Prize-winner and dissident: Andrey Sakharov. Sakharov recalled students, in temperatures below −20°F (−29°C), stealing lumps of coal from the locomotive to fuel the stoves in their wagons, which housed forty to each wagon in appalling conditions. It took them six weeks to reach Ashkhabad in Turkmenistan. Often trains would arrive after journeys of several weeks to find that there were no buildings ready.

Nevertheless, the astonishing wholesale evacuation of industrial plant succeeded. By its end, writes Braithwaite, 'five hundred factories and two million people had been moved from the city. It took over seventy thousand trains . . .' The operation was completed by 25 November – a miraculous achievement, and just in time for Zhukov's winter offensive.

The importance to the overall Soviet war economy can be understood from the statistics: by October, after only three months of war, the country had lost 62.5 per cent of its coal production (largely in the captured areas of the Ukraine), more than two-thirds of its pig-iron, steel and rolled metals (71, 68 and 67 per cent respectively) and 60 per cent of its aluminium. Before the war, half of the country's automobiles, half of its machine tools and instruments and more than 40 per cent of its electrical equipment had been produced in and around the capital. By November, as Stalin completed the evacuation of industries from Moscow, the loss of over 300 factories to the enemy deprived the Red Army of what had once been a monthly production of 8.5 million shell-cases, nearly 3 million mines and 2 million aerial bombs. The loss of chemical plants cut the output of explosives, causing a grave crisis because the Red Army had by then almost exhausted its pre-war stocks of ammunition. The relocation of Moscow's factories was, as the war historian John Erickson notes, something 'little short of an Industrial Revolution', carried out within a matter of weeks, an undertaking which itself created immense demands for fuel, raw materials and construction labour.

As panic took over in October, there were regular reports of parachutists landing in the middle of Moscow. Its guards having fled, even the British Embassy was looted. Backed by all the savage rigour of the NKVD, Zhukov introduced the most draconian measures. Martial law was declared. 'Suspicious' citizens were arrested and shot without pretext. Years later Beria would boast that, during the Battle of Moscow, 638,112 men had been detained and 505 'deserters' executed. On 30 October Zhukov issued an edict warning that 'cowards and panic-mongers' fleeing the battlefield and 'Provocateurs, spies and anyone fomenting unrest' would be shot on the spot. 'Not a step back!

Forward for the Motherland!' was the cry. Special 'blocking units' were introduced with orders to shoot at once any troops seen falling back without orders.

Military and police patrols appeared on the streets again. The panicky flight ceased. Ten thousand deserters and 25,000 people trying to evade military service were arrested. There were reports that, over the period 1941–2, a total of 157,000 Soviet servicemen were executed, the equivalent of more than fifteen divisions. According to Braithwaite, it was said that 'some executions were carried out by a murderous woman in a shed in the courtyard of the Moscow City Court'. On 16 October, more than 200 people were shot in Moscow by the NKVD, the biggest killing in a single day since the Great Purge of the 1930s. The lucky ones might escape immediate death by being sent to penal battalions charged with the task of clearing minefields in advance of an attack. Their expectation of life was not high. Another round in the purge of senior commanders took place. One of the Red Army's ablest tacticians, General Dimitry Pavlov, who had commanded the key Western Front in the first terrible weeks, the unfortunate general who on the eve of Barbarossa had been enjoying an evening out in Minsk, had already been executed in July, together with several other senior officers. Then, in October, among those liquidated was General Yakov Smushkevich, commander of the Soviet Air Force, an intrepid Jew who, having fought through the Spanish Civil War, had been in charge of Zhukov's aviation at the Battle of Khalkhin Gol, and made a Hero of the Soviet Union – now executed on the orders of Lavrenty Beria on 28 October 1941, the same day as Zhukov's predecessor General Shtern. There were suggestions of anti-Semitism, never far from the surface in Stalin's Russia.

Yet even in a totalitarian state victory could not be achieved through the rule of terror alone. By the end of October, to the frightened men inside the Kremlin, as well as the general populace outside the wall, it must have looked like the eleventh hour. Morale had never been more fragile. Zhukov's reserves were almost exhausted. And still the Germans kept on coming closer to Moscow. But, almost alone, Stalin refused to be panicked. Suddenly he managed to pull out of the hat a supreme trick. After all the disasters of the past four months, finally he made a decision of extraordinary courage which would go far to earning him a reputation as a great war leader. He announced to his inner team that he intended to mount a full-scale military parade in Red Square on 7 November to celebrate Red Army Day, as had been done every year in peacetime. Members of the Stavka reacted with horror. The Germans were at the very gates of Moscow, a couple of hours' drive away, and what if the Luftwaffe, with its superiority in the air, were to bomb the parade? Stalin remained adamant; he consulted Zhukov, who assured him that the city would hold, that the enemy was 'in no condition to organise a major attack in the next few days', and encouraged him to go ahead with the parade. Stalin did.

As in peacetime, Stalin took the salute atop the now empty Lenin Mausoleum, together with members of the Politburo who had not left for Kuibyshev. The Luftwaffe was conspicuous by its absence. The only thing that went awry was one tank which ran out of control, and turned in the wrong direction. That drew a laugh even from Stalin. To hold the parade, Stalin had had to scrape the barrel to gather up cadets, veterans and troops of an internal security division. They to-talled nearly 30,000 – or the equivalent of two large divisions. It was a demonstration of tremendous audacity. In a windy speech full of bombast, Stalin predicted that 'within little more than a year, Hitlerite Germany will collapse under the weight of its own crimes'. Needless to say, it was received with lengthy ovations.

What was particularly significant in his speech was his invocation of the example of 'our great ancestors – Alexander Nevsky, Dimitry Donskoy . . . Alexander Suvorov, Mikhail Kutuzov' – all of them victor-ious generals from the Tsarist era. It was an artful device for turning the war, switching from the existing propaganda image of the struggle of the Marxist-Leninist proletariat to one of historic nationalism. Such nationalism would inspire every patriotic Russian. Soon he would even be allowing, indeed encouraging, religion, that 'opiate of the masses', to flourish once again, because that was what he sensed the ordinary Russian now wanted. Here was born the notion of the Great Patriotic War. Rodric Braithwaite sees the November parade as 'a remarkable, perhaps foolhardy gamble. But unlike some of Stalin's other gambles in 1941 and 1942, it paid off in spades.' Morale soared, as Muscovites seemed to regain faith in themselves.

Nevertheless, by the beginning of November the defence belt

around Moscow was still dangerously incomplete. It had been hard to recover from the loss of 90 per cent of the Red Army's tanks in the first week of the war, let alone the loss of 3 million in prisoners of war, and possibly another 3 million killed. One-third of Russia's rail network was behind enemy lines. War production was starkly diminished. Stalin was reduced to handing out packets of fifteen tanks at a time to threatened sectors.

With frenzied speed Zhukov set about building concentric lines of defence around the capital. Some 600,000 citizens of Moscow – students, clerks, office workers, women, artists and pensioners – were conscripted into building new lines well into the city suburbs. At first they were despatched without spades or pickaxes, with neither food nor accommodation. Typifying the wasteful inefficiencies of the Soviet system, little was achieved. Alongside these were raised hastily formed *opolchenie* units, a kind of Home Guard. All they had by way of arms were antique foreign rifles, with an allocation of one for every two volunteers. It was hardly surprising that the *opolchenie* produced no more than 10,000 recruits.

Under Zhukov's forceful drive, backed with menaces and threats, the Moscow construction teams gradually achieved extraordinary results with their limited materials. Great anti-tank ditches, some of them thirty feet deep and supported by tetrahedrons of steel, blocked all the routes entering the city – a tactic which recognized that the Panzers were essentially a road-borne force. Skilfully placed earth revetments were dug, which a T-34 could run into and fire from, with only its heavily armoured turret visible. Nevertheless, with just 90,000 troops at maximum, and of mixed quality, now left available to defend a 150-mile-wide front, with open flanks at each end, Zhukov's force was stretched to the limit. As a political commissar remarked to a general, 'We are generals without troops.' Sometimes untrained units had to be thrown in piecemeal at appalling cost; one newly arrived cavalry division from Tashkent was massacred almost in its entirety, at nil cost to the enemy. Only a general with the standing and reputation for ruthlessness of Zhukov could get away with such casualties. By the beginning of December, the German Army commander Field Marshal Walther von Brauchitsch was reporting that the Red Army had 'no large reserve formations'; it was a spent force.

If the Wehrmacht, in continuing to push relentlessly towards Moscow, still seemed like an unstoppable, superhuman force, how did the scene seem to the Germans in the front line? In conquering the whole of western Russia, German casualties had amounted to 46,000 by the end of July. Yet another 118,000 had died in the battles for Kiev and Leningrad and in the advance on Moscow. By the end of November casualties would amount to 23 per cent of the effective overall strength of the Wehrmacht, or nearly three-quarters of a million.

By the end of that same, unusually cold November, when the temperature had reached 40°F below zero (–40°C), Bock was reporting that his men had still not received winter coats, often having to pack newspapers into their jackets. Soviet soldiers, in contrast, had warm, quilted uniforms, felt-lined *valenka* boots and fur hats. Hitler, in all his hubristic arrogance, had refused to consider that Barbarossa could possibly run on into the winter, and had effectively blocked cold-weather measures. Moreover, the Soviet partisans, by the end of 1941 increasingly well organized and fanatically committed as a consequence of German atrocities, were striking telling blows at the Wehrmacht's long lines of communication deep behind the front. Essential supplies of food, clothing, fuel and ammunition were simply not getting through. Soviet intelligence had noted, as early as the last days of September, that a German attack at Pulkovo, on the approaches to Leningrad, had been accompanied by no more than twenty tanks – which was taken as a sure sign of a slackening of effort.

This gave Zhukov a vital breather, at a moment of extreme crisis, in which to consolidate the defence structures, while organizing formations of newly arrived reserves. By now he had more or less completed three concentric defence lines circling the city.

On 6 November, the day before Stalin's triumphal Red Army Day parade, it began to snow again, and then swiftly to freeze, sheeting roads and fields with a hard surface on which a highly mechanized army could move. The mud solidified too. The attackers could resume their deadly advance. Bock still had almost as many men as Zhukov's defenders: and he had many more guns, and more than twice as many tanks. In mid-November the Germans' left hook managed to reach a point a mere fifteen miles north of the city. Their intention was to push the Third and Fourth Panzer Armies across the Moscow Canal, to envelop Moscow from the north-east. Guderian's Second Panzer Army would attack Tula and then close in on Moscow from the south: the second of two deadly German tentacles that were intended to reach around the rear of the city. As the Soviets fought the threat from the flanks, Fourth Army would attack the centre, straight down the high-way to Moscow. Facing them, Zhukov had the 5th, 16th, 30th, 43rd, 49th, and 50th Soviet armies, all of them fatigued and under strength.

On 15 November, after a day's ferocious battle, Zhukov's 17th Cav-alry Division had 800 men left; three of his divisions were no longer in touch with army HQ. The whole of his right wing was fighting desper-ately to hold off the growing threat of encirclement. In two weeks of relentless fighting, though lacking sufficient fuel and ammunition, the Germans slowly crept towards Moscow. By 19 November Lieutenant-General Konstantin Rokossovsky found that his 18th Army, which was blocking the vital Volokolamsk highway, was in danger of being out-flanked on both sides. Zhukov ordered him to fight where he stood:

> Kryukovo [a village twenty-five miles from Moscow] is the final point of withdrawal: there can be no further falling back. There is nowhere else to fall back. All and any measures must be taken quickly to win a breathing space, to stop the retirement. Each further step backward by you is a breach in Moscow's defences. All commanders, from juniors to seniors, to be in their places, on the battlefield.

Rokossovsky, convinced that he should withdraw, appealed against this order. Zhukov threatened to have his one-time superior in rank shot for disobedience. The Germans reached Yasnaya Polyana, the home of the revered Tolstoy, just south-west of Tula, on the road to Moscow. There were many heroic episodes, for instance that of Major-General Panfilov's 316th anti-tank men, ground to pieces while fighting German tanks on the Volokolamsk highway, where today a forty-foot statue still marks their stand. 'Even Stalin's nerves were shaken,' rec-ords Braithwaite, by setbacks in the defences of Moscow at this point. To the south, the weight of Guderian's northward thrust struck two divisions on 50th Army's left flank, the 413th and 299th, the latter no more than 800 men strong, while the reserve, 108th Tank Division, had 2,000 men and thirty old T-26 tanks. However, Second Panzer Army was blocked.

On the German side, General Halder was noting in his war diary that some German regiments were now led by an *Oberleutnant* (captain). On 19 November, a whole German division was reported to have panicked. It was the first time that such a thing had happened. The Germans now had no more battalions in reserve; nor, apparently, did Zhukov.

Stalin now played his second ace of the campaign. German intelligence officers were suddenly stunned to discover their forward units being counter-attacked with vigour by fresh and hitherto unidentified troops in large formations. They constituted the vanguard of some thirty divisions of Siberian troops just arrived from the Soviet Far East. They were tough and fresh, but seasoned with the battle-experience of having fought the Japanese to a standstill at Khalkhin Gol just two years previously – under Zhukov. No troops in the world were better acclimatized to the unprecedently harsh cold that was about to grip the Moscow front. They arrived with their own spanking new T-34s, painted white, supported by assault troops clad in white sheeting: a terrifying phantom army, thrown into battle by Zhukov almost immediately they decanted from the train after their long trip across the Trans-Sib. These Siberian reinforcements arrived just in time to reverse the tide of battle. Augmenting Zhukov's hard-pressed 49th and 50th armies, on 22 November they struck a savage and totally unexpected blow against Guderian's Second Panzer Army, which was attempting to encircle Moscow from the south. It inflicted a shock defeat on the Germans, a reverse on a scale that had not been seen since Barbarossa began. Bock wrote that he now saw himself facing 'a Verdun': 'a brutish, chest-to-chest struggle of attrition'.

However, the Fourth Panzer Army still managed to push the Soviet 16th Army back, splitting it from the 30th, and succeeded in crossing the Moscow–Volga Canal. From the northern tentacle the Third Panzer Army finally captured the important town of Klin after heavy fighting on 24 November. Zhukov recalled that it was at this time that Stalin asked him: 'Are you sure that we can hold Moscow? I ask you this with pain in my soul. Speak honestly, like a communist'. Zhukov replied: 'We can certainly hold Moscow, but at least two more armies will be needed, and if possible 200 tanks.'

By 28 November, the German 7th Panzer Division (the veteran

division General Erwin Rommel had led in the French campaign) had seized a bridgehead across the Moscow–Volga Canal, bringing them less than twenty-two miles to the Kremlin before the 1st Shock Army forced it back across the canal. Moscow was in sight, but the German forces were wearing out.

On the southern approaches to the city, Zhukov managed to hold the key city of Tula on the tip of Guderian's prong; the Wehrmacht never got closer to the capital from this direction. Frustrated by Soviet resistance on both the northern and southern approaches, on 1 December Bock attempted another offensive from the west, but it was soon repelled. On 2 December, one reconnaissance battalion actually managed to reach the Khimki railway station, only 11 miles from the centre of Moscow. They could clearly see the spires of the Kremlin. It would be the high tide of the German attack on Moscow. (Tourists arriving by air in Moscow today will be shown the monument marking the high tide of the German attack; it stands close to Sheremetyevo Airport, now well inside the city suburbs.)

A turning point in the battle – if not, with hindsight, a turning point in the whole war – had been reached. But by now the German attack was beginning to peter out. The Russian winter was about to add its weight to the balance.

So how had Stalin managed to acquire this vital infusion of fresh troops that would tip the precarious balance between Zhukov and Bock and save Moscow? It was the consequence of a piece of intelligence from the agent whom earlier in the year Stalin had condemned as a 'drunk and a pimp': Richard Sorge, in Tokyo. Despite the disheartening rebuff he had received for his highly accurate messages about the date of Barbarossa, throughout the summer of 1941 Sorge continued to supply his masters in Moscow with top-grade intelligence. What Stalin wanted to know from him, above all else, was whether there was any likelihood that Japan might seize on Soviet reverses in Barbarossa to launch an attack in the Far East, in revenge for the defeat at Nomonhan. As early as August Sorge had been reporting that this was unlikely: because Japan's proponents of 'go south' had won the day and were busy preparing the strike on Pearl Harbor. (This was not, however, a piece of information that Stalin would pass on to the United States, which he continued to distrust at least as much as he distrusted Nazi

Germany.) Later that month, Sorge sent in a very detailed report stating emphatically that Japan would not attack the Soviet Union until Moscow had been captured, 'the Kwantung Army's troop strength becomes three times that of the Red Army', and there were 'visible signs of internal collapse in the Siberian Army'.

From his travels in Manchuria, Sorge's agent Hotsumi Ozaki had passed to Sorge confirmation that 'The Kwantung Army has decided not to have a war with Russia.' This was all so specific and authoritative that even Stalin could not disregard it, though Sorge would claim that it was not until the end of September that Moscow did finally believe this report.

Thus, at a critical moment when the final, all-out German drive on Moscow was under way, Stalin took the calculated risk of despatching those highly qualified troops from Siberia – nearly a million in total – to reinforce Zhukov, their one-time commander. They would arrive just in time to tilt the balance.

As well as being perhaps the most valuable piece of intelligence Sorge would ever send, it was also to be his last. Stalin's cold-shouldering in the spring had imposed a strain on Sorge's nerves at an increasingly difficult time, just as the Japanese secret police were moving in on him. He took to drinking more heavily than ever, racing around Tokyo on his motorbike and throwing caution to the winds. The beginnings of the round-up of his ring had begun. Miyagi threw himself out of a police-station window, having come clean about Sorge. Sorge sent his last message to Moscow on 4 October, his forty-sixth birthday, and was arrested fourteen days later, together with Max Clausen. Apparently feeling that his mission had been completed, Sorge gave a full confession (according to Gordon W. Prange's account, he was not tortured – perhaps surprisingly, given Japanese predilections).

The trials of these agents were held through the summer and autumn of 1942, while Stalingrad was under siege, and continued until August 1943. The Japanese made three overtures to the Soviets, offering to trade Sorge for one of their own spies. However, the Soviets declined all offers, insisting that Sorge was unknown to them. Some historians have argued that Sorge's Barbarossa coup led to his undoing, because Stalin could not afford to let it become known that he had rejected warnings of the German attack in June 1941. Surprisingly, too, Sorge was kept alive in prison, and apparently treated reasonably well for another three years, only to be hanged on 7 November 1944.

It was not until the Khrushchev era, in 1964, that the Soviet Union officially acknowledged this extraordinary, German-born hero of the Great Patriotic War. The Soviet press claimed that, when he was about to be executed, Sorge had shouted: 'Long live the Communist Party, the Soviet Union and the Red Army.' It is hard to see how they might have acquired this piece of information. On 5 November 1964, Sorge was awarded the supreme decoration of Hero of the Soviet Union. A fulsome citation read:

> In this grave hour for our country ... Richard Sorge and his fearless comrades once again rendered invaluable service to the Soviet people. They reported that the Japanese militarists, confident that the Hitlerites would cope with the Red Army, were concentrating forces for unleashing war in the Pacific. This information made possible the transfer of Soviet divisions from the Far East, although the presence of the Kwantung Army in Manchuria necessitated the Soviet Union's keeping a large number of troops on the eastern borders ...

A street in Moscow remains named after him, while a postage stamp, value of four kopecks, was printed in his memory.

At the end of November 1941 the freeze which, earlier in the month, had hardened the ground, thus briefly enabling Hitler's Panzers to launch their final bid for Moscow, now turned fiercely against them. The mercury dropped to a record −58°F (−50°C), the coldest in Russian history. Nothing like this had ever been experienced by Napoleon. The Wehrmacht was not equipped for winter warfare. It lacked winter-grade lubricants; tank engines froze solid, motor transport was not better off, and even machine guns jammed in the cold. Horses died; so did the men. More than 130,000 cases of frostbite were reported, with Guderian signalling twice as many as battle casualties. Frozen grease had to be scraped off every shell before loading, and vehicles had to be heated for hours before use. Weather paralysed the Luftwaffe. For the first time since the catastrophe of 22 June, Russian aircraft were able to achieve something like local superiority. By 27 November, General Eduard Wagner, Quartermaster General of the German Army, would be reporting: 'We are at the end of our resources in both personnel and material. We are about to be confronted with the dangers of deep winter.' The Soviet troops, particularly the Siberians, were much better prepared for sub-zero warfare. T-34s, specially winterized, remained dangerously active.

It hardly strains the imagination to picture the Wehrmacht camp in the last days of November, as it strove to cover the last miles to Moscow. The young Germans in Bock's spearhead, now 1,500 miles or more from the *Gemütlichkeit* of home, found themselves in a frozen, dark, inhospitable land, where every inhabitant was possessed by one wish only: to kill the invaders. Cold and hungry, with their winter clothing not yet arrived or destroyed by partisans hundreds of miles behind the lines, and with the local villages burned to the ground on Soviet 'scorched earth' orders, scrupulously carried out, the Germans were left with neither shelter, food nor fuel. They watched daily the agony of the precious horses, essential even to a force as mechanized as the Wehrmacht; they died by the thousand, often left in their harnesses, bogged down inextricably in the *rasputitsa* mud or, later, frozen to death. At the same time they saw their Panzers simply worn out and not replaced, whereas a knocked-out T-34 always seemed to be replaced by three more.

So what kept the Wehrmacht soldier going? There were the two words fundamental to the German soldier over the ages: *Kamerad-schaft* (camaraderie: you never let your comrades down) and *Eidespflicht* (the duty which bound you to the military oath). Both were reinforced by fear – by fear of death at the front, and now by fear of the power of the secret police set up by the dictator who had first despatched the German soldier so deep into Russia. Yet there was manifestly another factor: a sense of exultation as forward recce units reported being within sight of the Kremlin's spires and towers. Here at last Bock's irresistible might was within reach of the Holy Grail. Moscow's fall, so Goebbels repeatedly told the *Frontsoldaten*, would inevitably be followed by the fall of Stalin, by the crumpling of the whole Soviet state – and, in consequence, by an end to the war.

The phenomenally icy weather continued into December, with some of the lowest mean temperatures ever recorded, day after day. For the ill-equipped Wehrmacht, prepared by the self-assured Führer for a short summer campaign only, it was impossible to carry on. The attempt to capture the Soviet capital ground to a halt. 'The offensive on Moscow failed ...' General Guderian admitted in his diary. 'We underestimated the enemy's strength, as well as his size and climate. Fortunately, I stopped my troops on 5 December, otherwise catastrophe would be unavoidable.'

This was not, however, how Zhukov intended to let matters rest. At the end of November he submitted a bold plan to Stalin for a major counter-offensive. Stalin agreed. The forces for the attack were cobbled together from all the available reserves in the Red Army, but with a backbone provided by yet more fresh troops arriving in Moscow from Siberia. The units available to Zhukov numbered over 500,000 men, together reportedly with 1,000 tanks and 1,000 aircraft, and on 5 December, the very day that Guderian issued his halt-order, they launched a massive counter-attack. Their main objectives, sensibly, were the two threatening German prongs to north and south of the capital. To great advantage, Zhukov employed the very Russian skill in *maskirovka* which had served him so well in Nomonhan against the Japanese. With negligible sources of intelligence available to them from a thoroughly alienated populace, Bock's spent forces were taken completely by surprise. Western armies, their officers had been taught at Potsdam, did not attack in winter. They rested up. Certainly they would not think of moving in sub-zero weather. Anyway, the Red Army's losses had surely been so great as to make any offensive out of the question.

Zhukov's counter-attacking infantry appeared clad in white camouflage capes, mounted on propeller-driven sleds and carrying Tommy guns. Even the T-34s were painted white; all that could be seen of them were great spumes of snow as they rushed forward. To the Germans it must have seemed like a great phantom army arising out of nowhere. Surprise was complete. Many of the T-34 squadrons had been formed up as much as 100 miles behind the front in some sectors, proving that mobile warfare was still possible in the Russian winter. All along the Moscow front German troops retreated. Soon after, the High Command in Berlin ordered a halt to all offensive operations. Bock wrote in his diary: 'The Russians, who have destroyed almost all facilities on the main roads, have been able to obstruct our transport arrangements to such an extent that the Army Group no longer has what it needs to survive and to fight ... Today we no longer have the possibility of significant manoeuvre.'

By 13 December, German forces had retreated more than fifty miles from the capital. On the 18th, Bock was relieved of his command. Army Group Centre, under his command, had come the closest the German Army would ever get to Moscow. Never again would the Soviet capital be threatened. To his diary Bock confided:

> All along, I demanded of Army High Command the authority to strike down the enemy when he was wobbling. We could have finished the enemy last summer. We could have destroyed him completely. Last August, the road to Moscow was open; we could have entered the Bolshevik capital in triumph and in summery weather. The high military leadership of the Fatherland made a terrible mistake when it forced my army group to adopt a position of defence last August. Now all of us are paying for that mistake.*

Over the next four weeks the Germans would be pushed back over 200 miles. By then Barbarossa had cost them over 210,000 killed and missing and 620,000 wounded, a third of whom had become casualties after the beginning of Operation Typhoon. On top of this came an unknown number of Axis casualties such as Hungarians, Romanians and Finns. On 5 December, Hitler ordered his troops to assume a defensive stance. Guderian believed that the current front line could not be held, but Hitler was adamant: there could be no withdrawals. Guderian objected and was soon dismissed, as were a number of other generals including Bock for 'medical reasons', though he was brought back a few months later. Some forty other high-ranking Wehrmacht officers were also relieved of their command.

The Soviet offensive continued for the best part of a month, with Zhukov attempting on a few occasions – and with varied success – to repeat the double encirclement of Nomonhan against the Germans.

Yet, by the time Zhukov's offensive ceased on 7 January 1942, the Moscow front had been pushed back up to 100 miles along 600 miles of front. Moscow was now safe, and the Germans had been dealt their first major defeat of the Second World War. The myth of the invincible

---

* Bock was killed in the last days of the war, by a British fighter strike, the only one of Hitler's field marshals to die in action.

Blitzkrieg had been shattered. It also provided a most important boost for Soviet morale. Hitler now had to prepare for a prolonged struggle. Operation Barbarossa had failed: stalled on the approaches to Moscow.

Hitler had conceived a low opinion of his regular Wehrmacht generals at various points in the victorious French campaign of 1940, when they had shown themselves to be indecisive or over-cautious. It was only his superior will and intuition that had carried them through to victory – or so he persuaded himself. Now all his misgivings had been given new shape by the failure to seize the enemy capital, which had been so clearly within his grasp by the beginning of December. From his distant eyrie, it was clearly just a matter of one more push. Then he would be recognized as the greatest warlord the world had yet produced. On 19 December Hitler took over direct command of the German Army from Walther von Brauchitsch. One of his first utterances was that 'The will to hold out must be brought home to every unit!' That meant that no tactical withdrawal, however militarily desirable, would henceforth be countenanced. It would bring doom to German armies from Stalingrad to Berlin.

Buried in his East Prussian forest hide-out, the Wolf's Lair, accessible only to his terrified toadies, Hitler was completely out of touch with his front-line generals. His vision of the world was comparable to that of a Panzer driver, closed down in his tank, able only to peer through a narrow slit. He would vent his contempt and rage on the generals after every check and setback encountered by the Wehrmacht. News filtered through to him very slowly, and was usually tinged with false optimism. General Halder would write up in his diary all his fears, but he would seldom dare broach them to the Führer. Consequently Hitler fed on the first (Japanese) tidings of Pearl Harbor, and believed that the American fleet was completely destroyed.

Hitler's conviction that he was a superhuman, however, now led him to commit one further act of supreme hubris. On 11 December 1941, four days after Japan struck at Pearl Harbor, he saw fit to declare war on the United States. Why? He did not need to; he was not bound by any commitment to the Mikado. Inexplicable as the act still seems, it could only have come from some self-sown belief that, with the fall of Moscow only one push away, and with it the final conquest of Russia, he was about to become Lord of the Universe. Why should he share his glory with a contemptible Asian country which in a matter of days, and with small losses, seemed poised to conquer a far larger empire than had Hitler and his mighty Wehrmacht? Why not seize this moment to display his contempt for the wobbling Anglo-Saxon powers?

After the great triumph of the winter offensive of December 1941, Stalin too – over-inflated by success – now went on to commit another of *his* calamitous mistakes. Encouraged by Zhukov's winter triumphs, he concluded that the Red Army was stronger than it really was, that one great push across the board would finish off the invaders. Accordingly he ordered a general offensive for the spring of 1942. Zhukov, knowing just how exhausted his troops were from the winter offensive, was horrified. In the event, the spring offensive proved an almost unqualified disaster. The Wehrmacht was still too strong. Masters of defence, the Germans had reinforced the lines they had retreated to in December with a system of 'hedgehog' strongpoints. With terrible casualties, the Russians exhausted themselves battering against these. Thus, when Hitler opened the new campaigning season with a thrust towards Stalingrad and the oilfields of the Caucasus, they had few fresh troops in reserve to meet the new threat. The new German summer offensive of 1942 split the Russian front into fragments on either side of Kursk. Three armies (Weich's Second Army, Hoth's Fourth Panzer, and Paulus's Sixth Army), along with eleven Panzer divisions, fanned out towards Voronezh and the Don River. Paulus's Panzer divisions reached the Don on either side of Voronezh on 5 July, approaching the fringes of the oil-rich Caucasus – and ultimately Stalingrad.

That August, Zhukov was sent to assume overall command of the sagging Russian front at Stalingrad. Here he found a great grey tongue of German troops licking towards the River Volga at Stalingrad. Zhukov, the victor of Moscow, went with orders to command and co-ordinate the battered defenders, with their backs to the river. As the enemy troops poured into the tongue of occupied steppe, he spotted an opportunity that he had seen at Nomonhan three years previously. Occupying a huge area, the over-stretched Wehrmacht had long and highly vulnerable flanks. Both north and south of the city, these flanks were defended by Romanian or Hungarian Axis troops: troops of indifferent quality and resolution, and poorly armed. This was reminiscent of the situation in Nomonhan where Zhukov had found flanks held by vulnerable and second-rate Manchukuoan troops. He thus applied the same tactics as at Nomonhan, though on a vast scale in which millions of troops, as opposed to tens of thousands, were involved. The ultimate result was the colossal defeat and total destruction of Paulus's army at Stalingrad. Over 90,000 Axis troops were marched into captivity, from which only a few thousand ever returned. It was the disaster that marked an irreversible turning-point in German fortunes in the Second World War. This was forever the battle with which Zhukov's name would be associated. However, it should be stressed that Stalingrad would almost certainly not have happened had it not been for Zhukov's victory in front of Moscow. Rodric Braithwaite notes judiciously:

> By one measure – the number of people involved – the Battle of Moscow was the greatest battle in the Second World War, and therefore the greatest battle in history. More than seven million officers and men from both sides took part, compared with the four million who fought at Stalingrad in 1942 ... This was a scale never matched in the fighting in Western Europe and Africa. The Battle of Moscow swirled over a territory the size of France, and lasted for six months ... The Soviet Union lost more people in this one battle – 926,000 soldiers killed, to say nothing of the wounded – than ... the combined casualties of the British and the Americans in the whole of the Second World War. This was the horrendous price they paid for inflicting on the Wehrmacht the first real defeat it had ever suffered.

These are statistics impossible to dispute. There remains one crucial issue, still much argued about among historians: if Moscow had fallen in the winter of 1941, would the Soviet Union have collapsed with it? My personal view is that it probably would have: apart from the city's huge importance as a communications hub, and – still, despite the evacuations – as an industrial complex, its moral significance as capital was unquantifiable, as indeed was Stalin's all-out commitment to its defence. Finally there was the proviso in Sorge's last message: if Moscow fell, Japan might be tempted to enter the war for some cheap gains in the Far East. Such a two-front threat would have demanded the certain return to Siberia of those formidable troops with which

Stalin had turned the tide at Moscow; leaving the rest of Russia a feeble prey to the Nazi hordes.

Could Hitler, then, have taken Moscow? Yes, if he had started Barbarossa earlier, and thereafter concentrated all his overwhelming force on that one objective. What a shattering reversal of arms for a hitherto omnipotent warlord, so steeped in hubris, and all its self-deluding conceits!

PART FOUR

MIDWAY, 1942

CHAPTER TWELVE

THE *KIDO BUTAI*

At 7 a.m. on Sunday 7 December 1941, Admiral Isoroku Yamamoto's carrier planes struck Pearl Harbor, perhaps the most written-up event in military history. Whether, as Japan claimed, a proper declaration of war got mislaid in the post is immaterial.* America was caught thoroughly by surprise, which of course made a Day of Infamy that much more infamous. As we have seen in Part One, Pearl Harbor should perhaps have been better prepared for such a sneak attack in the light of what happened at Port Arthur in 1904, when the Japanese attacked without declaring war and while diplomatic negotiations were still under way. But history's lessons are too often ignored.

In the five months following Pearl Harbor, Japan swept the board in the Pacific, contrary to US estimates that it would not be capable of mounting more than one major naval operation at a time. In short order Hong Kong, the Philippines, Singapore, the Dutch East Indies and Burma were seized, and the seemingly irresistible Japanese were knocking on the doors of India and Australia. In Malaya and Singapore, bicycle-riding shock-troops trained by that evil genius Colonel Tsuji in French Indo-China, rounded up some 130,000 British and Australian troops with minimal losses. In his history of the Second World War, Churchill called the fall of Singapore to the Japanese the 'worst disaster and largest capitulation in British history'. Mopping up British naval units in the Indian Ocean, together with the surviving remnants of the Dutch fleet, the Japanese Admiral Chuichi Nagumo had forced the abandonment of Ceylon (today's Sri Lanka) as a naval

---

* In Yamamoto's original plan it was stipulated that the attack should not commence until thirty minutes after Japan had informed the United States that peace negotiations were at an end. In 1999, however, a professor of law and international relations in Tokyo, Takeo Iguchi, discovered documents which pointed to a revealing debate inside the government and which in his view showed 'that the army and navy did not want to give any proper declaration of war, or indeed prior notice even of the termination of negotiations . . . they clearly prevailed'.

base. For the first time in its imperial history, the Royal Navy had to fall back on East African and South African ports, abandoning everything east of Durban.

As the historian Samuel Eliot Morison notes, only one major battle in which the US Navy was involved 'was decided by gunfire. All the others were won by ships' torpedoes, and by bombs and torpedoes delivered to the target by aircraft'. The true queens of the chessboard would prove to be the newfangled aircraft carrier. As of 7 December 1941, Japan had six fleet carriers; the US had only two that were battle-worthy, to cover the whole Pacific. A storm had providentially prevented Admiral Halsey and his *Enterprise* task force of aircraft carriers from reaching Pearl Harbor on the 7th.

Yet, far more powerful than the loss of life, and of all those battle-wagons, was the moral impact it had across the width and breadth of the United States. As Yamamoto is sometimes supposed to have said after the attack: 'All we have done is to awaken a sleeping giant and fill him with a terrible resolve.' Without warning, America's own territory had been brutally violated; 2,402 men had been killed and 1,282 wounded. The backbone of the navy's battle fleet appeared to have been destroyed.

Heartless as it may sound, however, in retrospect Pearl Harbor was the best thing that could have happened for the Western alliance. After Hitler's attack on Poland in September 1939, and until the fall of France nine months later, Britain had fought a desultory and half-hearted war. The mighty French Army did absolutely nothing to help the poor Poles. But in the United States after Pearl Harbor the country universally was galvanized to total war in a way that it had never been before, and never would be again. From being a nation at least half of whose people were dedicated to peace and isolation, America at once became passionate for war and victory. The commitment to global war even, coming as it did four days later, with Hitler's declaration of war, was greeted almost with relief, certainly with determined acceptance.

With it went an angry, racial hatred of the Japanese. The fighting in the Pacific would be fought with a savagery not seen on the Western Front in Europe. As the historian Alan Nevins put it, 'Probably in all our history no foe has been so detested as were the Japanese.' It was primarily 'the treachery of Pearl Harbor' that could never be forgiven, followed by the atrocities to the POWs on Bataan, and the murder of British nurses in Hong Kong and Singapore. Altogether it produced a 'rage bordering on the genocidal', says John W. Dowler in his excellent account of the struggle in the Pacific, *War Without Mercy*. It was exemplified by Admiral William F. Halsey's 'Kill Japs! Kill Japs! Kill more Japs!' At home such slogans would appear in movies or in the press, along with such sentiments as 'now you are going to get it – and it won't be finished until your detestable empire is wiped off the face of the earth.' As the war correspondent Ernie Pyle remarked, 'In Europe we felt that our enemies, horrible and deadly as they were, were still human . . . but out here [in the Pacific] I soon gathered that the Japanese are looked upon as subhuman and repulsive.'

This informed the personal conduct of the war. In the South Pacific the psychology became 'kill or be killed'. No prisoners were taken, and no quarter on either side was given. Often Japanese naval survivors would be shot in the sea, with the words, 'We can't be sporting in a war.' Equally no quarter was given to the wretched native Japanese living in the US, the 'Nisei' (second generation), most of whom had been loyal citizens for many years: on the American west coast, first- and second-generation citizens of Japanese ancestry were rounded up and committed to internment camps. Even the highly respectable Smithsonian Museum in Washington DC came out with such unscientific remarks as 'Japanese skulls are 2,000 years less developed than ours.' As Dower notes, 'the end results of racial thinking on both sides were virtually identical – being hierarchy, arrogance, viciousness, atrocity and death'. This was what a combination of Pearl Harbor and the twisted legacy of *bushido* had led otherwise civilized nations to. It was Japan's historic misfortune that American 'hate' would possess the ultimate weapon of vengeance, the atomic bombs dropped on Hiroshima and Nagasaki. Well might one wonder how the chivalrous Admiral Togo would have reacted had he been able to witness the way his noble victory of 1905 had become debauched in such a vicious war.

Yet, even amid the intense gloom that followed Pearl Harbor, for Americans – being Americans – there was always that spark of hope. That spark was turned into a flame when, on 17 April 1942, a tiny force of sixteen USAAF B-25 bombers, under Lieutenant-Colonel James H. 'Jimmy' Doolittle, struck back at the very heart of Japan – one of the most courageous, self-sacrificing and inspiring feats of arms undertaken by any Allied unit in the Second World War. It was just a pinprick, but it would hold important strategic implications for the subsequent course of the Pacific War.

Only two weeks after Pearl Harbor, Roosevelt summoned the Joint Chiefs of Staff to the White House to demand that a bombing raid on Japan be carried out as soon as possible, to restore battered public morale. The carrier decided upon was the 27,900-ton *Hornet*. A lightweight by comparison with Japan's *Akagi* and *Kaga*, both of them over 41,000 tons, *Hornet* was a brand-new ship, currently undergoing sea trials off the Virginia coast. She had a green crew, many aged no more than eighteen, recruits fresh from bootcamp, some of whom had never seen the ocean. On 2 February 1942, they were stunned to see two experimental B-25s loaded on board. Then, after setting out to sea, they watched them take off – the first ground-based medium bombers ever to do so in the history of aviation. They were unable to return. Having completed their bombing mission the B-25s were to overfly Japan and land on airfields in Russian Siberia or in China. Although Soviet Vladivostok would have been the nearest field, Moscow – fearful of getting embroiled in war with Japan – refused permission. The additional mileage imposed in reaching China meant that the bombers would be straining for their last drops of fuel.

It was, however, the Chinese who suffered most from the barbaric Japanese retribution that followed the Doolittle Raid. An estimated 250,000 Chinese from the areas which had helped US airmen were reported to have been executed by way of reprisal. This horrifying figure has never, to my knowledge, been disputed; but if accurate it must make it the most savage reprisal in all of the Second World War.

Of course, all sixteen of the valuable B-25s were lost. Ten thousand navy personnel were involved in the operation. Two of Halsey's indispensable carriers – the *Hornet* and *Enterprise* – were put at risk. So was it all worth it? In the United States, battered after months of unrelenting bad news from the Pacific, the impact on morale was tremendous. Here, for the first time, America was hitting back at the very heart of the Japanese war machine. The raid's impact was enhanced by Roosevelt's mysterious declaration – most alarming, by implication, to the Japanese – that the raiders had come 'from Shangri-la'. It would be twenty-six months before American bombers would be striking again at Japan. By then, with development of the B-29 Superfortress, each carrying ten times the bomb-load of Doolittle's B-25s, the results would be devastating – culminating in the dropping of the atom bombs on Hiroshima and Nagasaki.

Though only a pinprick, the Doolittle Raid had a powerful influence on Yamamoto's thinking. He warned that the raid could be a 'taste of the real thing' that was to come. It meant that the defensive island perimeter which Japan had created around itself in those first heady weeks after Pearl Harbor was still not large enough. To make Japan safe, it would surely have to be pushed still further out. Admiral Nagumo's raiding force, which had been sweeping the Indian Ocean as far west as Ceylon, was summoned home. Fighter units which had been earmarked for the Solomon Islands and the drive on Australia were withdrawn to protect the homeland.

More decisive in the war as a whole was the effect that the raid had on Japanese plans for attacking Midway Island (really an atoll embracing two islands) – the nearest US base to Japan. Two weeks before the Doolittle Raid, when Yamamoto presented his plan for the seizure of Midway, its feasibility had met with strong criticism from the army. Now, persuaded by its potential threat to the homeland, the doubters came around to support Yamamoto's Midway plan, and the operation was brought forward with urgency and excessive haste: to be launched at the beginning of June 1942.

In the spring of that year, the tide of war was running strongly against the Allies. In the Pacific, the seemingly irresistible Japanese were knocking hard on the doors of India and Australia. Never had an empire been acquired in so short a time, certainly with such a huge perimeter. Its quest for raw materials, especially those essential to the unending war in China, now looked assured. Swiftly the guarding outposts that protected that empire were being powerfully entrenched, and reinforced, by Japanese arms. Gained in but a few weeks, how many months if not years would it take to roll it up again? Allied planners must have asked themselves countless times in head-scratching despair. How long before the great base of Singapore, captured by the Japanese in weeks, would once again fly the Union Jack? And where now were the bases from which such a return could be made?

There were few enough of these left, now that the juggernaut of Japanese aggression had been, at least temporarily, halted in its relentless momentum. At one end there was distant Australia, plus a handful of islands in the Solomons and a tenuous grip on the south-eastern tip of inhospitable New Guinea. At the other end, the tiny atoll of Midway Island, a solitary US outpost on the way to Japan, 2,600 miles away – and 1,300 miles distant from Pearl Harbor. For Japan, Midway was an essential stepping-stone to the capture of Hawaii, itself particularly vulnerable to invasion, and a threat to the west coast of the United States. For America, for those very same reasons, Midway had to be fought for, and held, at any cost.

At the far west of the sprawling Hawaiian archipelago, and the hardest part to defend, the tiny atoll of Midway measures less than twice the area of New York's Central Park. In early May, Japanese and US carrier fleets fought out a bitter engagement in the Coral Sea, between the Solomons and New Guinea. It was the first naval battle ever to be fought when the opposing fleets were never in sight of each other. American losses were heavier, in that they lost the carrier *Lexington* (more through American carelessness than enemy skill), while the *Yorktown* suffered heavy damage and, in Tokyo, was reported sunk. But the Japanese lost forty-three aircraft and their hard-to-replace veteran crews. Most significantly, the drawn battle persuaded the Japanese to abandon their plans to seize New Guinea's Port Moresby, the jumping-off point for invading Australia.

Nevertheless, the early summer of 1942 and the year's run of amazing successes presented the Japanese warlords with almost a surfeit of strategic options. In the prevailing state of Allied debility, most of them were enticing ones – and all of them involved a naval initiative. They could have resumed their thrust westwards across the Indian Ocean, occupying Ceylon; or the drive southwards, to take Fiji and Nouméa, New Caledonia, severing US links with Australia. They could strike north-eastwards to occupy the Aleutian archipelago and threaten the United States via Alaska. Or they could drive on Hawaii, by first taking its solitary outpost of Midway Island. The only vector they would no longer contemplate was the north-western one, into Soviet Siberia. Nomonhan in the summer of 1939 had taught them a salutary lesson: to avoid a swipe from the freshly revitalized Russian

Bear. The new Japanese empire – or what its leaders liked to call the Greater East Asia Co-Prosperity Sphere – had a gigantic perimeter to defend, which presupposed a continuing superiority at sea. That in turn depended upon a strategy of aggressive defence; and as long as the US Navy was undefeated that defence could not be static.

The man on whose shoulders all these monumental options rested was the fifty-seven-year-old Admiral Isoroku Yamamoto, Commander of the Combined Fleet, architect and executor of the raid on Pearl Harbor. Born in a simple wooden house in Nagaoka, in one of the harshest parts of Japan, Yamamoto had had a tough upbringing. He was the youngest son of an impoverished samurai family, so badly off that they farmed him off to be brought up in another household. Always cold towards him, his father Sadayoshi, a poorly paid schoolmaster, seems to have been unusual even by contemporary Japanese standards. The boy was given the name Isoroku, which means 'fifty-six', for the simple reason that his father was that age at the time. When another son died, Yamamoto's father declared that he wished it could have been Isoroku instead. Understandably, the boy left home as soon as he could to join the navy, graduating with honours from the Naval Academy in 1904, just in time to participate in the Russo-Japanese War. His mother sent him off to war with a specially embroidered handkerchief on which his father had inscribed: 'Please fall for the Emperor and your country. Even when the flower of the warrior falls, it will still have a beautiful fragrance ...'

As a young lieutenant, Yamamoto had fought and been wounded – losing two fingers on his left hand – at Tsushima in 1905, as well as sustaining numerous other injuries which left permanent scars to the rest of his body. It was officially recorded that he had been wounded by a Russian shell hitting his cruiser, *Nisshin*; but the truth seems to have been that it was a 'cook-off' caused by unstable Japanese explosives within the breech of one of the cruiser's own guns. He had then accompanied his admiral, Togo, to the hospital bedside of the wounded and humiliated enemy admiral, Rozhestvensky. It was an encounter that clearly left a deep impression on Yamamoto, as indeed had the extraordinary Japanese triumph at Tsushima.

As noted earlier, Admiral Togo became a national hero and Tsushima a sanctified touchstone of national policy. Yamamoto, like most

Japanese of his time, was brought up venerating Togo, and felt humiliated by the fetters which he saw the West once more attempting to
place upon post-1905 Japan, notably in the treaties of the 1920s and
1930s, which would place limitations on the growth of the Japanese
Navy.

Yamamoto was an early exponent of carrier warfare, and under
his influence Japan in the 1930s, ignoring treaty restrictions, built up
the world's most imposing and most modern carrier fleet at a time
when most navies were still wedded to the notion of big-gun warship supremacy.* He was also a passionate gambler, never missing an
opportunity to play poker, and he would open a book on almost any
event, even betting a dozen bottles of beer on the sinking of the two
British capital ships off Malaya in December 1941, *Repulse* and *Prince
of Wales*. He once all but broke the bank at Monte Carlo, and would
joke that he would love to retire from the navy and spend the rest of
his life there. Though married with a family, for most of his life he
enjoyed the adoration of a geisha mistress, Chuyiko, whom he would
visit even on the eve of shipping off to war. A small man of five foot
three, Yamamoto was taciturn and modest in speech, yet every once in
a while he could not resist showing off, often by perilously performing
a handstand on a ship's rail, even sometimes when he was an admiral.

Unusually, in the early 1920s he was sent to study at Harvard, and
served twice as a naval attaché in Washington. He took the opportunity to travel widely, visiting the automotive industry in Detroit and
the Texas oilfields. 'Because I have seen the motor industry in Detroit
and the oilfields of Texas [he wrote to a friend], I know Japan has no
chance if she goes to war with America, or if she starts to compete in
building warships.' Yet his US immersion would fail him when it came
to assessing how American character would react under the challenge
of total war.

---

* The big guns on warships of twelve inches calibre and more could wreak terrible havoc on
even the most heavily armoured ship. They would seldom sink it in one salvo, unless there
was a lucky shot, as with *Bismarck* sinking HMS *Hood*. The drawback in modern warfare was
that the battleship had to close within twenty miles or so for its guns to be within effective
range. In contrast, the carrier-borne torpedo bomber and dive bomber – as seen at the Battle
of the Coral Sea, Pearl Harbor and in the sinking of *Repulse* and *Prince of Wales* – could strike
a devastating blow at 300 miles distance with its torpedoes and armour-piercing bombs: the
kind of warfare in which capital ships never saw each other.

In 1932 Yamamoto was put in charge of the technical manufacture of naval aviation. One result of this collaboration was the Zero, which was to prove the best carrier-borne fighter aircraft on either side in 1941. The following year he was given command of the First Aircraft Carrier Squadron, flying his flag in the carrier *Akagi*. Then in 1936 he became Deputy Minister of the Navy. Though it was a position which offered little influence on policy, he celebrated the appointment by giving a party for journalists, at which he performed a handstand. He found politics in Tokyo to be overlaid with menace and violence. He tried his best to slow the march to war with the United States and Great Britain. But he became so convinced that he himself stood in danger of assassination at the hands of pro-war zealots that in August 1939 he readily accepted appointment as Commander-in-Chief of the Combined Fleet, in order to go to sea for his own safety.

A vigorous opponent of the aggressive army clique which had embroiled Japan in the unending war with China and had taken supreme power under General Hideki Tojo in October 1941, Yamamoto had serious misgivings about the consequences of war with the United States. (Even before Pearl Harbor he remarked, 'I shall run wild for the first six months or a year, but I have absolutely no confidence for the second and third years of the fighting.') The author of the standard Japanese biography of Yamamoto, Hiroyuki Agawa, judiciously entitled it *The Reluctant Admiral*. Like many of the peace-lobby in Japan in the late 1930s, Yamamoto seems to have been swept along by the tide of events.

As war became inevitable in 1941, he now put all his energies and talents into planning it as vigorously as possible. For him there was no question of resignation: the samurai code demanded his obedience. In May 1939, when he feared assassination, Yamamoto had drafted his will: 'For a warrior, dying for one's country is the most honourable thing. It makes no difference whether the death is on the battlefield or at home. It is easy to die like a warrior on the battlefield but it is difficult to die for a principle. The grace of the Emperor is great, and the Japanese history is as long as eternity. I cannot help but think about Japan's future. My personal honour, life or death is of no concern.'

Recollections of Togo's triumph at Tsushima swayed the gambler in

Yamamoto, an exponent of airpower over the battleship, into hoping that one decisive battle, shattering the US battle fleet at anchor in Hawaii, would neutralize America and permit Japan to carry out its quest for empire in the Far East. Contrary to what he might have learned from his years in the United States, by the spring of 1942 Yamamoto had rashly persuaded himself that 'the American fleet was a beaten, demoralized outfit that would need to be coaxed towards its own annihilation'. He could not see that the surprise attack on Pearl Harbor had ensured the implacable hatred of the US, coupled with a grim determination to destroy the attacker. 'Remember Pearl Harbor' had become a slogan that would encourage Americans to extraordinary acts of courage, revealing in them unexpectedly vast reserves of energy and ingenuity. As already noted, it also ensured that the Pacific War would be fought with unbridled ferocity and no quarter given on either side.

With the strike on Pearl Harbor having turned out at best an incomplete victory, in March 1942 Yamamoto now proposed a twin-pronged operation. The objective would be to seize Midway, and at the same time lure out the residue of the US Pacific Fleet, which would be destroyed in one decisive engagement – as Togo had done to Russia in 1905. At first the army (which would have to supply the Midway invasion forces) resisted. Then came the Doolittle Raid on Tokyo of 18 April (which, in the words of one senior Japanese naval officer, 'passed like a shudder over Japan'). It provided a major shock to Japanese security and was a personal affront to the Emperor, which gave Yamamoto just the winning hand he needed.

Symbolically, the Midway operation would be launched on 27 May, Japan's national day commemorating Togo's 1905 triumph. This was but a further indication of how obsessed the Japanese mentality was with this past triumph, and Yamamoto's determination to repeat it. The scale of the operation was monumental, and entirely hubristic in conception, incorporating virtually the whole of the Combined Fleet; far bigger than the assault on Pearl Harbor, and in its complexity it was described by one US historian as 'Byzantine'.

Once Nagumo's bombers had softened up the defences of Midway (which were confined to a tiny area divided between its two small islands), Rear-Admiral Raizo Tanaka's Transport Group would land

5,000 invasion troops. Covering them would be Vice-Admiral Takeo Kurita with four heavy cruisers;* and further out still would lurk Vice-Admiral Nobutake Kondo's main body, comprising four more heavy cruisers and two battleships.

Behind would come, some 600 miles from Midway, at least a day's sailing apart, Yamamoto's Main Body with no fewer than five battleships. He himself would command the battle from the colossal *Yamato*† – at 72,800 tons the biggest battleship ever built, whose 18.1-inch guns could outrange any existing Allied ship, and sink them with shells each weighing more than 3,000 pounds, at an extreme (and unheard-of) range of twenty-six miles. This overwhelming force would trap, and in one decisive action smash – according to Tsushima principles – the US fleet after it had sailed to defend Midway.

Finally, as a completely separate operation, and in no way a diversionary action, Vice-Admiral Moshiro Hosogaya's Northern Force would be sent north to invade three inhospitable islands in the US-owned Aleutian chain (the first US mainland territory to be taken). This alone mounted three heavy and three light cruisers, twelve destroyers and two light carriers.

The fleet assembled to carry out these multiple tasks numbered some 200 ships. It must have presented a remarkable spectacle as the main force slid out of a mist-bound Inland Sea. But the warships were to be spread over a vast area of North Pacific waters, and here would lie the gravest weakness of Yamamoto's elaborate plans: dispersal. Offending all the principles of concentration preached in the nineteenth century by the American Admiral Alfred Thayer Mahan, the various components would be too far apart to support each other. Yamamoto's own

---

* Throughout the Pacific War the Japanese heavy cruiser was perhaps the IJN's best weapon – sturdily constructed, able to take huge punishment, packing a powerful punch, and superior to most of her US Navy counterparts.

† Commissioned a week after Pearl Harbor, *Yamato* had been constructed in great secrecy and in clear breach of the existing naval limitation agreements. Her nine mighty guns fired just a few shots before she was sunk by US torpedo planes in April 1945, with the loss of most of her crew of 2,332. Her sister ship *Musashi* had an equally inglorious fate, sunk at Leyte Gulf the previous year. Their demise defined a clear end to the reign of the battleship, or superdreadnought. The *Yamato* designs were approved by the Japanese Naval High Command; in all, five *Yamato*-class battleships were planned, over strong objections by naval aviators, who argued for the construction of aircraft carriers rather than battleships. It was fortunate for the Allies that Japan's battleship advocates won out.

Main Fleet would be lurking 600 miles north-west of Midway, and over 3,000 miles from home waters. The Aleutian element of the plan was to prove a particularly wasteful drain on resources. Great military brains from Napoleon to Clausewitz had stressed repeatedly: 'Never have more than a single objective.' In war the simplest operations are the most successful. Yamamato had too many objectives: he saw too many things. But then he was not destined to be a Napoleon, nor even another 'Nelson of the East'.

On 1 May, battle manoeuvres were held aboard the mighty *Yamato*. But they were phoney, sycophantically designed to please the C-in-C. With nine 'hits' scored, both *Akagi* (once commanded by Yamamoto himself) and *Kaga* were sunk – but Chief of Staff Ugaki quickly reversed the umpire's decision and *Akagi* was 'refloated'. It was one more display of what the Japanese themselves identified as the 'victory disease', which would distort all Japanese planning that spring.

Against such a dread armada as the *Kido Butai*, the cutting edge of Japan's main naval strikeforce, what had the battered US Pacific Fleet to offer? First and foremost, it had its commander, the fifty-seven-year-old Chester W. Nimitz, known as CinCPac (pronounced 'sink-pack'), the commander-in-chief of the Pacific Fleet. Growing up in Texas, a state not often associated with the sea, Nimitz enjoyed the homely pastime of 'pitching horseshoes'. His grandfather had served as a sailor in the Imperial German merchant marines, and Nimitz himself spoke German, which he used when studying marine engines in Germany before the First World War. The future C-in-C graduated seventh from a class of 114, but blotted his copybook when, as a young ensign, he ran a destroyer aground in the Philippines. He received a reprimand, but redeemed himself a few years later when he saved a rating from drowning. Nimitz became a leading US Navy authority on submarines, which was to serve him in good stead from 1942 onwards, but he had little experience of carrier warfare. When he assumed command of the Pacific Fleet in December 1941, Nimitz did so, appropriately enough, in a ceremony aboard the US submarine *Grayling*; normally this would have taken place on a battleship, but there were none left afloat at the time. The new commander combined, remarkably, the attributes of both boldness and caution, and listened to his advisers. Good at delegating authority, Nimitz was immune to panic; he commanded authority in the most adverse of times.

Upon his appointment, Nimitz had written to his wife, 'I will be lucky to last six months. The public may demand action and results faster than I can produce.' In fact, he was to shine as one of the few Allied commanders to provoke almost no criticism. In contrast with the Japanese, his assets were slender. Without a single battleship after Pearl Harbor he had in hand just two undamaged aircraft carriers, *Enterprise* and *Hornet*. As we have seen, the latter had a largely green crew, while many of the aviators had never taken off from a carrier. His third available carrier, *Yorktown*, *Hornet*'s sister ship, limping back after taking a battering in the Battle of the Coral Sea, was being repaired feverishly in dry dock in Pearl Harbor.

But his most telling weapon lay in the realm of intelligence. Led by a back-room genius, Commander Joseph J. Rochefort Jr, a top-secret team known as Station Hypo had broken the Japanese naval code, JN-25. Admiral Ernest J. King, Commander-in-Chief, United States Fleet, and Chief of Naval Operations (COMINCH-CNO) throughout the Second World War, had doubts about the navy intelligence teams, but Nimitz trusted them. From Rochefort's intercepts Nimitz learned that a massive Japanese assault was in the offing; he knew its components, and the rough date, but not its objective. That appeared in the Japanese code as 'AF'. Nimitz and Rochefort suspected that it stood for Midway, but were not sure. So, in a clever ruse, an unencrypted signal was sent, reporting a shortage of fresh water on the island. Instantly the Japanese fell into the trap, reporting in their compromised code that 'AF' was low on water.

One important additional feature was that the Japanese ships lacked the radar with which US vessels were equipped. From Rochefort's code-breaking, Nimitz could predict attacks scheduled for 28 May. He assessed that 'Japanese conquest of Midway would give their bow-shaped homeland a steel tipped arrow aimed straight at the heart of Hawaii ...'. The intelligence estimate was to prove only five minutes, five degrees and five miles off. Nimitz's subordinate at Midway, Rear-Admiral Raymond A. Spruance, would say of him: 'not only did he accept the intelligence picture, but he acted upon it at once'.

One immediate setback for Nimitz was that Vice-Admiral William F. 'Bull' Halsey, his pugnacious carrier chief, was hospitalized with painful psoriasis. As his replacement, to Nimitz's surprise, Halsey nominated Rear-Admiral Spruance, with Vice-Admiral Frank Fletcher in overall command. A 'black shoe'* sailor who had never commanded a carrier force before, Spruance was a cool, meticulous and careful commander, schooled on destroyers, and hating any form of publicity. Indeed, in many ways he stood at the opposite pole to the fiery Halsey. As things turned out at Midway, it may be that his replacement of Halsey was a blessing in disguise. Halsey was not nicknamed 'Bull' for nothing; on occasion (and dangerously) he would be the bull in the china shop. The orders Spruance received from Nimitz included the characteristic injunction: 'You will be governed by the principle of calculated risk . . .'

With foresight, and in contradistinction to Yamamoto who rashly placed all his carriers in one basket, Nimitz divided his three into two task forces, TF 16, under Spruance, comprising *Enterprise* and *Hornet*, and TF 17, centred around the damaged *Yorktown* with an escort of two heavy cruisers and five destroyers. In command of TF 17 was Frank Fletcher, an experienced cruiser and battleship commander who had brought *Yorktown* through the Battle of the Coral Sea earlier in May.

Meanwhile a small covering force was sent to Dutch Harbor, in the Aleutians, under command of Rear-Admiral Robert A. ('Fuzzy') Theobald, aged fifty-eight.

On 15 May, Nimitz set his modest force in motion. Repairs on *Yorktown*, estimated to require three months, were rushed through by a workforce 1,400 strong, the shipyard gangs actually taking to sea while completing their work aboard the carrier. The great ship could only move at a reduced speed. But she could launch and recover aircraft. That was enough.

Fletcher won the first hand by managing to slip his force past the submarine cordon despatched by Yamamoto to track US naval movements out of Pearl Harbor. Arriving too late, the Japanese literally missed the boat. So, although (thanks to Hypo) Nimitz had a good idea of where major units of the Japanese fleet were heading – namely to a rendezvous 200 miles north-west of Midway – Yamamoto and, more importantly, Nagumo had no idea where the American force

---

* Aviators were distinguished by being permitted to wear brown shoes.

was, nor how many carriers it contained. They had persuaded themselves that two US carriers had been sunk in the Coral Sea, and had no idea that *Yorktown* could in fact be sailing towards Midway.

Fletcher's and Spruance's objective was to rendezvous at a map reference codenamed, optimistically, Point Luck, north-east of Midway, whence they intended to ambush Nagumo's invading fleet from its left flank.

Both Nagumo's submarine and aerial reconnaissance were sloppily carried out. Had they been otherwise, Fletcher's carriers would almost certainly have been spotted, with dire consequences. The sloppy reconnaissance was all part of the prevailing Japanese 'victory disease'.

The Japanese armada, the greatest ever to put to sea, had set off 'majestically', its crews in high spirits. In his diary, Captain Yoshitake Miwa, the Combined Fleet's air officer, wrote of this 'greatest expedition': 'Everybody in the fleet, from the head down to the men, entertains not the least doubt about a victory. Whence comes such a spirit that overwhelms the enemy before the battle is fought?'

Then the armada ran into a thick North Pacific fog. With visibility less than 600 yards, speed was reduced to twelve knots, on a dangerous zig-zag course. All that many could hear was the deep blast of *Yamato*'s foghorn. For security, Nagumo issued orders that pilots would have to return to their flat-tops on their own, and could not expect any radio help.

Spirits rose again as the fleet emerged from the fog near Midway. 'But where is the enemy fleet?' asked Nagumo. Meanwhile, in a Catalina PBY flying-boat, at 0900 on 3 June, a young ensign, John Reid, shouted, 'My God, aren't those ships on the horizon? I believe we have hit the jackpot.' In fact this was not Nagumo's carriers, but Tanaka's invasion fleet.

At 0700 that same day, a Japanese invasion force, under Rear-Admiral Kakuji Kakuta, with the light carriers *Ryuo* and *Jun'yo*, struck Dutch Harbor in the Aleutians, and occupied two islands, Kiska and Attu. Though the first US mainland territories to be seized by the enemy, they were in fact icy and barren outposts, of little strategic value. But a less well-informed and judicious commander than Nimitz might well have been taken in by what seemed like a ploy, designed to distract his gaze from the main attack.

The following morning, at 0545, the curtain went up on Midway with another PBY, piloted by Lieutenant William Chase, rattling off the warning: 'Many planes heading Midway. Bearing 320, distance 150'. Bristling with defences that had been urgently reinforced by Nimitz, Midway at once sent all its aircraft aloft to meet the enemy – and so as not to be caught on the ground as at Pearl Harbor. Totalling 124 planes, they consisted primarily of a squadron of seventeen Army Air Force B-17 Flying Fortresses and a mixed bag of some three dozen Marine Corps fighters, Wildcats, Vindicators and Brewster Buffalos. These fighters were largely obsolete; the pilots nicknamed the Vindicators 'Vibrators' or 'Wind-Indicators', and the stubby little Brewster Buffalos 'Flying Coffins'. One Marine captain said of them damningly: 'any commander that orders pilots out for combat in an F2A-3 [Buffalo] should consider the pilot as lost before leaving the ground'. Some of the planes, non-metal antiquities from peacetime, had the fabric peeling back; others developed engine failure. Was it not a disgrace to send young men to fight and die in such ancient aircraft?

Up against these planes were some of the most experienced aviators in the business, who had flown in China, in the Pearl Harbor raid, the Coral Sea and the Indian Ocean. In addition they flew the best carrier fighter in the world, the deadly Zero (or Mitsubishi A6M). Lethally nimble and faster than any US equivalent, with a remarkable range of 1,600 miles, it would later be reckoned to have shot down more than 1,500 US planes in the course of the war. Its Achilles heel was that, designed expressly for attack, it lacked protective armour, which was to prove its undoing as later US fighters evolved.[*]

Bombers based on Midway made several attacks on the Japanese carrier fleet. These included six TBF Avengers from *Hornet*'s VT-8,[†] their crews on their first combat operation, and four B-26 Marauders armed with torpedoes. Major Lofton Henderson, killed while leading his inexperienced squadron of SBU-3 Vindicator dive bombers, was

---

[*] One of the unexpected bonuses of the Aleutian campaign was that a Zero, attempting to force-land at Akuta, ended on its nose in a tundra bog, breaking the pilot's neck but itself remaining intact. The Zero was swiftly dissected by American engineers to find its secrets and weaknesses.

[†] US Navy carriers were designated by their commissioning date: so for example VB-3 was the bomber squadron from *Yorktown*; VT-6 the torpedo planes from *Enterprise*; VT-8 the torpedo planes from *Hornet*.

the first Marine aviator to die during the battle. He was posthumously honoured by having the main airfield at Guadalcanal named after him in August 1942. The Japanese shrugged off the attacks with almost no losses (perhaps no more than two fighters), while destroying all but one TBF torpedo bomber and two B-26s.

Out of the 108 planes Nagumo sent against Midway in that first wave, only a third were bombers. With mistaken caution, in case he should meet the naval targets that Yamamoto was counting on, he held the rest in reserve. The result was that, though shooting the US fighters out of the sky (only two remained flyable), he failed to cause more than ephemeral damage to the island's defences. The crucial airstrip remained virtually untouched; perhaps, in their certainty of success, the Japanese were hoping to use it themselves. At the same time, unexpectedly accurate anti-aircraft fire had downed a large number of the attackers. Midway could still easily resist any landing.

At 0705 on 4 June the Japanese attack leader, Lieutenant Joichi Tomonaga, flying off *Hiryu*, sent an unhappy Admiral Nagumo this message: 'There is need for a second attack wave.' At first hesitant – to Yamamoto's displeasure – Nagumo complied. As no warning of the proximity of enemy carriers had reached him and with ground targets in mind, he passed down the order to replace the reserve aircraft's torpedoes with fragmentation bombs – not an operation that could be accomplished in a few minutes.* At about the same time Nagumo had a close brush with death when a US Marine plane, crippled by anti-aircraft fire from his flagship *Akagi*, crashed into her deck, narrowly missing the tightly packed bridge where he stood. Nagumo's order stood in direct contradiction of Yamamoto's: to keep the reserve strike force armed for anti-ship operations. But he was encouraged by this comforting message from Yamamoto: 'there is no sign that our intention has been suspected by the enemy'.

With such minute-by-minute actions taking place, it may be hard to decide at what point fortune began to switch sides. But Nagumo's order at 0715 on 4 June to switch missiles may have been the moment when

---

* Torpedoes were only of use in attacks on naval units, while fragmentation bombs were effective on airfields and troops. Even in a naval attack, it was sensible to arm dive bombers with armour-piercing bombs, which exploded below decks, instead of with fragmentation bombs, which would cause only extensive surface damage.

Yamamoto's complex plan started to unravel. For if any of Yamamoto's seven battleships and heavy cruisers had been available to hammer Midway's defences with their massive guns, not to mention the mighty 18.1-inch shells of *Yamato*, they could surely have swiftly rendered the tiny atoll's defences untenable. But, under Yamamoto's scheme, they were being uselessly held back in reserve hundreds of miles away, for the decisive action, the reprise of Tsushima, which would never take place. Another factor with serious implications for Japanese success was that the larger warships in Yamamoto's and Kondo's forces carried scout seaplanes, an essential reconnaissance and intelligence tool denied to Nagumo.

At about this time Nimitz was reporting gloomily to Admiral King that, with a 'great force of about 80 ships' now converging on Midway, 'Most of Midway's fighters, torpedo planes and dive bombers ... were gone ...' Yet, for all this sacrifice of lives and planes, not a single hit had been scored. Lieutenant-Colonel Walter Sweeney's squadron of B-17s now entered, making several sorties. Bombing from 20,000 feet warships which were, with utmost skill, twisting and turning at twenty-five or thirty knots has been described by one writer as like 'dropping a marble from eye height on a scampering cockroach'. Again, not a hit. Nevertheless, as was the custom with strategic bombing throughout the war on all fronts, exaggerated claims were made: at least one battleship was reported seriously damaged.

The B-17s dropped 322 bombs without scoring. But they did achieve one important thing: they delayed Nagumo's jinking, zigzagging carriers from heading straight upwind at the steady twenty-five knots that was essential for launching and collecting aircraft, minutes when a carrier would be at its most vulnerable.

Meanwhile, on learning that Nagumo's carriers had been identified, Fletcher, who had been holding back from committing his planes, instantly ordered an all-out attack with everything that was available. He thought it essential to get a strike in before Nagumo's superior force could land on him. Disjointedly, at 0700 *Hornet* began her launches, followed promptly by *Enterprise*. *Yorktown*'s planes took off ninety minutes later, at 0838. But whereas the skilled Japanese crews had got off in fifteen minutes, it took the green *Hornet* teams an hour to do so. *Hornet* was to be an unlucky ship almost throughout. In the confusion of inexperience, planes had to circle, wasting precious fuel; so the first attacks went in piecemeal, and unco-ordinated, the slow and obsolete torpedo bombers disastrously unprotected by fighter cover – and many of them carrying useless torpedoes.

For all the US intelligence advantages, Fletcher still did not know where precisely in all the Pacific vastness lay Nagumo's four carriers. Worse still, led by a self-assured commander Stanhope C. Ring, the *Hornet* attack group followed an incorrect heading of 263 degrees rather than 240, which had been angrily, but in vain, insisted on by Lieutenant-Commander John C. Waldron, in command of Torpedo Squadron 8 (VT-8, from *Hornet*). Nicknamed by historians 'The Flight to Nowhere', the bombers of Ring's Air Group Eight totally missed the Japanese carriers, returning to *Hornet* with all bombs 'still neatly tucked under the wings'.

With insubordination worthy of a Nelson, Waldron broke formation from Ring to follow what he believed to be the correct heading. It was to cost him his life, and the lives of all but one man of his squadron. Sighting the enemy carriers, Waldron began attacking at 0920, followed by VT-6, from *Enterprise*, at 0940. Waldron's last orders were: 'If there is only one plane left to make the final run in, I want that man to go in and get a hit.' With dauntless courage, he was last seen going in 'just as straight to the Japanese Fleet as if he had a string tied to them'. Without fighter escort, all fifteen TBD Devastators of VT-8 were shot down by hordes of Zeros without being able to inflict a single torpedo hit. Waldron's brave head-on attack did, however, cause Nagumo to reverse course, out of the wind, thus delaying his ability to put up more of his planes.

Ensign George H. Gay Jr, aged twenty-five, the only survivor of VT-8, from his ditched plane saw Waldron stand heroically in the cockpit of his downed plane as the water closed in. Until that terrible morning Gay had never carried a torpedo in a plane, let alone taken off from a ship while carrying one. Moreover he had 'never seen it done'. Now, hiding afloat under his rubber dinghy, for the next few hours Gay uniquely had a view of the whole battle from the front stalls, observing Japanese decks full of planes with fuel hoses scattered all over the place – what a target! Gay was wise to play possum, his escape remarkable: three other downed US airmen were hauled aboard Nagumo's ships, brutally interrogated and then dumped overboard – their legs attached to five-gallon canisters filled with water.

One of the three, Ensign Osmus, was evidently forced to reveal the whole US order of battle. But the revelation that he was facing three operative enemy carriers, not just two, led Nagumo into making his second fatal error. He now ordered the frantic, exhausted deck crews to switch *back* to torpedoes. The unloaded bombs were left casually on the decks, along with exposed fuel lines.

The suicidal VT-8 attack was described by one writer as 'equivalent to a stone thrown into a group of pigeons'. Off *Enterprise*, VT-6 met with a similar fate to VT-8, with no hits to show for its efforts, thanks in part to the abysmal performance of its (US) Mark 13 aircraft torpedoes. Most travelled feet beneath their targets; or their detonators failed to explode; or they simply fell apart in the water. It would take US Navy experts many costly months yet to trace the faults, and come up with a weapon half as efficient as the Japanese Long Lance torpedo. Many brave airmen would lose their lives in vain.

An hour after the VT-8 and VT-6 strikes, the veterans of VT-3 off *Yorktown*, Fletcher's last reserve, struck with greater efficiency. Under Lieutenant-Commander John Thach, the planes deployed Zero-defeating tactics, known as the Thach Weave, which they had developed from experience in the Coral Sea. Thus *Yorktown*'s force was the only one to arrive over target and effect a co-ordinated attack. At a countdown, it was assessed that 'Of the forty-one Devastator torpedo planes launched from three American aircraft carriers that morning, only four made it back . . .'

Despite these horrific losses, not a single enemy target was hit. The Japanese had shot down most of those planes and sent the rest fleeing. A final disaster occurred on the *Hornet*, when a wounded pilot upon landing triggered his guns accidentally, raking the island structure and killing several personnel – including the son of the C-in-C Atlantic, Admiral Ingersoll. But the American torpedo attacks had not been totally in vain. They had set the Japanese combat air patrols off course and had denied the Japanese carriers the time and ability to launch a counter-attack. Better discipline, and employment of all the Zeros aboard, might well have enabled Nagumo to succeed. And Lieutenant-Commander John Waldron's attack had caused Nagumo to reverse course out of the wind, thus delaying his ability to put up more of his planes.

Nagumo had still not managed to get the planes of his own strike force up on to the flight deck for launch. To do so, all he needed was a short respite. He was not going to be allowed it.

CHAPTER THIRTEEN

FORTUNE TILTS

With their carriers outnumbered and Yamamoto's vast fleet waiting in the wings to pounce, at this point the battle might well have looked lost to the Americans. But events were moving fast. The true miracle was about to occur. Within less than half an hour the whole course of the Pacific War would change.

At 0745 hrs from *Enterprise* had taken off her oldest pilot, the thirty-nine-year-old Lieutenant-Commander Wade McClusky Jr, commanding a squadron of SBD Dauntless dive bombers. He was convinced, emotionally, that there was 'not a chance in the world' of his being killed: 'Not me, anyone else but me . . ."* Each plane carried one lethal armour-piercing, 1,000-pound bomb. But, on the imprecise bearings given, they were running low on fuel because of the time spent hunting the enemy. Some bombers ditched from fuel exhaustion before the attack commenced. McClusky himself had never yet dropped a bomb from an SBD.

Enter US submarine *Nautilus*, a giant vessel which had been doggedly pursuing Nagumo. Spotted by Japanese destroyer *Arashi*, *Nautilus* was depth-charged relentlessly, but unsuccessfully, and chased out of Nagumo's 'box'. *Arashi* then returned at full speed to the Japanese fleet, throwing up a broad, white V-shaped wake. From the air McClusky caught sight of the wake and followed it. *Arashi* provided a fateful signpost, an arrow, leading McClusky directly to the enemy carriers.

There, clustered vulnerably close (since Nagumo's protective box had been disrupted by the earlier plane strikes), were *Kaga*, *Akagi* and *Soryu* – the gems of the *Kido Butai*. From 15,000 feet, throwing his bomber into a near-vertical dive, McClusky selected the 38,000-ton

---

* Awarded the Navy Cross, he would indeed survive the war, to become a rear-admiral.

monster *Kaga*. He narrowly escaped collision with the thirty-one-year-old Lieutenant Richard H. Best, aiming for the same target.

They went in unchallenged, the defending Zeros having been brought to low altitude by the ill-fated torpedo planes. The sacrifice had paid off. At 1022 McClusky's planes bombed the *Kaga*, killing her captain, Jisaku Okada, and the ship's senior officers. The resulting fires detonated the 80,000 pounds of explosives which had been left strewn across the hangar deck during Nagumo's rearming process. A series of devastating multiple fuel-air explosions spread with terrifying speed through the great ship. Lieutenant-Commander Thach later declared, 'I have never seen such superb dive bombing. It looked to me like almost every bomb hit.'

Swiftly correcting from his near-collision with McClusky, four minutes later Jimmy Richard Best moved with his two wingmen to attack the 35,000-ton *Akagi*, Nagumo's flagship. The first bomb missed, and the second bomb landed in the water. But the last bomb pierced the flight deck and exploded in the midst of a pack of bomber planes. The *Akagi* was finished.

At nearly the same time, dive bombers of *Yorktown*'s VB-3, led by Lieutenant-Commander Max Leslie, hit and fatally damaged *Soryu*.

Scenes on the stricken ships beggared description. Instantaneously *Kaga* lost 269 mechanics on her hangar deck, while 419 of *Soryu*'s were similarly immolated. Fires turned the lower decks to red heat, trapping engine-room crews so that they were roasted or scalded alive. The destruction revealed basic faults in Japanese carrier design. Their flight decks were wooden, as opposed to armour-clad.* Compared with stalwart structures like *Yorktown*, or even the lost *Lexington*, the enemy carriers were gimcrack affairs, highly inflammable with poor fire-fighting capacity, to say nothing of poor discipline, with fuel left sloshing around from an unsecured system and the bombs and torpedoes not stacked properly away. The vessels were also lacking in flash-proof doors. Like the Zero fighter, the Japanese carriers reflected the *bushido*-oriented national philosophy: everything was designed for a swift, aggressive war, the minimum being done for defence, or for the protection and wellbeing of crews.

* The harsh realities of naval warfare in Europe had led the Royal Navy to sheet over flight decks with armour plate. After Midway the US would follow suit.

On *Akagi*, the proud ship Yamamoto had once commanded now afire and dead in the water, her propeller drive destroyed, one important witness was Commander Mitsuo Fuchida, the national hero who had led the attack on Pearl Harbor. Confined to hospital quarters by a sudden appendix operation, he contrived to break out and stagger on to the flight deck just as Best's bomb struck. Narrowly escaping the blast, at the bridge he ran into Captain Minoru Genda, one of the architects of Pearl Harbor, who remarked laconically: '*Shimatta!*' ('We goofed'). It said everything. Fuchida escaped, the last man down a rope-ladder, breaking both legs. In the lifeboat with him was a broken Admiral Nagumo, transferring his suddenly shattered command to the light cruiser *Nagara*. *Akagi*, the queen of flat-tops, the very symbol of Japanese air power, was scuttled before dawn the following day.

Of the *Soryu* attackers, Max Leslie, commanding VB-3, and his wingman Lieutenant (Junior Grade) P.A. Holmberg, ditched near USS *Astoria* after running out of fuel, by which time their parent carrier, *Yorktown*, was under enemy attack. Leslie, Holmberg and their gunners were rescued by one of the escorting cruisers' whaleboats.

None of *Akagi*'s planes, assembled and reloading, had had a chance to take off. Had they done so, and launched a revenge attack on Fletcher's carriers, the day might well have ended differently for the US.

Moving back into the fray, the dauntless *Nautilus* fired three torpedoes into *Kaga*. All failed. One split in two and was used as a rescue float by a floundering Japanese sailor. *Kaga* and *Soryu* both sank later that evening. Meanwhile that afternoon, the fourth of Nagumo's carriers, *Hiryu*, had been pinpointed by a scout aircraft from *Yorktown* at an estimated 110 miles distance. Spruance promptly ordered Lieutenant W. Earl Gallaher on *Enterprise* (who had taken over from a wounded McClusky) to launch her final strike of dive bombers, plus some from *Yorktown* – a total of twenty-four, all that were still flyable. It was just after 1700 hours. Despite being assaulted by more than a dozen Zeros, the attack landed four, possibly five bombs on *Hiryu*, leaving the carrier ablaze like the others. Her forward elevator was flung up against the bridge, rendering the carrier unable to launch, or receive, her aircraft.

A strike from *Hornet*, launched late because of a communications error that followed the 'Flight to Nowhere', concentrated on the remaining escort ships, but failed to score any hits. The day had been an undiluted fiasco for *Hornet*, the brave but unlucky ship from which only weeks previously the Doolittle Raiders had struck Tokyo.

After futile attempts at firefighting, *Hiryu* stayed afloat throughout the night of 4 June. In an elaborate ceremony, accompanied by shouts of '*Banzai!*', the Emperor's portrait was reverently removed from the ship. Despite physical attempts to rescue him, Rear-Admiral Tamon Yamaguchi, flag officer of 2nd Carrier Division (*Hiryu*, *Soryu*), insisted on staying aboard, in ancient naval tradition. Japanese legend has it that he and *Hiryu*'s captain, Tomeo Kaku, went down while calmly admiring the moon. In Yamaguchi the Imperial Japanese Navy lost possibly its most competent, and best-loved, carrier commander. His valedictory words, apparently, were: 'I have no words to apologise for what has happened. I only wish for a stronger Japanese Navy and revenge.'

Yamaguchi, and *Hiryu*, however, would not go entirely unavenged.

Once *Yorktown*'s location had been revealed, down like a swarm of angry bees came the Japanese torpedo planes and bombers. To Captain Buckmaster on the bridge the bombs looked 'like a small keg of nails coming down'. Out of eighteen bombers attacking, seven managed to score three telling hits. Fire sucked down by the ventilator shafts killed the engine-room teams, leaving the ship limping in the water. Reporting the fierce fire, Japanese aircrew declared the *Yorktown* sunk. Follow-up flights took off to sink another US carrier that had been spotted, but it was still the same, incredibly robust *Yorktown*, already a semi-invalid from the Coral Sea. Operating with an efficiency not seen on the attacked Japanese carriers, Buckmaster's damage-control personnel managed to extinguish the fires and get *Yorktown* back in action in less than two hours, able to make nineteen knots.

Leading one of the Japanese waves was Lieutenant Joichi Tomonaga who, full of the 'victory disease', had bombed Midway earlier in the day. He was shot down by Thach.

Prudently, at 1313, Fletcher transferred his flag of command to the cruiser *Astoria*; he then handed over command of the joint task force to his better-placed junior, Spruance. A short time later, a strike of torpedo planes off *Hiryu* (a last gasp before destruction overtook her) connected with deadly effect. A brilliantly executed run unleashed two torpedoes into *Yorktown*'s portside, ripping 'a single giant 60 x 30 foot hole in the *Yorktown*'s starboard side'. Almost stationary, she began to list to an alarming 26 degrees. At about 1500 hours, Buckmaster reluctantly gave the order to abandon ship. But still the sturdy vessel did not sink; so effectively was she patched up that the second wave's torpedo bombers mistook her for *Enterprise*, convincing the High Command that two US aircraft carriers had in fact been knocked out.

Hours later, in fact not until the afternoon of 6 June, an intrepid Japanese submarine, *I-168*, slipped in to administer the *coup de grâce*. Almost all the survivors of *Yorktown* had been removed to her escorting destroyer, *Hammann*. But there remained one more tragedy for the US Navy: a torpedo aimed at *Yorktown* instead struck the destroyer, splitting *Hammann* in two. As she sank, her fused depth-charges exploded, killing scores of survivors struggling in the water. Valiant *Yorktown* finally went down, but most of her crew were saved, at dawn on 7 June.

The Battle of Midway was over. Upon the servicemen who had fought in it, the young ensigns, lieutenants, lieutenant-commanders and ordinary GI armourers, Nimitz would heap just praise: 'I firmly believe [they] have already changed the course of the war.'

Thanks to the radio silence he had imposed, the fog of war and a good measure of Japanese 'victory disease', Yamamoto in his ivory tower of the gigantic *Yamato* remained supremely out of touch with reality until the very last minutes of the battle. Parallels might be found with Hitler immured in his Wolf's Lair the previous December. At 1915, well after the last of his four carriers had been put out of action, Yamamoto sent an absurd Combined Fleet Signal No. 158:

1. The enemy fleet, which has practically been destroyed, is retreating to the east.

2 Combined Fleet units in the vicinity are preparing to pursue the remnants and at the same time, to occupy AF.

With a crucial time-lag between his distant command and Nagumo, Yamamoto still seems to have been fantasizing about his Tsushima-style naval Armageddon. Though the battle at sea was already lost, and all his carrier planes gone, Yamamoto persisted in a half-hearted attempt on Midway, sending in heavy cruisers to shell it. In the course of it two cruisers collided in the dark. Both were seriously damaged, *Mikuma* later being sunk by USS *Dauntless*. At last facing the facts, at 0255 on 5 June Yamamoto ordered his immense *Kido Butai* to turn about and head for home.

In sharp contrast, Nimitz back at Pearl Harbor was throughout reckoned to be on top of events. Like Yamamoto, the victorious but prudent Spruance also decided to pull back his task forces. He had been left with only three operational torpedo bombers in the whole Pacific Fleet. For his withdrawal, he was criticized at the time; doubtless Bull Halsey would have rushed in. But as he reported to Nimitz, '... I did not feel justified in risking a night encounter* with possibly superior enemy forces, but on the other hand, I did not want to be too far away from Midway next morning. I wished to be in a position from which either to follow up retreating enemy forces or to break up a landing attack on Midway ...' But history would vindicate Spruance: in the words of the US Navy's official historian, '... Spruance's performance was superb ... [he] emerged from this battle one of the greatest admirals in American naval history.' He would go on to command the Central Pacific Force, and later succeed Nimitz as CinCPac.

His fleet sunk around him, Nagumo had offered to take the traditional way out, but Yamamoto declared icily, 'I am the only one who must apologise to his Majesty,' adding, 'If anyone is to commit harakiri because of Midway, it is I' – but he didn't. According to the ethics of *bushido*, perhaps he should have done. In two historic battles, Pearl Harbor and then Midway, Yamamoto had led his nation to ruin, a ruin from which it would never recover. But such was the legend surrounding him that he was unsackable. The following year fate would catch up with him, when he was intercepted in an aerial ambush and killed over Bougainville in the Solomon Islands. In July 1944, during the last stages of the Battle of Saipan, Chuichi Nagumo committed suicide – not in the traditional way, but with a pistol to the temple, dying miserably in a cave.

Spurious reports that two American carriers had been sunk had

---

* It was a form of naval warfare in which the Japanese had, so far, excelled.

briefly raised morale in the *Kido Butai*. Meanwhile US escort vessels were picking up its survivors. As late as 18 June, an American PBY flying boat saved thirty-five valuable crew-members from the sunken *Hiryu*. Having given up information, none of them wanted to return to Japan, preferring to be recorded as lost with their ship.

Despite the menace of submarines, US vessels diligently kept up the search for survivors, both of ships and of downed aircraft. Ensign Gay was plucked safely from his hiding place beneath his aircraft's rubber float. Machinist Albert W. Winchell, shot down off *Enterprise* together with his gunner, Aviation Radioman Douglas M. Cossett, survived seventeen days of drifting; they were the last to be rescued.

Worse was the fate, and disgracefully so, of the brave veterans of Midway repatriated to Japan, many wounded or suffering appalling burns. Officers aboard *Yamato* refused to allow any of the wounded to be taken on, on the grounds that the sight of blood might cloud the C-in-C's judgement. So they were promptly transported, amid total secrecy, to a hospital ship under cover of darkness, and then segregated from the rest of the country, forbidden to receive mail, telephone calls or even visits from wives. Indignant, Fuchida thought it was 'Just like we are in an internment camp!'. On recovery most of the men were shipped off to the Solomons, many never to return home or see their loved ones again.

This was all done so that Imperial Japan, shunning, under its rigid *bushido* code, any sense of shame at a defeat, could declare in banner headlines: 'NAVY SCORES ANOTHER EPOCHAL VICTORY'. The Japanese would not learn the true story of Midway till much later in the war, when it was already lost. Even in the worst days of late 1944 their military leaders would never admit that they had lost a single battle. A total of 3,057 Japanese sailors and airmen had died at Midway. The IJN's four most powerful carriers had been sunk: *Akagi*, with 267 dead; *Kaga*, 811; *Hiryu*, 392; *Soryu*, 711. In the last phase of the battle, the heavy cruiser *Mikuma* had been sunk, with 700 crew; and *Mogami* badly damaged. Two hundred and forty-eight planes had been destroyed, the loss of their pilots representing the whole of a year's graduating class. US losses totalled one already damaged carrier (*Yorktown*), one destroyer and 150 aircraft; a total of 307 men were killed.

It was indeed a Tsushima, but in reverse.

Bare statistics, however, don't tell the whole story. The loss of those four top aircraft carriers in the twenty minutes at Midway permanently ruined what had been the most successful Japanese naval weapon system of the war. In no way could Japan's relatively backward industrial base ever catch up with US production. More critically, the Japanese would never recover from the loss of so many planes and trained pilots. By late 1943 there would emerge an entirely new US Navy that more than made good the losses of 1941–2. The US would never lose another battle in the Pacific.

With the brilliance of hindsight, there is generally a good time to end a war which one side is losing. For instance, after the first Battle of the Marne in September 1914, Moltke knew that Germany could not win the war; but he failed to grasp the nettle. Realizing as Yamamoto did, after Midway, that the war was lost for Japan, this would have been a good moment for Tokyo to sue for peace. In which case, the hideous doomsday weapon, in the form of 'Little Boy' and 'Fat Man', might have remained in their boxes at Los Alamos for ever.

On strictly mathematical reasoning, Yamamoto, with his 4:3 ratio in carriers manned by crack crews, and his massive back-up in battleships and cruisers, should have won at Midway. In fact, he had lost before the engagement began. Instead of concentrating his forces on the main objective, as Napoleon would have done on land, Yamamoto with his ambitiously complex plans dispersed them on trivial targets such as the strategically worthless Aleutians. The two light carriers Yamamoto despatched there could well have tipped the balance at Midway, and once Midway had been taken or neutralized the Aleutians would have fallen into his pocket for the asking.

But, despite his veneration in Japan, Yamamoto was no Napoleon, certainly no Nelson, and no Togo; he was outclassed by Nimitz all along the line. Damned by the rigidity of Japanese command structures, inflated by the insidious 'victory disease', he – the only man out of his 40,000-strong command actually to have served at Tsushima in 1905 – rashly allowed himself to be seduced by that old phantasmagoria. If ever there was a case of hubris affecting the course of a battle further down the lane of history, Midway was it.

Had Yamamoto succeeded at Midway, however, would it have

changed the course of the war? It would certainly have prolonged it – though, as was not known then, the atom bomb was always at the end of the tunnel (the Manhattan Project began in August 1942). The A-bomb, and the devastating conventional raids on the Japanese homeland that preceded Hiroshima in 1945, were the natural consequence of US supremacy in the skies that had first been won at Midway. But, had Midway fallen into Japanese hands, and with Hawaii under constant menace, west-coast Americans would naturally have been prey to biting insecurity, which could well have manifested itself in terms of pressure to reverse the strategy of 'Hitler first', with the Pacific War taking second place. Across the Atlantic, the consequences of such a reversal would have been incalculable. Hitler would have been left to consolidate his grip on Europe; Soviet Russia and even England might well have succumbed. Such a Europe would have been beyond the reach of reconquest by the United States alone. Had the war run on beyond 1945, without a shadow of a doubt the atomic bomb would have been used on Germany first.

Studies have been written describing Midway as a 'miracle' – or simply a gauge of skill. Perhaps it combined both. Certainly McClusky spotting, in the whole wide Pacific, the wake of the Japanese destroyer *Arashi*, like an arrow pointing directly to the Japanese carriers, seems little less than miraculous. Great luck was certainly involved at several points. It will be recalled that Napoleon always insisted that his generals should be lucky. But that notion of luck also incorporates a great deal of skill, and a detailed study of opportunities. Napoleon would not have thought highly of Yamamoto: the unlucky Admiral who did not understand the art of concentration.

Midway was indeed a most extraordinary victory. The historian Craig L. Symonds has described it as 'the most complete naval victory since Horatio Nelson's near annihilation of the Spanish and French fleets at Trafalgar in 1805, and like that battle, it had momentous strategic consequences ... the Japanese never again seized the strategic initiative; their only hope was to hold out long enough for the Americans to tire of the struggle.'

In terms of the history of naval warfare, 4 June 1942 was a stunning vindication of the pioneers' belief in the carrier and its aircraft as the future queen of the oceans. Midway saw the eclipse of the mighty *Dreadnought* class as the capital ship of navies; both the super-battleships *Musashi* and *Yamato* would be sunk by carrier planes, having scarcely fired a shot from their gigantic guns. From Midway on, the line would run directly to Hiroshima in 1945 – and beyond that to the establishment of the United States as the world naval superpower.

PART FIVE

KOREA AND DIEN BIEN PHU, 1950–1954

CHAPTER FOURTEEN

THE AMERICAN CAESAR

As the Pacific War, which Japan had thrown itself into so rashly, waged so savagely and lost so catastrophically, came to an end in August 1945, there were some rough edges, some unfinished business, left in parts of the Far East where the Japanese had once held sway. Rough edges, unfinished business: one such legacy was in Japan's former colony of Korea. In June 1950, egged on by Stalin, Kim Il-sung's North Korean People's Army invaded the South. At roughly the same time, organized guerrilla warfare was taking hold in France's colonial territories of Indo-China. There the Japanese capitulation had created a vacuum into which communist guerrillas, under a chieftain called Ho Chi Minh, had moved before the restored French regime and France's armed forces, barely recovered from the war, could resume control. In both conflicts, elements of hubris would display themselves in different roles, manifested in ways most challenging to Western interests.

Following the Japanese capitulation, by tacit agreement between the victorious US and Soviets, that part of Korea north of the 38th Parallel was left to communist control, under a Stalinist puppet, Kim Il-sung; while the south in effect became an American satellite state, the Republic of Korea (ROK), controlled from Japan, with its capital at Seoul dangerously close to the border. At the head of the ROK was Syngman Rhee, an unpleasantly authoritarian figure whose declared intention was to restore national unity by force of arms. However, his small American-trained army lacked heavy weaponry and amounted to little more than a lightly armed gendarmerie. Kim Il-sung's Democratic People's Republic of Korea by contrast had inherited the armour and artillery left behind by the Soviets after their August 1945 conquest of Manchuria – that is, all that had not been passed on to Stalin's fellow communist Mao Tse-tung. Over the late 1940s a series of progressively bloody border incidents had taken place, disquietingly reminiscent of the events in Manchuria which had led to Nomonhan in 1939.

On 25 June 1950, the North Korean Army surged across the 38th Parallel, led by its battle-proven Russian T-34s, carrying all before them, sowing panic and murdering prisoners of war and political 'suspects'. Horrific stories reached the American press of wounded GIs (a small contingent of US-supporting troops had been sent hastily from Japan) thrown on to bonfires by Kim Il-sung's horde. Seoul fell, and the North Koreans barrelled on, scattering the ROK forces before them. They employed, with resounding success, the double-envelopment strategy which Zhukov had first pioneered, not so far away, at Nomonhan in 1939. By July the South Korean Army and its courageous American allies were penned into the south-eastern corner of the peninsula, their backs to the historic Straits of Tsushima. Representing only 10 per cent of the area of Korea, the corner came to be known as the Pusan Perimeter.

Not for the first or last time, US intelligence had been caught asleep at the tiller. At this nadir of relations with Stalin in the Cold War there were serious fears that Korea might be just a feint, a deception, while the Soviet Army, with its huge preponderance of forces, was planning the greatly feared 'Big Push' into a disarmed Western Europe. In Britain army reservists were called back to the colours (one of whom was the present author).

With great courage President Harry S. Truman, who had started work humbly as a Missouri haberdasher and had unexpectedly found himself at the White House on the death of Roosevelt in April 1945, picked up the gauntlet. He brought the North Korean invasion before the UN Security Council. The Soviet Union had vacated its seat (it was peevishly boycotting the council on account of the UN's refusal to offer a place to communist China) – so, without the customary Soviet veto, the Security Council, on 27 June, was able to pass Resolution 82, which authorized a UN force to assist South Korea.

Thus the US and its Western allies could wage a war under the banner of the United Nations, a state of affairs which would never arise again. The UN empowered the American government to appoint a commander, and General Douglas MacArthur was selected. He thus became Commander-in-Chief of the United Nations Command

(UNCOM), while remaining Supreme Commander for the Allied Powers (SCAP) in occupied Japan, which he had effectively controlled since accepting the surrender aboard USS *Missouri* in September 1945. MacArthur had rejected calls to have Hirohito arraigned for war crimes along with his generals, and in thus preserving the Emperor in line with age-old Japanese customs, had come to be widely regarded almost as a kind of deity in Japan, second only to the Emperor. It was paralleled with the veneration he received in America as the glorious victor of the Pacific War.

All South Korean forces were also now placed under MacArthur's command. The *New York Times* praised his appointment. 'Fate could not have chosen a man better qualified to command the unreserved confidence of the people of this country.' It would soon be eating its words. As the ROK Army retreated before the North Koreans, MacArthur received permission to commit US ground forces. Most GIs instinctively disliked Korea from the start. They saw it as 'a nation of sad people – oppressed, unhappy, poor, silent, and sullen'. They called these people, Northerners and Southerners alike, 'gooks', and it was not a term of endearment, let alone respect. Ever present was the smell of human excrement; and one roadless mountain was followed by another. A typical GI remark was: 'I'll fight for my country, but I'll be damned if I can see why I'm fighting to save this hellhole.' Yet the first US division sent to plug the 'hellhole', General Dean's 24th, only 20 per cent of whose soldiers had seen action in the Second World War, fought with conspicuous valour, though it was outnumbered and poorly equipped. All it could do was to put up a fighting withdrawal, falling back to the Pusan Perimeter, that toehold in the extreme southeast of the country.* It looked like a final stand. But retreat was not a word in MacArthur's vocabulary.

Promoted in the victorious days of the Second World War to become one of America's five-star Generals of the Army, Douglas MacArthur had never been an ordinary general. A number of commanders in that war, such as Eisenhower and Marshall, had never seen action (Patton was a rare exception), but not one had experienced as much as MacArthur. In the fighting on the Western Front during the First World

---

* The 24th Division suffered 3,602 dead and wounded and 2,962 captured, including the division's commander, Major-General William F. Dean.

War, he had risen to the rank of brigadier-general, was nominated for a Medal of Honor and was awarded the Distinguished Service Cross twice and the Silver Star seven times.

On the retired list from 1937, MacArthur was recalled to active duty in 1941 as commander of United States Army Forces in the Far East, based in the Philippines. A series of disasters followed Pearl Harbor, starting with the destruction of his air force on 8 December 1941, and the invasion of the Philippines by the Japanese. MacArthur's forces were soon compelled to withdraw to Bataan, where they held out until May 1942. In March 1942, MacArthur, his family and his staff left the nearby fortress of Corregidor Island in PT boats and escaped to Australia. There MacArthur became Supreme Commander, South-west Pacific Area. For his defence of the Philippines, he was awarded a Medal of Honor, which made him and his father, Arthur MacArthur Jr, the first father and son to be so decorated. After more than two years of fighting in the Pacific, where he was in command of all Allied ground forces, he fulfilled a promise to liberate the Philippines. It was MacArthur who officially accepted Japan's surrender on 2 September 1945.

During the Second World War MacArthur was *the* outstanding war hero. With his battered service cap, filmstar dark glasses, rumpled khaki shirt and pants, and his homely corn-cob pipe, his face was always in the news; he was, in fact, the pin-up of all Americans. Later, as Supreme Commander, South-west Pacific Area, his renown continued as he pursued the strategy of island-hopping which led to the Japanese homeland. The reticent Nimitz, deserving of equal laurels for his consistent series of brilliantly executed naval triumphs, was often put in the shade. However, MacArthur's star dimmed as his faulty strategies led to grievous casualties, especially among the indigenous population, in the reconquest of the Philippines in 1944–5. Many conceived the costly campaign as an ego trip as he sought to justify his declaration of 1942, 'I shall return.' In this campaign MacArthur was awarded his third and fourth Distinguished Service Medals.

There is no doubt that MacArthur remains one of the supreme geniuses of the Second World War. But it was a genius flawed by an overweening, indeed hubristic vanity, which led to one of the most humiliating disasters in US history. His biographer William Manchester entitled his book *American Caesar.* Certainly he bestrode the Pacific like a colossus for ten years; and such was his grandeur and sheer battle experience that there were few brave men in his entourage who would stick their heads above the parapet and say: 'No, sir.' He was, as one of his commanders once remarked, 'senior to everyone but God'.

At the time of the Korean invasion of June 1950, MacArthur was seventy, but with the vigour of a man half his age. In an attack, he would always be up front with the lead platoon, or in the prow of a landing craft. He was constantly at the battle front, making seventeen observation flights over enemy lines. When MacArthur had arrived, virtually unescorted, to accept the Japanese surrender in August 1945, Churchill commented that '[Of] all the amazing deeds of the war I regard General MacArthur's personal landing at Atsugi as the bravest of the lot.'

By August 1950, the North Korean attacks on the perimeter of Pusan had run out of steam, their forces and supplies exhausted. Fresh UN troops were arriving. Already MacArthur was planning a counter-offensive. Not for him a strategy of slogging back up the mountainous peninsula, mile by mile. Instead, recollecting the success of his island-hopping strategy of the Pacific War, which pinpointed linchpins in the Japanese defence structure while simply bypassing others, he planned a bold coup that would strike far behind the North Korean lines. Origin-ally codenamed Bluehearts, then Chromite, it would land a powerful force of US Marines and armour, totalling some 75,000 troops and backed by over 250 naval vessels and airpower, at Inchon, the port for Seoul and more than 100 miles behind the enemy lines at Pusan. It stood also on the narrow waistline of Korea, and driving across it MacArthur intended to trap the broken remains of the North Korean People's Army as it reeled back from the Pusan bridgehead, severing their lifeline from the North. It seems that when drawing up his plans, MacArthur noted the Japanese invasions at Inchon in 1894 and 1904, and saw how from there they had seized all Korea, before swiftly pur-suing the enemy across the Yalu River into Manchuria. There is no evidence, however, that he studied Kodama's campaign or made use of it for his own. But then MacArthur usually preferred his own counsel.

One of the remarkable aspects of the planning of this daring en-terprise, dependent as it was on total surprise, was the lack of security surrounding Chromite. Officers on MacArthur's staff talked about it widely and loosely. Had the North Koreans picked up on this, they could surely have sent the Inchon landings reeling back into the sea. What was their intelligence, and that of the Soviets, doing? There were no Richard Sorges any more in Japan; yet one must recall that 1950–1 represented the apogee of effectiveness of the Burgess–Maclean–Philby axis of British spies working for the Soviets. Philby, the most accomplished and deadliest spy of all, was then MI6's man in Washington, while Burgess was Second Secretary in the British Embassy. Donald Maclean was about to take over as head of the American Department in the Foreign Office in London. One much respected US general serving at the time, James 'Jumpin' Jim' Gavin, recalled that 'the enemy repeatedly displayed an uncanny knowledge of UN troop deployment'. While preparing his book, William Manchester was assured by that expert on fictional espionage John le Carré that 'It can be assumed that (1) anything we in our government knew about Korea would have been known at the British Embassy and (2) that officers in the Embassy of the rank of these three [Burgess, Maclean, Philby] would have known what the Embassy knew.'

Was this just a lapse on the part of what was at the time the world's most effective spy system? Or could there have been a more sinister explanation? Namely, that Stalin refused to communicate vital intelligence to Kim Il-sung because he actually *wanted* the UN troops to invade North Korea, so that Mao would be forced to intervene? Or, more simply, that the headstrong MacArthur would be lured into a trap which couldn't be resisted? Given the Machiavellian deviousness with which Stalin had acted in August 1939, neither seems impossible.

When MacArthur first put Chromite to the Joint Chiefs of Staff, he encountered strong opposition. Its chairman, General of the Army Omar Bradley, who had led US armies in Europe from D-Day onwards, but always spoke with the voice of caution, had recently predicted that 'large-scale combined amphibious operations . . . will never occur again'. This was distinctly the mood of the brass assembled to discuss Chromite. There were concerns about Inchon's daunting natural defences: its approaches were two narrow passages, which could be easily blocked with mines. It had one of the highest tides in the world – thirty-two feet, exceeded only by the Bay of Fundy north of

Maine. But MacArthur argued powerfully that the North Koreans, equally conscious of Inchon's formidable defences, would accordingly be surprised and caught off-guard by an invasion there.

He bombarded the Pentagon with his arguments. On 23 August, the Joint Chiefs flew from Washington to hold a meeting at Mac-Arthur's headquarters in Tokyo. At the briefing, members of the staff of Vice-Admiral James H. Doyle, who was in command of all naval operations during the Korean War, criticized every single technical aspect of Chromite. It was quite simply impossible, and the navy didn't want to do it.

But MacArthur responded with an address of historic eloquence. He compared his plan with that of General James Wolfe at the Battle of the Plains of Abraham, in 1759, brushing aside the problems of tides, hydrography and terrain. Like the defeated French commander Louis-Joseph de Montcalm, 'the North Koreans would regard an Inchon landing as impossible. Like Wolfe, I could take them by surprise.' He would 'cut the enemy's supply line and seal off the entire southern peninsula. By seizing Seoul I would completely paralyse the enemy's supply system – coming and going.'

MacArthur ended by laying praise unsparingly on the US Navy for its triumphs in the Pacific War. Admiral Sherman, Chief of Naval Operations, then rose to declare that he had heard 'a great voice in a great cause'. That was it: Inchon, the greatest amphibious landing since D-Day in 1944, was on. None of the military potentates present that day would foresee that victory at Inchon would make the Generalissimo appear invincible and the Chiefs impotent.

MacArthur, to his constant embarrassment, suffered appallingly from sea-sickness. Nevertheless, on 15 September 1950 he was up in the prow of the first ship of the armada as his forces landed at Inchon, on schedule. It was, he remarked, 'Just like Lingayen Gulf.' His appreciation proved correct – the North Koreans were taken totally by surprise. UN casualties were light – 536 dead, 2,550 wounded – but 30,000–40,000 North Koreans were caught in the savage US naval and aerial softening-up. That other pugilistic man-of-war of the Pacific, Admiral 'Bull' Halsey, called it 'the most masterly and audacious strategic course in all history'. The beachhead was consolidated two days later. But the capture of Seoul for a second time (and there would be a third, and then a fourth, before the war ended) was not well managed; in fact it was all but disastrous. It took MacArthur two days longer to capture Seoul from his Inchon landings than it had taken General Kodama's Japanese in 1904, despite the advantages of surprise, huge superiority of force and 1950s standards of mobility. The US Marines leading the thrust were no longer the battle-hardened men of Tarawa and Iwo Jima, but mostly post-war rookies, for whom coming up against one of the dreaded T-34s was a fearful experience. As a consequence, the escape route of the People's Army to the north, not unlike the Falaise Gap* in Normandy of August 1944, was only partially closed. The coastal road to the east remained open to the fleeing North Koreans. Though all South Korea was now liberated within fifteen days, and though the remains of Kim's broken invasion force around Pusan fell back in disarray, some 30,000 escaped, to form cadres for a new army to be retrained in the North. Their hearts were filled with a desire for vengeance.

Before Operation Chromite was even launched on 15 September, Truman issued a directive to General MacArthur which – in the blinding light of twenty-first-century hindsight – comes across as one of the most disastrous ever issued by a democratically elected leader to his military commander. The consequences are certainly still with us today. Truman now authorized MacArthur to advance beyond the 38th Parallel. It was a fatal door to open to the American Caesar, his head bursting with self-confidence. His wise friend and political adviser (with ambassadorial rank) William J. Sebald had been warning him of a Japanese proverb – 'In the moment of victory, tighten your helmet-strap.' But MacArthur was unheeding. He preferred to quote that other grandiose warlord, Bernard Law Montgomery, who pronounced that 'Generals are never given adequate directives.' So it was incumbent on the recipient to interpret the edicts of the 'First Consul'. According to William Manchester, 'Washington never told MacArthur exactly what he was expected to do' – just as long as he was winning. (Here, in another context, one might detect echoes of Hitler and the German generals, limp and unquestioning after the triumphs of 1940.)

* In August 1944 General Patton's sweeping advance out of Normandy had trapped the bulk of the German Army. But the net was only partially closed, so that an important element of the survivors were able to escape and fight another day.

From now on President and Generalissimo were no longer singing from the same hymn-sheet. On 27 September, MacArthur received the top-secret National Security Council Memorandum 81/1 from Truman reminding him that operations north of the 38th Parallel were authorized only if at the time 'there was no entry into North Korea by major Soviet or Chinese Communist forces, no announcements of intended entry, nor a threat to counter our operations militarily . . .'

Now how should Caesar, triumphant at the battle front, be expected to interpret such a 'directive' from distant Rome? (That same day, in Moscow, Stalin at an emergency session of the Politburo, condemned the incompetence of the People's Army command and held Soviet military advisers responsible for the defeat – for which he was largely responsible.) On 29 September MacArthur restored the government of the Republic of Korea under Syngman Rhee. The following day Defense Secretary George Marshall sent an eyes-only message to MacArthur: 'We want you to feel unhampered tactically and strategically to proceed north of the 38th parallel.' (We may wonder if the eyes of Philby and Co. also saw this message.)

What of the role of Harry S. Truman in all this? Acting under the umbrella of the UN, did the President of the US, and his Defense Secretary, the great General Marshall, really have the authority to grant such powers to MacArthur? Of course, the US was providing 88 per cent of the 341,000 international soldiers, as well as paying most of the costs.*

Fate had certainly dealt Truman a rough hand. In 1944 he had been selected to be Roosevelt's fourth-term running-mate, largely through the wheelings-and-dealings of US domestic politics, and not least because of distrust of the extreme left-wing orientations of FDR's 1940 running-mate, Henry A. Wallace. Failed for West Point (on account of his eyesight), and one of the few twentieth-century presidents not to have a college degree, he came of humble Missouri stock, his knowledge of the outside world limited to service as a captain of a National Guard artillery unit in France in the First World War, where he served

---

* On 29 August 1950, the British Commonwealth's 27th Infantry Brigade arrived at Pusan to join the UN Command, which until then included only ROK and US forces; it became the third biggest force throughout the war. Among the others were France, with 1,119 men; Colombia, with 1,068; Luxembourg, with 44.

in the Meuse-Argonne offensive. There he gained respect for the efficiency and courage with which he had commanded his artillery battery. On returning home to Kansas City he set up a haberdashery store, but it crashed. He then went into local Democrat politics, making his reputation as an unrelenting foe of corruption and corporate greed. He was elected to the US Senate in 1934.

Sworn in as Vice-President on 20 January 1945, in the three remaining months of the ailing President's life, Truman was kept at a disdainful arm's length. The President and Vice-President met alone together only twice during those months. FDR, sick and patrician, rarely contacted Truman, even to inform him of major issues or decisions. Truman certainly received no briefing on the development of the atomic bomb, or on the growing difficulties with Stalin and Soviet Russia. He had been Vice-President for only eighty-two days when President Roosevelt died on 12 April 1945. Now the most powerful leader on earth, knowing virtually nothing about foreign or military affairs, he told reporters, 'I felt like the moon, the stars, and all the planets had fallen on me.'

Truman's first awareness of the Manhattan Project's successful development of an atom bomb seems to have come at the Potsdam Conference, of July 1945; there Stalin revealed, with a smirk, that he knew more than the President of the US did. The following month Truman, and Truman alone, would have to face up to the awful decision to explode the new weapon over Japan. A short while later – in 1949 – he would be confronted by the fact that Stalin had also constructed an A-bomb.

From then on problems would descend thick and fast, like lava from Vesuvius, on the head of the untried new President. On 5 March 1946, Truman's home state of Missouri, a visiting Winston Churchill (though now out of power) proclaimed the reality of the 'Iron Curtain' which Stalin had slammed down across Europe. Then, in 1947, came Soviet threats to Turkey and Greece (Truman responded by calling forth the aid programme that would bear his name). The following year provided the most serious Soviet threat to date, when the Russians blockaded the western sectors of Berlin in 1948. Powerfully backed by Britain, Truman launched a massive airlift to supply Berliners until the Russians backed down. Then, in 1949, under Truman's aegis was created the defensive military alliance which would come to be known as NATO. Meanwhile, as if there were not enough trouble abroad, at home Truman was beginning to be gnawed at by the phenomenon known as McCarthyism. Then, in 1950, came the thunderbolt of Korea. All this in little more than one term of office.

If Truman would be marked in history as the 'brave little man', he should also go down as feisty, fearless – and extremely pugnacious. Typical of the latter quality was the letter he wrote, as an outraged father, to a music critic who had panned a recital given by his daughter Margaret: 'Some day I hope to meet you. When that happens you'll need a new nose, a lot of beefsteak for black eyes, and perhaps a supporter below ...' So, on all these accounts, the American Caesar was eventually going to find himself up against a boss of mettle.

For such a master of grand strategy, MacArthur adopted a plan of action to move up into North Korea that could hardly have been more flawed, certainly as compared with the skilful campaign conceived by the Japanese generals Kodama and Kuroki back in 1904. Admittedly their objectives were somewhat different, but not entirely. Kuroki's had been to seize a back-door entry to Port Arthur, by crossing the Yalu River near its mouth in the west, and incidentally thereby to secure the whole Korean peninsula for Japan. After capturing Seoul, he had thrust north for the lower reaches of the Yalu.

In contrast, MacArthur sent his motley forces up to the Yalu through the mountains, dividing his already stretched command to make a further seaborne landing at Wonsan on the opposite coast to Inchon. Into the rugged middle, he pushed the newly re-formed ROK Army, still shaky from its June drubbing. Between the various components were the numerous lateral and trackless valleys, making it virtually impossible for one unit to render assistance to its neighbour; but, on the other hand, ideal for the infiltration of a largely foot-borne army from across the Yalu. Ahead of the spreadeagled UN forces stretched the highly porous border with Chinese-held Manchuria, formed largely by the Yalu River. Here was North Korea at its very widest: almost a thousand rugged miles, reaching to within a few miles of Soviet Vladivostok in the north-east, compared to the narrow waistlines of the peninsula of little more than 100 miles at Seoul or Pyongyang (the North Korean capital), each side of the 38th Parallel. An offensive–defensive position on either of these lines might have commended itself to a less incautious commander than MacArthur. But the Julius Caesar of the Orient was not such a one. Already he was proclaiming 'Home by Christmas', and an impatient US public, barely recovered from the exertions of four years' war, expected him to deliver.

In the first week of October 1950, just days since the liberation of Seoul, MacArthur's UN forces moved northwards across that famous 38th Parallel. Meanwhile, ominously, on 30 September, China's Foreign Minister Chou En-lai had warned, through the medium of the Indian Ambassador to China, K. M. Panikkar, that if the UN crossed the parallel China would 'send troops to defend North Korea'. Mao's troops, in their guise as a 'People's Volunteer Army', now began to slip over the Yalu in their thousands. They went unobserved by US intelligence. There followed another warning, from the Indian Prime Minister Jawaharlal Nehru himself. But as US–Indian relations were strained at this time, neither warning was heeded.

On 15 October, on the tiny Pacific atoll of Wake Island, which had heroically though vainly held out against the Japanese in December 1941, there took place one of the most extraordinary top-level meetings of the twentieth century. President Truman flew nearly 7,000 miles to meet his Generalissimo and confer about the state of the war – the site selected by MacArthur in order to be close enough to *his* command base so as not to be away from *his* troops in the field for too long. In the days of short-hop piston-engine planes, the twenty-five hours' flying would have constituted an appreciable effort on the part of the sixty-six-year-old Truman. MacArthur's seemingly discourteous refusal to meet the President on continental US territory prompted much unfavourable press comment. The patrician and fastidious Secretary of State, Dean Acheson, declined to go along, later explaining, with exquisite diplomatic style, that 'While General MacArthur had many of the attributes of a foreign sovereign . . . and was quite as difficult as any, it did not seem wise to recognize him as one.' Acheson sent his Assistant, Dean Rusk, along instead. Also in the entourage were Ambassador John J. Muccio, Secretary of the Army Frank Pace Jr, Ambassador-at-Large Philip C. Jessup, General of the Army Omar Bradley and the ubiquitous diplomat W. Averell Harriman. With MacArthur came CinCPac, Admiral Arthur W. Radford.

Photographs of the two leaders meeting each other are revealing. It was their first encounter. The former haberdasher arrived after his long flight nattily clad in tie and dark city suit, MacArthur as usual in open shirt and khaki slacks, the corn-cob pipe not far off. Was he demonstrating rank, that while he had commanded as a one-star, West Pointer in the First World War, Truman had been a mere captain from the Missouri National Guard? Whatever his motive, Truman took instant umbrage at MacArthur's sloppy attire; also, instead of saluting his Commander-in-Chief, as protocol-minded General Marshall and other five-stars would have done, MacArthur shook hands, equal to equal.

Starting at 0736, with the formal proceedings ending at 0912, Wake Island time, this historic encounter took place without any agenda. Truman seemed unusually taciturn, venturing few interventions, manifestly discomfited by MacArthur's towering imperial demeanour, which seemed designed to overawe and disarm lesser mortals. MacArthur started in by offering reassurance:

I believe that the formal resistance will end throughout North and South Korea by Thanksgiving. There is little resistance left in South Korea – only about 15,000 men – and those we do not destroy, the winter will . . . The North Koreans are making the same mistake they have made before. They have not deployed in depth. When the gap is closed the same thing will happen in the north as happened in the south. It is my hope to be able to withdraw the Eighth Army to Japan by Christmas . . .

He was 'no longer fearful' of Chinese intervention: 'We no longer stand hat in hand. The Chinese have 300,000 men in Manchuria. Of these probably not more than 100/125,000 are distributed along the Yalu River. Only 50/60,000 could be gotten across the Yalu River. They have no Air Force. Now that we have bases for our Air Force in Korea, if the Chinese tried to get down to Pyongyang there would be the greatest slaughter . . .'

MacArthur went on to reject an Indian proposal to inject Indian and Pakistani troops along the Korean–Manchurian and Korean–Soviet frontiers, as a buffer between these countries and the US forces in Korea: 'It would be indefensible from a military point of view. I am

going to put South Korean troops up there. They will be a buffer . . .
The ROK troops can handle the situation . . .'

After some exchanges about the current 'puzzling' performance of
America's French ally in Indo-China, the Wake Island meeting ended.
Truman declared it 'a most satisfactory conference'. There was a not
very dignified little ceremony at the close, when Truman pinned a
(fifth) Distinguished Service Medal on MacArthur. 'You have set a
shining example of gallantry and tenacity in defence and of audacity in
attack matched by but few operations in military history,' he declared,
before clambering back into his plane for the long flight home. On 30
October, MacArthur wrote to Truman, in true imperial style: 'I left
the Wake Island conference with a distinct sense of satisfaction that
the country's interests had been well served through the better mutual
understanding and exchange of views which it afforded. I hope it will
result in building a strong defense against future efforts of those who
seek for one reason or another (none of them worthy) to breach the
understanding between us.'

That was not quite how the world would come to see it. As William Manchester noted: 'Nehru in New Delhi, for example, could have
provided better answers than MacArthur on Wake.' In fact each of
the two principals had heard what he wanted to hear, a true dialogue
of the deaf. On 19 October, four days after the conference ended, the
US forces captured Pyongyang. That same day, the 13th Army Group
of the Chinese People's Volunteer Army (PVA) began pouring across
the Yalu River, 250,000 strong.

Given that the CIA with all its electronic paraphernalia was unable
to spot either Egypt's march on Sinai in 1973 or the outbreak of the
Iraq–Iran War seven years later, US aerial reconnaissance in 1950 might
be excused for not sighting the PVA units in daytime. It was an army
that moved, and supplied itself, on its feet. They marched at night and
were well-camouflaged during the day. This huge army travelled the
nearly 300 miles from Manchuria to the combat zone in nineteen days.
Napoleon's Grande Armée could not have done better. The US military historian S.L.A. Marshall describes the PVA's approach march as
'a phantom which cast no shadow'.

Meanwhile, co-ordinated with his Inchon (Chromite) strategy,
MacArthur had landed his hastily cobbled-together X Corps at

Wonsan and Iwon behind the North Korean lines, far up on the other – eastern – side of the peninsula. His aim was to trap, and wipe out, the remains of Kim's retreating army in a giant pincer movement, pinning them against the Yalu. This was enough for a paper at West Point, maybe, but it did not suffice given the daily changing facts of life at the front in Korea. It meant that, as they progressed northwards towards the Yalu, MacArthur's forces would find themselves in the widest part of Korea, and the wildest. They would spread out on the longest front in modern warfare. And MacArthur was operating with indifferent troops: the ROK troops which had just about been reconstituted after the summer disasters, and green US units which had never operated together.

On 25 October the PVA 13th Army Group launched its First Phase Offensive, hitting the UN forces near the Sino-Korean border. The Chinese and US military finally met on 1 November. Deep in North Korea, thousands of bugle-blowing soldiers from the PVA 39th Army encircled the US 8th Cavalry Regiment (part of the 1st Cavalry Division), assaulting the Americans from three sides.

The 1st Cavalry Division had fought under MacArthur tenaciously through the recapture of the Philippines in 1944, but after 1945 had been stationed in Tokyo. There its members became known scornfully as 'MacArthur's pets', on account of their ceremonial rather than active role. Many were in their early twenties, wanting free education in return for brief military service, under the GI Bill of Rights, but never expecting to be thrown into one of the nastiest wars of the twentieth century. They were poorly trained and totally unprepared by cushy ceremonial duties in Tokyo, so it was not surprising they would not perform well under front-line conditions. The low quality of the '1st Cav' however could not be blamed on MacArthur; rather it was the fault of the post-1945 US administration, which, pressured by popular opinion, had demobilized US forces recklessly and prematurely, at a time when the threat from aggressive world communism was at its apogee. After the Unsan debacle, other army and Marine units disparagingly described the 1st Cav shoulder insignia as representing 'The shield they never carried, the horse they never rode, the bridge they never crossed, the line they never held, and the yellow is the reason why'. Yet the overall casualty statistics show a less unflattering picture:

while in all the battles of the Second World War the 1st Cav lost 734 killed in action and 3,311 wounded (236 died of wounds), in Korea they would amount to 3,811 killed with 2,086 wounded.

The effect on the US troops of this first PVA attack is vividly described by the twenty-year-old Private Carl Simon, of G Company, 8th Cavalry, who in the darkness heard firing, bugles and shouting. No effective resistance was offered: 'There was just mass hysteria,' said Simon. 'It was every man for himself. The shooting was terrific, there were Chinese shouting everywhere. I didn't know which way to go. In the end I just ran with the crowd. We just ran and ran until the bugles grew fainter.'

The historian Max Hastings describes how Simon found himself 'among thirty-five frightened fugitives, in the midst of Korea without a compass. The officers among them showed no urge to exercise any leadership. The group merely began to shuffle southwards. Most threw away their weapons. They walked for fourteen days, eating berries, waving their yellow scarves desperately but vainly to observation planes.'

Simon and his companions represented but a small part of the disaster for the US forces. On 1 November, continues Hastings, 'Strong [Chinese] forces had hit them with great determination, separating their units, then attacking them piecemeal. Batteries in transit on the roads, rifle companies in positions, found themselves under devastating fire from small arms, mortars and Katyusha rockets.' By dawn only six of 8th Cavalry's officers and 200 enlisted men were still able to function. More than 170 were wounded, and the number of dead or missing uncounted. It soon ceased to exist as an organized force.

What Simon experienced would now run through a whole army: the 'Great Bug-Out' contagion, with soldiers fleeing in all directions like bugs from beneath a lifted stone. The surprise attack forced UN troops back to the Ch'ongch'on River, but the Chinese PVA, somewhat surprisingly, did not pursue them. Perhaps like good tacticians they were probing the enemy front for points of weakness; certainly the skill with which the PVA conducted its later Second Phase Offensive would suggest that. A key date may have been 21 November, when Soviet spy Donald Maclean was appointed head of the Foreign Office's American Desk. From there he would have been able to inform his masters in Moscow, for onward transmission to Peking, that the British Prime Minister Clement Attlee would veto any US deployment of the A-bomb in Korea, or any Caesarish adventures into China proper. Meanwhile, from his GHQ in Tokyo, MacArthur was telling the Pentagon that he needed no more reinforcements. He treated the annual phenomenon of the Yalu freezing over, and becoming a highway for Chinese infantrymen, with complete disregard. At the front, US units, scattered all over North Korea, celebrated a miserable Thanksgiving on air-dropped frozen turkey. So much for MacArthur's autumnal expectations.

Brought about by hubris on the part of one of its greatest commanders, the Bug-Out debacle was one of the most shameful episodes in US military history. One may recall the 60 per cent losses suffered by some GI units in the Battle of the Bulge: during the Bug-Out US casualties at their highest never exceeded 25 per cent. But then the US forces were no longer a band of brothers. Morale could hardly have been lower. The young, inexperienced GIs who found themselves suddenly on the receiving end in North Korea were terrified of being taken prisoner by the 'Chicoms', this strange phantom army of men in padded jackets. US fears of Chicom captors were largely unjustified. For all the fearsome din of bugles, drums and shouts, the Chinese were less cruel than the North Koreans; in captivity, about the worst POWs suffered was the harsh communist 'Re-education Programme'.

In the US, critics of the war on both sides were firing off salvoes. James 'Scotty' Reston in the *New York Times* reasoned that Chinese intervention might have been forestalled if, when Pyongyang had been captured, the United States had offered to allow a UN peace commission to 'take over a buffer zone on the Korean side of the Chinese frontier'. On the other hand, Peking would have heard other, more bellicose voices, such as Syngman Rhee's saying, 'The war cannot stop at the Yalu River,' and the hard-line Senator William F. Knowland of California asking, 'Why not a neutral zone ten miles north of the Yalu River?' On 24 November, the day after a joyless Thanksgiving at the front, MacArthur launched his 'Home for Christmas' offensive towards the Yalu River.

The following day the PVA struck with its Second Phase Offensive. Swiftly it overran the ROK II Corps at the Battle of the Ch'ongch'on

River, and then decimated the US 2nd Infantry Division on the UN forces' right flank. Nevertheless MacArthur continued to urge his field commanders forward four days after the first enemy breakthrough. But, on the 28th, the US Eighth Army commander Lieutenant-General Walton 'Bulldog' Walker, at sixty-one a veteran of both world wars, announced the UN offensive at an end – apparently without orders from MacArthur. That same morning in Washington, a shocked Truman told his personal staff in the White House: 'General Bradley called me at 6.15 this morning. He told me a terrible message had come from General MacArthur ·... The Chinese have come in with both feet.' This was the day, he recorded later, 'when the bad news from Korea had changed from rumours of resistance into certainty of defeat'.

This may well have been the day that Truman, progressively disillusioned with, and irritated by, MacArthur, determined to get rid of his American Caesar. MacArthur's vainglorious promises of speedy and complete victory had abruptly turned into a major catastrophe for the United States' arms, and those of its UN allies up the line. MacArthur made a desperate plea for more troops. The only unit available was the 82nd Airborne Division. MacArthur asked to be allowed to deploy men from Chiang Kai-shek's Nationalist Army. On both scores he was refused. He was thinking of a 'counter-invasion against vulnerable areas of the Chinese mainland'. There was talk of unleashing an atomic response; but America's allies, notably Britain's Attlee, would have none of it. Much as Truman might then have wished to be rid of MacArthur this was virtually impossible. For all the disaster he had unleashed by his drive to the Yalu, he was still far too popular among the American public. And still he enjoyed the support of his fellow military on the Joint Chiefs of Staff.

At the beginning of December, the UN Command retreated in disorder – its two main components, Walker's Eighth Army in the west and General Edward Almond's X Corps in the east, cut off from each other by the main mountain ranges of North Korea, and thus destroyed in detail by the relentless PVA. The Eighth Army's retreat was the longest and most humiliating in US Army history. Max Hastings records one American colonel, Paul Freeman of the 23rd Infantry, observing bitterly to a subordinate: 'Look around here. This is a sight that hasn't been seen for hundreds of years: the men of the whole United States Army fleeing from a battlefield, abandoning their wounded, running for their lives.'

In ten days, troops of the US Eighth Army retreated, or ran, 120 miles. By 30 November, the PVA 13th Army Group had driven the Eighth Army from all of north-west Korea. On 5 December, UN troops abandoned Pyongyang. Walker ordered his Eighth Army to retreat to below the 38th Parallel. The Eighth Army was back across that border by mid-December. 'We're bugging out' became the slogan of the day. Some observers reckoned that the debacle matched the collapse of the French Army in 1940.

Yet among the displays of confusion and downright cowardice, there were actions of great courage. A US Regimental Combat Team and the US 1st Marine Division were caught unprepared by a three-pronged encirclement by the PVA at the Chosin Reservoir in brutal wintry weather. Pulling back from Chosin to the port of Hamhung, the US Marines fell into a deadly ambush and had to fight desperately to break their way out to the sea. Losing much of their heavy weaponry, they suffered 4,418 battle and 7,313 non-battle casualties, the latter from frostbite – against which, in the savage North Korean winter, MacArthur's forces had been little better equipped than Hitler's before Moscow in December 1941.

Meanwhile one of the greatest supply dumps in Korea was destroyed as the mass evacuation from Hamhung was effected. Nearly 200 shiploads of UN Command forces and matériel were evacuated to Pusan. Before escaping, the UN Command forces razed most of the city, notably the port facilities. They had been there little more than six weeks. In driving the US X Corps headlong out of North Korea, Mao could boast a signal triumph. US airpower and technical superiority could avail nothing against the hordes of footslogging, bugle-blowing men in their amorphous padded jackets.

In Washington there was serious talk of pulling out of the whole of Korea. On 16 December 1950, President Truman declared a national emergency. UN morale hit rock bottom on 23 December when General Walker, the popular commander of the Eighth Army, was killed in an automobile accident. On 4 January 1951, South Korea's capital of Seoul, now largely destroyed by US fire in the course of the Inchon landings, fell for a third time, its wretched citizens subjected once more to the mass executions and torture of their northern neighbours. The entire UN front was ruptured. At home Dean Acheson brooded on the prevalent 'stench of spiritless defeat, of death of high hopes and broad purposes'.

In war the pendulum swings, however. Walker's successor, Lieutenant-General Matthew B. Ridgway, a Virginian, was one of the most outstanding Allied leaders to emerge from the Second World War. There he had led the US 82nd Airborne, and was greatly respected by fellow Americans and allies alike. On taking over from the deceased Walker, on 27 December 1950, Ridgway was told by Mac-Arthur: 'Eighth Army is yours, Matt. Do what you think best.' It was an act of characteristic imperial grandeur, but a wise one. Acquiring the nickname 'Old Iron Tits' as a result of his habit of wearing hand grenades attached to his chest harness, Ridgway restored the morale of the beaten UN forces with astonishing speed. Now dependent on a huge back-up supply system for its vast forces, and dangerously over-extended, the PVA in turn had become vulnerable to unchallenged US airstrikes. Its casualties were immense, unacceptable even to Mao and to China's seemingly bottomless manpower reserves.

General Bradley described Ridgway's success in turning the tide of the Korean War as 'the greatest feat of personal leadership in the history of the Army'. A resuscitated Eighth Army struck north again in January 1951, inflicting heavy casualties on the Chinese and recapturing the ruins of unhappy Seoul (the fourth time it had changed hands) in March that year. There Ridgway sagely paused.

With the improved military situation, Truman saw the opportunity of proposing a negotiated peace. But then, on 24 March, MacArthur threw his bombshell into the works: he publicly called upon China to admit defeat. He was thus simultaneously challenging both the Chinese and his own superiors. Truman's proposed announcement was shelved. On 5 April, Representative Joseph William Martin Jr, the Republican leader in the House of Representatives, read aloud on the floor of the House a letter from MacArthur critical of Truman's Europe-first policy and limited-war strategy in the Far East. The letter concluded with the clarion call: 'We must win. There is no substitute for victory.'

This was an intolerable act of insubordination, by a general to his democratically elected Commander-in-Chief, and would be unacceptable to any head of state. MacArthur described his démarche as merely a 'military appraisal'. But it was, in fact, an ultimatum to the enemy, 'an attempt to intimidate Peking on pain of sanctions which neither the United States nor any other member of the UN was prepared to apply', in the words of William Manchester. Within the top echelons of government in Washington, anger was universal. General Ridgway thought MacArthur had 'cut the ground from under the President, enraged our allies, and put the Chinese in the position of suffering a severe loss of face if they so much as accepted a bid to negotiate'. All agreed that MacArthur must go. Dean Acheson declared: 'there was no doubt what General MacArthur deserved; the sole issue was the wisest way to administer it'.

President Truman decided. At the back of his mind was the historic dispute between President Lincoln and his over-ambitious Civil War General George B. McClellan – another intolerable challenge to executive leadership.* On the morning of 6 April 1951, he called a meeting in his office with Marshall, Bradley, Acheson and Harriman to discuss what should be done. Harriman was emphatically in favour of MacArthur's relief. Acheson personally supported relieving MacArthur, but kept quiet. Generals Bradley and Marshall opposed it, on military principles and as fellow Second World War soldiers. Marshall asked for more time to consider, while Acheson, lawyer, statesman and politician, warned Truman that he would be facing 'the biggest fight of your administration'. On 8 April, the Joint Chiefs met with Marshall in his office. Each of the Chiefs in turn expressed the opinion that MacArthur's relief was desirable from a 'military point of view', but they recognized that military considerations were not paramount. They were concerned that 'if MacArthur were not relieved, a large segment of our people would charge that civil authorities no longer controlled the military'.

The four military advisers met with Truman in his office again on 9 April. By this time Truman, according to his memoirs, had already made up his own mind; Bradley informed the President that the Joint

---

* Though there the situation was somewhat reversed, with Lincoln wanting to attack and McClellan to hold back.

Chiefs all agreed that MacArthur should go, and Marshall now added his own assent.

On 11 April 1951, Truman drafted an order to MacArthur:

> I deeply regret that it becomes my duty as President and Commander-in-Chief of the United States military forces to replace you as Supreme Commander, Allied Powers; Commander-in-Chief, United Nations Command; Commander-in-Chief, Far East; and Commanding General, U.S. Army, Far East.
>
> You will turn over your commands, effective at once, to Lt. Gen. Matthew B. Ridgway. You are authorized to have issued such orders as are necessary to complete desired travel to such place as you select.
>
> My reasons for your replacement, will be made public concurrently with the delivery to you of the foregoing order, and are contained in the next following message . . .

As sometimes occurs with earth-shaking events in US history, there was an embarrassing slip-up between decision and the actual delivery of the lethal order. It was decided that it should be properly delivered to MacArthur via the Secretary of the Army, Frank Pace. But Pace was away at the front in Korea. A press leak resulted in MacArthur hearing of his sacking first via the media. This rather ensured an untidy and demeaning end to a great soldier, a humiliation which the American Caesar and his very articulate supporters would play up to. It was a botched execution, which, noted William Manchester, 'could scarcely have been administered more unwisely'. One of MacArthur's senior officers, Colonel Paul Freeman, observed: 'I thought his sacking was disgraceful. Sure, he had it coming. He should have been relieved. But it should have been done in a dignified way. He was an actor and an egoist, but he had been a very great man.' MacArthur told his faithful friend William Sebald that what most hurt was to be 'publicly humiliated after fifty-two years in the Army'. In Tokyo the deposed Generalissimo relayed the news simply to his wife: 'Jeannie, we are going home at last.' He would return home a martyred hero.

In Tokyo the departure of the revered Caesar was received with dismay. Prime Minister Shigeru Yoshida declared that he had been 'looked upon by all our people with the profoundest veneration and affection. I have no words to convey the regret of our nation to see him leave.' The press felt the same way. *Asahi* declared, 'Japan's recovery must be attributed solely to his guidance. We feel as if we have lost a kind of loving father,' and the *Mainichi Shimbun*: 'MacArthur's dismissal is the greatest shock since the end of the war. He dealt with the Japanese people not as a conqueror but a great reformer. He was a noble political missionary.'

As the fallen chieftain returned to his homeland, a terrific rainstorm lashed its countryside. It seemed symbolic. Professor Arthur Schlesinger wrote: 'It is doubtful if there has ever been in this country so violent and spontaneous a discharge of political passion as that provoked by the President's dismissal of the General ... Certainly there has been nothing to match it since the Civil War.' Unexpectedly and disastrously, with the flames fanned by McCarthy and his allies on the extreme right of the Republican Party, Truman became the most hated man in America. From having been a popular president, re-elected on his own merits just two years previously, Truman saw his rating fall to 23 per cent, lower than Richard Nixon's low of 25 per cent during the Watergate Scandal in 1974, and Lyndon Johnson's of 28 per cent at the height of the Vietnam War in 1968. In the *Chicago Tribune*, Robert A. Taft, the powerful Republican leader in the Senate, called in the most vitriolic terms for immediate impeachment proceedings against Truman: 'President Truman must be impeached and convicted. His hasty and vindictive removal of General MacArthur is the culmination of a series of acts which have shown that he is unfit, morally and mentally, for his high office. The American nation has never been in greater danger. It is led by a fool who is surrounded by knaves.'

Across America there was fierce criticism of the 'bankrupt haberdasher' and his 'traitorous' State Department. At public events Truman was booed. Veterans sent back their medals. Constituents flooded their representatives on Capitol Hill with intemperate telegrams such as: 'IMPEACH THE IMBECILE; WE WISH TO PROTEST THE LATEST OUTRAGE ON THE PART OF THE PIG IN THE WHITE HOUSE; IMPEACH THE JUDAS IN THE WHITE HOUSE WHO SOLD US DOWN THE RIVER TO THE LEFT WINGERS AND THE UN ...' When invited to address Congress on his return to Washington that April, MacArthur made a thirty-four-minute speech which was interrupted thirty times by standing ovations. One Congressman, overcome by emotion, shouted: 'We heard God speak here today . . .!'

As one Senator observed, the whole country was 'on a great emotional binge'. The climax came with the hero's cavalcade accorded to MacArthur in New York City. Experts on such detail noted that the ticker-tape was 'four times Eisenhower's record for dumping of litter'. There were many serious Americans, deeply worried by the Sino-Soviet threat of communist world domination as evinced by the June 1950 attack on South Korea, and who thought that victory had been within MacArthur's grasp before the Chinese intervened. Later they would note that 60 per cent of the UN losses in Korea – over 80,000 of them Americans – actually followed MacArthur's recall. But this ignored the realities: MacArthur never had sufficient forces to drive up to, or hold a line on, the Yalu, let alone embark on any more ambitious offensive enterprises, even with the support of nuclear weapons. Nor did he have the backing of America's major allies, such as Britain, or of the other components of his UN force. It was all very well for MacArthur to trumpet that limited war 'was like limited pregnancy'. But, only five years in from the most costly war in its history, was the US public – when it put on its thinking-cap, and its emotions back in the box – really prepared to face a fresh major conflict in the Far East? And what about the potential threat to an exposed and largely undefended Europe from Stalin's Red Army? In the end, few Americans would doubt that Truman, the elected President, had been obliged to strike MacArthur down.

The conflict in Korea would drag on, inconclusively, for more than another two years of grim positional warfare, more reminiscent of the First World War than the early fluid moves in the campaign.

Repelling several Chinese offensives, on a series of well-prepared defensive lines at immense cost to the attackers (PVA losses in the whole war were 400,000 killed and 486,000 wounded), Ridgway pushed on to the 38th Parallel. In the latter stages of the war, amid scenes of cowardice and incompetence, there were some bright moments, such as the British Gloucester Regiment's heroic defence on the Imjin River. There Ridgway sagely paused.

At last, on 27 July 1953, three years after the war had begun, a kind of armistice, but no peace treaty, was signed. A demilitarized zone ran roughly along the line of the 38th Parallel, where it had all started. Calculations of total losses reach horrendous proportions: for both the Koreas, possibly 4 million dead out of a pre-war population of some 30 million. Writers like Jon Halliday who are generally sympathetic to the North reckon that about 500,000 North Korean soldiers were killed, and over 2 million civilians. Persistent bombing reduced the whole of the North to rubble, its industry and infrastructure totally destroyed, in scenes that made the US wartime bombing of Japan look like amateurs' work. If ever there was a case of bombing a nation 'back into the stone age', as General Curtis LeMay allegedly once threatened in Vietnam, this was it; certainly nothing in Vietnam would quite match it. As for UN losses, US deaths were put at 54,246, of which roughly 20,000 were rated as 'non-battle' fatalities. The total of battle deaths among the other UN contingents came to 3,194, of which 686 were British.

Who won? In the words of Jon Halliday and Bruce Cumings, 'Each side proclaims that it won, yet each actually seems to feel that it lost.' They concluded that it was 'an unmitigated disaster for the Korean people of North and South' – though, with the passage of time, the 'disaster' looks increasingly unequal as the South emerges as one of the economic miracles of Asia, while the crazy, impoverished, pariah North of Kim Jong-un seems to slip ever further backwards.

Few acts of hubris in the twentieth century were punished more savagely or more swiftly than MacArthur's was, after that remarkable triumph at Inchon went so catastrophically to his head. Thrusting on to the Yalu in pursuit of total victory was a huge risk, which proved to be a frontier too far, a risk that was unjustified, the costs to world equilibrium unwarranted. Its consequences were legion, casting long shadows beyond the actual conflict of the Korean War. Korea was the first war fought by the United States which did not end in a clear-cut American victory. As far as it had involved a United Nations commitment this proved an experience unlikely to be repeated. When it came to Vietnam in the 1960s, the British Prime Minister Harold Wilson swiftly made it clear that British troops were not going to help out this time. Rather as happened with President Johnson in 1968, as a consequence of the unpopularity that the war, and specifically the sacking of MacArthur, had brought him, Truman declined to run for the White

House again. He would be succeeded by another great Second World War warlord, General Dwight D. Eisenhower.

Henceforth, at least until Iraq and Afghanistan came along, the US would confine itself to waging wars with limited objectives only. As Vietnam and the First Gulf War of 1991 would demonstrate, its leaders would pay fastidious attention to not transgressing national borders. There would be no invasion of Hanoi, nor pursuit of the Iraq Republican Guard over the Kuwaiti border. Probably the unyielding ferocity with which the Korean War was waged led to a hardening and a prolongation of the Cold War; to a worsening of the split with China, which would not begin to heal until the Nixon–Kissinger initiative of the early 1970s; and to a consolidation of Maoism and all its attendant evils. The spectacle of a modern Western army fleeing before Mao's cotton-clad divisions was not lightly to be forgotten in the Orient, no more than had been that of the destruction of Tsarist forces in 1905 Manchuria. In the eyes of much of the world, it was Korea 1951 that made a great power of Mao's China.

From the Western point of view, was it in fact worth fighting at all? 'If the Korean War was a frustrating, profoundly unsatisfactory experience,' writes Max Hastings in the closing words of his 1987 account, 'more than thirty-five years later it still seems a struggle that the West was utterly right to fight.' That surely remains true today. If the brave, raw troops of General Dean's US 24th Division had not been rushed to South Korea to meet Kim Il-sung's onslaught in June 1950, who knows what apocalyptic, speculative ventures Stalin might have been tempted to try with the overwhelming power of the Red Army presence in Europe.

Could the Korean War have been fought differently? Might a more satisfactory outcome have been achieved, leading for instance to a peacefully reunited Korea, if MacArthur had stopped on the 38th Parallel? Over sixty years later the jury is still out.

CHAPTER FIFTEEN

ECHOES OF VERDUN

When MacArthur learned of the Korean armistice on 27 July 1953 he-declared: 'this is the death warrant for Indochina'.

At the opposite end from Korea of the great, opaque landmass of Mao's China lay the beckoning, fertile territories of Indo-China, another restive peninsula pendant from the main body of East Asia. Ever since its associated states and kingdoms came under French rule from the 1880s onwards, the rich lands of *l'Indochine* had constituted the true jewel in France's imperial crown. But from the 1940s they had been racked by war, revolt and guerrilla activities. Following the fall of France in 1940, the colony had been administered by Vichy France. Then Japanese forces invaded, developing Indo-China as a jumping-off base for the invasion of Malaya, but leaving Vichy administrative authority nominally intact until taking full control in the last months of the war. As early as May 1941, the Viet Minh, an independence movement led by Ho Chi Minh (who had started his career as a pastry-cook in Paris), opened a campaign against French and Japanese rule. In Saigon, the anti-communist State of Vietnam, led by former Emperor Bao Dai, was belatedly granted independence in 1949. However, by the time the long-protracted armistice had been concluded in Korea in July 1953, what would come to be known as the First Indo-China War between Viet Minh guerrillas and the French Far East Expeditionary Corps had already been dragging on for seven years with no signs of resolution. It looked unwinnable, but also – given the modern power of the post-war French Army – unloseable. Yet, within six months, France would suffer a defeat just about as humiliating and as decisive as that inflicted upon it by the Wehrmacht in 1940, and at the hands of ill-equipped little orientals striking out of the jungle. This would change the whole structure of realpolitik in south-east Asia and impel the US into another role in the area, which it would not welcome. Nor would it succeed there any better than in Korea.

During the closing stages of the Wake Island Conference on Korea (15 October 1950), almost as an afterthought Admiral Radford, C-in-C the Pacific Fleet, had raised another issue:

ADMIRAL RADFORD: . . . The situation in Indo-China is the most puzzling of all as to what we can do or what we should do . . .

GENERAL MACARTHUR: . . . The situation in Indo-China is puzzling. The French have 150,000 of their best troops there with an officer of the highest reputation in command. Their forces are twice what we had in the [Pusan] perimeter and they are opposed by half of what the North Koreans had. I cannot understand why they do not clean it up. They should be able to do so in four months yet we have recently seen a debacle. This brings up a question of far deeper concern. What is the capacity and calibre of the French Army? In the first world war they were excellent. In the second world war they were poor. The present French soldier is doubtful. If the French won't fight we are up against it because the defence of Europe hinges on them. They have the flower of the French Army in Indo-China and they are not fighting. If this is so, no matter what supplies we pour in they may be of no use. The loss of territory in itself is nothing but the French failure is broader than this. I cannot understand it.

THE PRESIDENT: I cannot understand it either.

ADMIRAL RADFORD: The French seem to have no popular backing from the local Indo-Chinese. The French must train native troops. The rest of Southeast Asia – Burma, Siam – is wide open if the Chinese Communists pursue a policy of aggression. We probably have more chance of assisting in Indo-China than anywhere else. We must stiffen the backbone of the French.

MR HARRIMAN: The French hold a key position both in Europe and Asia. I have been told by officers who were there that the French fought well in Italy. This is a matter to which we must give close thought. The French must change their attitude relative to Indo-China.

THE PRESIDENT: We have been working on the French in connection with Indo-China for years without success . . . This is the most discouraging thing we face. Mr Jessup and others have worked on the French tooth and nail to try and persuade them to do what the

Dutch had done in Indonesia* but the French have not been willing to listen. If the French Prime Minister comes to see me, he is going to hear some very plain talk. I am going to talk cold turkey to him. If you don't want him to hear that kind of talk, you had better keep him away from me.

ADMIRAL RADFORD: Recently there were some French ships in Hawaii. I had the impression they were not anxious to go to Indo-China and were dragging their feet. They would have stayed in Pearl Harbor for six months if I had invited them . . .

This exchange speaks volumes about the new front which had already opened in the Far East, and which would eventually drag in the US for another bloody and costly twenty-five years.

The humiliating defeat that the flower of the French Expeditionary Corps was to experience at the hands of 'Vietnamese peasants', in the distant valley of Dien Bien Phu, would shake the confidence of the Western world in its conventional forces and redraw the map of Indo-China. What lay behind this disaster of spring 1954 was also a kind of hubris, but of a different flavour to that which had brought defeat to MacArthur on the Yalu, or Yamamoto at Midway, or Hitler before the gates of Moscow. To post-war Indo-China certainly the soldiers of France's reconstituted army brought with them the still prevailing sense of racial superiority, of the European over the Asiatic, to which the 1941–2 defeats at the hands of the Japanese had caused shock but little modification. Yet on top of that there was inlaid something more subtle. Since 1940 the proud French Army had suffered nothing but defeat; now it sought redemption. To compensate for the humiliations of the 1940s, there were battles, campaigns, which now *had* to be won. And to win them French commanders perforce searched back into history to latch on to victories and triumphs of the past that might by some magic of alchemy lead the way to victory in the unpromising present. One such would be the Battle of Verdun in 1916.

Verdun remains almost unique among the First World War battlefields as the one where the ghosts refuse to die. They have been preserved largely by the character of the battle itself, which remains the longest in any war. Its sinister fame as history's most atrocious also

* That is, grant independence.

derives from the sheer concentration of the battlefield, where, over a period of ten months from February to December 1916, an area smaller than Manhattan was subjected without let-up to the most intensive artillery bombardment ever known. The strategy behind the German assault in February 1916 was a bizarre one; it was not to break through, or even to capture a key French city, but to lure the French Army into a trap where it would simply be 'bled white' by superior German firepower. That choice of words by the German commander, General Erich von Falkenhayn, in itself suggested the image by which Verdun would forever be associated. In the event the battle was to bleed the attacking Germans almost in equal measure. Yet, well beyond the war of 1914–18, Verdun would stand out in French memories as *the* amulet signifying supreme courage and supreme sacrifice.

On the handful of hills bordering Verdun on the sleepy River Meuse, just 150 miles from Paris, the big guns of either side exacted over 800,000 French and German casualties over the ten months of battle, and so tortured the soil that whole strips of the countryside defied all attempts to return them to cultivation. Most *poilus* fought and died there without ever seeing the enemy. A factor peculiar to Verdun is that, whereas the fighting elsewhere on the Western Front took place in trenches which came to be all but effaced by the passage of time, here it swirled around a series of massive concrete forts which gave the city its 1914 reputation as the world's most powerful citadel. Two of them, Forts Vaux and Douaumont, scenes of some of the most lethal fighting of the battle, are kept open to the public. Battered and crumbling, they stand like Shelley's statue of Ozymandias, monuments to the folly, pride and heroism that epitomized what we still call the Great War.

Each year visitors in their thousands troop through the rugged casemates of Douaumont; one French writer, Jean Dutourd, taken to Verdun as a boy, claims that 'No historical remains I have seen since, however impressive, not even the Colosseum or the Temples of Paestum, moved me so profoundly as the Forts of Vaux and Douaumont.' Near by stands the spooky *ossuaire*, housing heaped in vaults visible to the casual eye the bones of 100,000 unidentified victims of the battle.

Over the post-war years, Verdun justly came to be regarded as

France's finest hour. Through Marshal Philippe Pétain's *noria* system of rotating units into and out of the front line, some three-quarters of the 1914–18 French Army passed through *l'enfer de Verdun* and were exposed to its unforgettable horrors. Of the French Army leaders of the 1950s, Raoul Salan and Henri Navarre, both fought on the Western Front as teenagers in 1917 and would have been forcibly indoctrinated in the glory represented by Verdun the previous year, as well as in its pyrrhic horrors. Jean de Lattre de Tassigny, the elitist cavalryman, fighting in Salonika as a young lieutenant (he was twice wounded), had no direct association with Verdun, but he too would certainly have heard every detail from *copains* who had served there. Meanwhile, in the inter-war period veterans' associations like Ceux de Verdun kept alive its memories.

At the same time, because of the horrifying losses suffered at Verdun, its symbolism also came to play a baneful role in the defeatism that brought France low in 1940. The remarkable success with which Forts Vaux and Douaumont had stood up to bombardment by Krupp's heaviest guns suggested to the Secretary of War, André Maginot, an *ancien combattant* who had lost his leg at Verdun, that the only way France could survive another war would be to surround itself with a chain of such forts. But this 'Maginot Line' coupled a defensive strategy with defeatism. Hitler's smart young generals, such as Heinz Guderian, tackled the problem of Verdun-like static warfare with a Blitzkrieg technique of fast-moving armoured warfare. They went round the side and back of Maginot's fortresses, forcing them to capitulate without firing a shot.

And yet the myths, and the slogans, of Verdun, chimeric as they were, would persist in the heart of the French Army well into the 1950s. By some deep twist of fate, in 1953 the French at Dien Bien Phu would find themselves in a predicament much as Falkenhayn had devised for them in 1916: *Hell in a Very Small Place* was the title that the scholarly war correspondent Bernard B. Fall gave to his account of the battle.* Only this time it was a place of the French Army's own choosing, and the enemy objective would be attained: to seize the French strongpoint, at whatever the cost (General Giap's Vietnamese troops

---

* Published 1966, a year before the author was killed with US forces in Vietnam.

would prove to be a great deal more contemptuous of losses than were Falkenhayn's Brandenburgers or Bavarians).

As we have already noted, by the autumn of 1953 the war in Indo-China had been dragging on for seven years. It had been born in the vacuum created between the withdrawal of the defeated Japanese in 1945 and the return the following year of the French colonial rulers, who – in the eyes of their Eastern subjects – had suffered an even more humiliating defeat at the hands of fellow orientals less than five years previously. A comparable vacuum had not occurred in countries such as Burma and the Philippines where British and American forces, bearing with them early prospects of independence, had expelled the Japanese. A combination of French intransigence towards decolonization, the corruptness of local rulers and military aid from Red China had progressively imposed the stamp of orthodox communism upon what had begun, typically enough, as a nationalist, anti-colonial revolt. The effective leader of the Viet Minh (League for the Independence of Vietnam) was now the sixty-three-year-old Ho Chi Minh, who claimed to have learned the meaning of revolution when in Paris in the 1920s. His military lieutenant was a forty-three-year-old doctor of political economy and former history master, General Vo Nguyen Giap, who had waged guerrilla war against the Japanese and now employed it against the French, whom he had every reason to hate. For not only had he been imprisoned in French jails, his sister had been executed by the French and his wife, sentenced to hard labour for life, had died in a French prison.

The war had so far cost France over 11,000 nationals killed, together with another 12,000 Foreign Legionnaires and African troops and 14,000 Indo-Chinese. More than 120,000 were either wounded or missing. Since the politicians refused to send national servicemen to Indo-China, it was the cream of the French regular cadres that bore the brunt. Every three years consumed an entire class of Saint-Cyr officers. Six hundred billion francs were spent on the war each year – far more than the capital value of France's remaining commercial installations there. In what Charles de Gaulle dubbed 'this absurd ballet', governments of the post-1945 Fourth Republic trooped on and off the stage with depressing regularity. In 1950, Georges Bidault was followed by Henri Queuille, who was followed by René Pleven; then Queuille returned, to be followed by Pleven again. Those hapless French leaders were weak men, presiding over a broken, divided and bankrupt country – and plagued perpetually by the cancer-like presence of the most powerful Communist Party in Europe, which commanded roughly one-third of the seats in the French Assembly. Finally, in 1953, came Joseph Laniel, who was followed by Pierre Mendès France, the courageous Sephardic Jew who would take the unpopular but inevitable course of getting France out of Indo-China, thus ending what most Frenchmen called the *sale guerre*, or dirty war.

So eighteen successive governments had come and gone in the Fourth Republic and none had found a way of ending the war. France's current Premier, in 1953, was Joseph Laniel, a weaver from Calvados known to his associates simply as 'poor Joseph', whose ministry has been described by one French historian as 'manufactured, like his speeches, with scissors and paste'. In Indo-China the war was run, with little direction from Paris, by an army as anxious to redeem the honour it still held to be tarnished from the capitulation of 1940 as it was to crush the Viet Minh. It had been constantly denied the men and equipment it demanded. In leadership, victory in 1945 left France with two military giants, Jacques-Philippe Leclerc and Jean de Lattre de Tassigny. Both were sent to try their hand in Indo-China. Each had the vision, and stature, to conclude negotiations with the rebel forces. They might have succeeded while France was still relatively strong vis-à-vis the Viet Minh, but, tragically for France – and maybe for the West as a whole – Leclerc was killed in 1947, in a plane crash over the Sahara. De Lattre, vainglorious and one of the most arrogant Frenchmen ever to wear a *képi*, outrageously overbearing to subordinates, came to Hanoi claiming that his presence was worth a division of French troops (which, of course, the Fourth Republic didn't have). Nevertheless, only Marshal de Lattre, with his immense prestige as France's most distinguished Second World War soldier, could have succeeded in bullying extra resources from the overstrained economy. He had devoted these resources chiefly to the construction of a miniature Maginot Line of blockhouses guarding Hanoi and the Red River delta. He saved Hanoi in 1951, and seemed to be turning the war around; he was perhaps France's best hope in Indo-China.

Then a double tragedy struck. De Lattre had a heroic young son called Bernard, who aged fifteen had engineered his father's escape from the clutches of pro-German Vichy. By the end of the Second World War Bernard had become the youngest officer ever to receive the *Médaille Militaire*, given for outstanding courage on the battlefield. In 1949 he volunteered for duty in Indo-China, where he swiftly made a name for himself in battle. In May 1951 Marshal de Lattre proudly bestowed the *Croix de Guerre* on his son. A few weeks later Bernard was killed in a Viet Minh mortar attack, his body riddled with shrapnel wounds. Marshal de Lattre never recovered. The following January he died of cancer.

General Raoul Salan succeeded de Lattre as Commander-in-Chief in Indo-China. Rather than having any distinction as a field commander or strategist, Salan was a specialist in intrigue and manipulation. Nicknamed 'the Mandarin' on account of his affinity for opium-puffing, under him any serious effort to regain the initiative in Indo-China went by default. With a characteristic curl of the upper lip, he dismissed Giap 'as a non-commissioned officer learning to handle regiments'. His officers tended not to like the Mandarin or to trust him; witness the fact that, in 1957, as soon as he was moved on to take command in Algeria, there was a mysterious attempt to assassinate him by firing a bazooka into his office, killing one of his staff officers. Meddling in politics, Salan in 1958 headed an insurrection which resulted in the return of General de Gaulle at the head of the new French Fifth Republic. But de Gaulle had little use for machinators like Salan and brought him home from Algiers. Then, in 1961, Salan emerged again as leader of the putsch targeting de Gaulle and his endeavour to bring about a negotiated peace in Algeria.

When the putsch collapsed, Salan went into hiding. He rose again as leader of the criminal, underground Organisation de l'Armée Secrète which over several years committed a series of criminal terrorist attacks, in both Algiers and Metropolitan France. In 1962 he was caught and sentenced to death; the sentence was later commuted to life imprisonment, and he was finally amnestied in 1968.

In May 1953 Salan was succeeded by the three-star General Henri Navarre, the seventh and final French commander in Indo-China. With the war going badly for the French and increasingly unpopular in Paris, Navarre was charged with bringing it to an honourable end.

A fighting soldier who had won the *Croix de Guerre* in both world wars, he switched French strategy from defensive to offensive operations, forming mobile strike forces. He had no experience in the field in Indo-China. An uncommunicative figure with a fondness for cats, on taking up his command he declared: 'I shall not make the same mistakes as my predecessors.' His boast was to be fulfilled – certainly no other French commander erred on quite so grandiose a scale as he would.

One of Navarre's first appointments was to promote a giant brigadier, René Cogny, an artillery officer, to command the key northern sector. Taken prisoner by the Germans in 1940, Cogny escaped several times to join the French Resistance, but was recaptured and repeatedly tortured, which left him with a permanent limp. Out in Indo-China, the war in the south, around Saigon, had deteriorated into one of ambush and attrition; while in the north the French, defensively based on de Lattre's blockhouses, had the delta fairly well under control. But, further inland, it seemed to Navarre that Giap might be mounting a serious threat to the French-controlled kingdom of Laos. Otherwise the French generally held the initiative throughout Indo-China, and Giap appeared indecisive. During the summer of 1953, more French troops had become available, and tens of thousands of Vietnamese recruits were joining the French Union forces. In addition United States military aid was pouring in. On the other hand, with the end of the Korean War in sight, it seemed clear that Red China would shortly be free to concentrate its resources, especially in American artillery pieces that had been captured in Korea, to aid the Viet Minh.

Towards the end of 1953, Navarre began to formulate a strategy aimed at both relieving the threat to Laos and inflicting a major defeat upon the Viet Minh before Chinese aid could become effective. He would lure General Giap into the kind of copybook setpiece battle taught at Western staff colleges ever since Napoleon, and then crush him thanks to superiority of equipment and firepower. It would also bear a curious resemblance to Falkenhayn's 'bleeding white' strategy at Verdun in 1916. It seems, however, that Navarre and Cogny pursued fundamentally different strategies: Cogny envisaged a light, mobile base of operations, while Navarre was thinking in terms of a much more permanent, heavily defended fortress. By following this latter course, it seemed that a modern, highly mobile army would be sacrificing this mobility to lock itself away in a kind of P.C. Wren (viz. *Beau Geste*) fortress. As a consequence of this fundamental strategic discord, relations between the two French commanders progressively deteriorated.

On 21 November, a strong French paratroop force led by three generals dropped on the isolated village of Dien Bien Phu deep in Viet Minh country and astride Giap's main lines of communication with China. Navarre's plan was to bait the trap by establishing a powerful and aggressive garrison there. The attraction of Dien Bien Phu lay in its possession of an airstrip (built by the Japanese) and its location in the largest valley in the area, which appeared too big to be easily sealed off. But it was less than 100 miles from the Chinese border, and almost 200 from the French bases around Hanoi, with the result that supply aircraft would be operating at extreme range. Over the exceedingly rugged intervening terrain, land communications with Hanoi were non-existent, so the Dien Bien Phu garrison would have to be sustained entirely by air. Aerial reconnaissance had been carried out during the dry season, and no account had been taken of the heavy rainfall at Dien Bien Phu or of the tendency for fog to fill the basin between the surrounding hills. Moreover, it seems that Navarre had been warned categorically by his air transport chief, Colonel Jean-Louis Nicot, that his service would not be in a position to maintain a permanent flow of supplies to the garrison. So, like Arnhem in the Second World War, this was to be an airborne battle. Encouragingly for the French, General Giap had no air force.

Despite these factors, and without going into the logistics of the operation too thoroughly, Navarre was confident that he could achieve his ends. He knew that Giap had artillery, but he had hitherto deployed nothing bigger than Japanese and Chinese 75mm field guns, and he had never marshalled more than a few scattered light anti-aircraft weapons with which to harass dropping operations. Finally, Navarre's intelligence officers estimated that Giap's primitive supply system over the tortuous jungle trails would be incapable of provisioning any force attacking Dien Bien Phu with more than 25,000 shells for its guns or with sufficient rice.

This assessment was based on the simple rationalization that

European troops could not do it. So Operation Castor now got under way. Right from the beginning, the elliptical Navarre never seems to have made it clear to Cogny, his subordinate, that he intended Dien Bien Phu to become a fortress designed to withstand a regular siege. Nevertheless, unlike the beaver, or *castor*, from which the operation derived its codename, the French forces at Dien Bien Phu failed to dig themselves in with sufficient depth to withstand a siege. Cogny conceived of it more as a base for guerrilla operations against Giap's rear links, although heavy enemy concentrations in the area made it an improbable choice as an anchor for such light mobile forces. Navarre disposed of a total of 100 battalions, though all but twenty-seven of these were absorbed in the static defences of the de Lattre Line protecting the Red River delta. However, with his professional soldier's low esteem for the potential of Giap's irregulars, he further divided his forces by attempting a simultaneous large-scale operation in south Vietnam. Thus only nine battalions remained by Dien Bien Phu, whereas it would probably have required at least fifty to safeguard so large a perimeter as that delineated by the chain of hills dominating Dien Bien Phu's wide valley.

This then was the situation when the first paratroopers launched Operation Castor on 21 November 1953. By Christmas a series of costly failures had made it clear to the French that Dien Bien Phu could not be used as a base for offensive operations as General Cogny had hoped. The French next undertook a second battle, designed to dislodge the enemy from dangerous look-out points they had established on the surrounding heights, from which the whole valley, and its essential airstrip, could be kept under constant observation. In the first attack, misdirected French artillery fire killed fifteen of their own Algerian colonial troops. By mid-February 1954 this second battle had also been lost, with the garrison abandoning the crucial heights. On the 17th, Cogny gave the order that attacks out of Dien Bien Phu were henceforth to be limited to 'light reconnaissance'. The fact that simultaneously two Viet Minh columns were striking in both north and south Laos clearly demonstrated that Dien Bien Phu had already forfeited any usefulness as a base for active counter-insurgent operations. From now on its role would be purely defensive.

Meanwhile, General Giap had willingly accepted Navarre's

challenge. With superhuman efforts some 50,000 coolies, living off a few pounds of rice a day and wheeling specially strengthened bicycles (an idea inherited from Tsuji in Malaya in 1941–2) that could carry 450-pound cargoes, were methodically moving up a siege train of over 200 guns. Many of them were American 105mm medium pieces, captured by the Chinese, either during the Korean Bug-Out or earlier from Chiang Kai-shek's defeated Kuomintang, and heavier than anything yet used by Giap. Using the utmost ingenuity and industry, Giap's gunners burrowed through the crests of the hills wrested from the French. Thus the muzzles of the guns poked out of small tunnels, pointing directly down on to the French garrison, and presenting targets almost impossible to hit. When the defenders had been asked what would happen if the Viet Minh installed their artillery on the forward slopes facing Dien Bien Phu, the response was that this had never been done since Napoleon.

While Giap was slowly mustering his siege forces, the French could still have used their air mobility to withdraw the garrison, and, having pinned down the bulk of Giap's forces, gain a tactical victory elsewhere. But Navarre, hubristically confident in the superiority of his arms over a guerrilla force in a pitched battle, was determined to sit it out at Dien Bien Phu. His sappers, however, estimated that it would take five months to fly in the materials alone for constructing the necessary fortifications. Then it was discovered that, though it was surrounded by jungle woodlands, the actual valley of Dien Bien Phu was completely denuded of timber, essential to the construction of deep dug-outs. And while Giap's men burrowed into the surrounding hills, the French did little to make Dien Bien Phu more tenable. Their reluctance to dig in, in contrast to the British and the Germans, had been noted ever since the First World War. 'The trenches were often dug only to knee level,' a survivor stated after the battle, 'there were no shelters, no blockhouses, nothing. Even the latrines were unsandbagged.' Worse still, the guns and mortars were not properly dug in and, glinting in their open firing positions, were strikingly visible to the Viet Minh up on the hills. Colonel Charles Piroth, the one-armed artillery commander at Dien Bien Phu, had refused offers of extra artillery. 'I have more than I need,' he declared, adding, 'We know to the nearest gun what they have got. We shall win because we have some 155s with plunging fire.'

When questioned by the visiting Minister of Defence, René Pleven, about the threat from Viet Minh artillery, another colonel retorted, 'We shall fight as at Verdun'. With all its pyrrhic glory, Verdun seems to have been never very far from French minds at Dien Bien Phu, and it was certainly the horrors and carnage of that battle that were to be evoked there. Nominated to command the outpost, General Christian de Castries remarked to General Cogny that the situation was 'somewhat like Verdun'. Yet this was only partially a valid analogy, since French forces besieged at Dien Bien Phu had to be entirely resupplied by air on an exposed landing strip that was within range of Viet Minh artillery fire. In stark contrast, the French forces at Verdun had been resupplied by roads and railways that were largely beyond the reach of German long-range artillery. On another occasion, General Navarre told the US Ambassador, Donald R. Heath, that Dien Bien Phu was 'a veritable jungle Verdun which he hopes will be attacked as it will result in terrific casualties to the Viet Minh and will not fall'. To Bernard Fall, author of the seminal account of Dien Bien Phu, it was 'Verdun transported into a tropical setting'. A more recent author likened the effect of the dense shelling to that of Verdun, in that the steady rain of projectiles 'ground the whole top layer of soil into fine sand and caused bunkers and trenches to implode'.

Finally, at the official commission of 1955 inquiring into causes of the disaster, the question was raised, poignantly, as to whether the 'fortifications . . . were as good as Verdun'. To us of the twenty-first century it may seem bizarre that soldiers fighting a battle in 1954 would hark back so frequently to the circumstances of forty years previously. But there it was. Constantly repeated in that deadly valley was the brave slogan of 1916: '*Ils ne passeront pas!*'

The fifty-one-year-old Colonel Christian Marie Ferdinand de la Croix de Castries, in command of the French fortress as the battle began, was, like de Lattre, a dashing and courageous cavalryman, of aristocratic lineage, trained at the elitist cavalry school at Saumur. In 1940 he had been captured by the Germans, but escaped to rejoin the French Army and fight with the Allies through North Africa and Italy and in the South of France landings of 1944. Already wounded during the Italian campaign, when he was captured once more but made repeated escape attempts, he had been wounded again by a landmine in

Indo-China which had smashed both his legs. He had then spent a year recuperating in France. Like Cogny, he walked with a cane and a limp. Always wearing the flashy fore-and-aft scarlet cap of the Spahis, he was described by contemporaries as a 'swashbuckling' figure, with a passion for equestrian sports and women. Each of the outposts at Dien Bien Phu was given a female name – such as Isabelle, Gabrielle and Huguette – reputedly after ladies in the commander's life. But was a cavalryman the ideal choice for command of an immobile front-line fortress?

On 13 March, as twenty-eight Viet Minh infantry battalions, comprising 37,500 men, braced themselves for battle, Giap opened his bombardment. Simultaneously numerous explosive charges were detonated so as to deceive Piroth's gunners as to the location of the Viet Minh guns, which, in their underground positions, proved to be almost invulnerable to both gunfire and air strikes. Terrible destruction was wreaked almost immediately on the ill-prepared French positions, and that very same day the Beatrice strongpoint fell to mass attacks by Giap's shock troops. Two days later the Gabrielle strongpoint was captured. The fanaticism of Giap's men, who used the still-living bodies of their own casualties as duck-boards, to avoid being blown up on the French mines, greatly impressed, and demoralized, its Algerian defenders. The same day Colonel Piroth, who had guaranteed that no enemy cannon 'would be able to fire three rounds before being destroyed', was so overcome with remorse that he blew himself up with a hand-grenade. By 31 March, Isabelle, consisting of a quarter of a square mile in which 1,800 men fought permanently in waist-deep swamp water, was isolated from the main garrison.

As Giap's noose drew ever tighter round de Castries' besieged camp, in Paris the politicians were wrangling over the niceties of German rearmament and the proposed European Defence Community. The Foreign Minister Georges Bidault was in an advanced state of alcoholism. In London his counterpart, Anthony Eden, was poised to rebuff any suggestion of British intervention, let alone deployment of nuclear weapons. In the US the Secretary of State John Foster Dulles and the Joint Chiefs of Staff talked vaingloriously about dropping a few nukes or air strikes on the Viet Minh lines gripping Dien Bien Phu. All this talk led to serious disillusion in France, which later turned to angry resentment. On 4 April, 'poor Joseph' Laniel addressed a desperate cry for help, in the form of direct US Air Force intervention from carriers in the region. The State Department temporized, amid much speechifying about the 'domino theory', which held that if one country succumbed to communism, neighbouring countries would do so too. About the only aid sent was in the form of Secretary Dulles to an unenthusiastic London.

Meanwhile throughout April conditions for the defenders became progressively more horrifying. They were particularly bad for the wounded, for whom there were no adequate medical supplies, hospital space or doctors, and matters were worsened by Giap's deliberate refusal to pick up his own wounded. These problems were compounded by the heat and tropical diseases, and of course as the siege grew tighter the gravely wounded could not be evacuated. In charge of Dien Bien Phu's so-called Mobile Surgical Unit was a fifty-four-year-old army doctor, Major Paul-Henri Grauwin.* Once the airstrip was put out of use in April, Grauwin found his surgical bunker overwhelmed. The bald statistics speak for themselves: over the two months of the siege, his unit registered 6,215 admissions, 739 operations, 324 evacuations and 252 deaths; in one night he and another surgeon amputated twenty-three limbs and repaired ten abdominal and ten chest wounds. There was a saying among the German Legionnaires, '*Magen Schuss, Kopf Schuss – ist Spritzer*' ('Belly shot, head shot – then it's an overdose job') – meaning a lethal injection of morphine.

As if these appalling conditions, with dwindling supplies, were not enough, there were the all-pervasive black ants; rats that would gnaw undeterred at the wounded; and maggots that throve on gangrenous flesh. Grauwin could never quite persuade his revolted patients that the fat white scavengers were beneficial to healing, in that they cleaned up the dead tissue. By the end of the battle in May, ankle-deep in evil-smelling mud, with no electricity and 1,300 wounded, so crowded together that their limbs overlapped, Grauwin was forced to operate by candle-light.

Like an episode from a more romantic era, the ugly saga of Dien Bien Phu was modulated by the presence at Major Grauwin's right

---

* Having survived the battle, and imprisonment by the Viet Minh, Grauwin wrote a searing account of his experiences, translated as *Doctor at Dien-Bien-Phu* (London, 1955).

hand of the only female nurse, Lieutenant Geneviève de Galard-Terraube, who was to become lauded as 'the angel of Dien Bien Phu'. Lieutenant Galard, who was qualified as an in-flight nurse with the French Air Force, was accompanying battle casualties back to Hanoi from Dien Bien Phu on 28 March when the C-47 on which she was the *convoyeuse* was damaged on landing, and was unable to take off again. At daylight the Viet Minh artillery destroyed the C-47, damaged the runway beyond repair and left Geneviève de Galard stranded. She volunteered to work in the field hospital alongside Grauwin, her special status as the only female nurse in the camp granting her (in lieu of a bedroom) a small cell lined with parachute silk and furnished with a cot and chair. Overcoming male prejudices, she gained immense respect for the selfless way in which she comforted the dying, and was placed in charge of a forty-bed room housing some of the most gravely wounded.

Incongruously, in addition to the brave Geneviève, also present at Dien Bien Phu were a number of Vietnamese and North African prostitutes, brought there to staff the essential army *bordel*. These unfortunate women were also conscripted into helping in Dr Grauwin's lazarette.

The defenders – paratroops, Legionnaires, Algerians and Indo-Chinese detachments* – continued to fight back with extraordinary courage and endurance. By early April Giap's men had already suffered some 10,000 casualties – representing half of the total Viet Minh forces – and their morale showed signs of ebbing as the *tricolore* still waved at Dien Bien Phu. Giap was concerned that 50 per cent of all his effectives were committed to the siege. In the view of at least one American writer, 'The People's Army came much closer to military failure at Dien Bien Phu than is generally believed.' If only the French means, and will, had not been lacking.

Although the French at home were by and large sick to death of the war in Indo-China, those on the spot tended – as previously noted – to continue to regard Dien Bien Phu, spiritually, as something of a

---

* It is not correct to speak only of 'French' defenders. Many in fact were Foreign Legionnaires, of whom a majority were Germans escaping from the debacle of war at home. In addition, there were substantial numbers of colonial Algerian *tirailleurs*, who fought with varying degrees of determination in what was for them an unpopular war.

requital of honour; but if the heroism of the troops more than made up for the humiliations of 1940, the same could hardly be said of their senior commanders, some of whom, worse than the Bourbons, seem to have learned nothing and forgotten everything. Bernard Fall's remark that they (and the politicians in Paris) spent their time writing memoranda 'concerned with covering themselves more against personal responsibility than against enemy attacks' has a nasty ring of the Third Republic about it. By mid-March, unappeasable hatred had grown between the cat-like Navarre and the bull-like Cogny, in a style all too reminiscent of Lords Lucan and Cardigan in the Crimean War a century earlier. Working in the same building, they communicated only by memoranda or via intermediaries, and Navarre seems never to have made his intentions properly clear to any of the executants.

Colonel de Castries, though certainly not lacking courage, displayed a patrician distaste from another age, for mud and blood. After his chief of staff had broken down and had been flown out, de Castries was not often seen outside his command post. According to Colonel Jules Roy, author of *The Battle of Dienbienphu*, de Castries, for all his known personal courage, 'timidly used his reserves to stop gaps or mend holes, not to strike. In reality he could not get them together because there were no shelters large enough to contain them.' A sapper, or at least an infantry commander, might indeed have been a better choice for Dien Bien Phu than a cavalryman.

The quartermaster's branch was a mess, and air supply inept – partly, it seems, because a certain national arrogance impeded the French from benefiting from United States experience. On the other hand, the French Air Force was undoubtedly deceived by its American colleagues (as indeed they would deceive themselves in the 1960s) as to the efficacy of interdiction bombing against an Asiatic enemy in Korea. Swiftly Giap's guns made the vital airstrip at Dien Bien Phu unusable. Now the second of the major French miscalculations began to exert its lethal influence. From China, Giap had amassed a formidable array of anti-aircraft weapons, shipped in from Korea where they were no longer needed. Transport pilots flying into his murderous flak 'envelope' compared it unfavourably with wartime experiences over Germany. Losses, hard to replace from the French Air Force's slender resources, mounted steadily. Day by day the Viet Minh dug out trenches like tentacles towards the French strongpoints, gradually encircling them in preparation for the final assault. Although Dien Bien Phu still held out with incredible heroism, and continued to receive small paratroop reinforcements, there was now no hope of escape for the beleaguered garrison. Moreover, much of the arms and ammunition parachuted in fell into Giap's hands.

Conceivably more and better tactical air support could have saved Dien Bien Phu, and at least have ensured a more durable peace in Indo-China. (It is worth noting that whereas during the 167 days of siege at Dien Bien Phu air sorties totalled 10,400, in 1966, during the Second Vietnam War, the weekly American total alone often exceeded 25,000.) In 1954, the only source which could have provided this extra air cover was the United States, and France pleaded repeatedly for assistance. Admiral Arthur W. Radford, the US Chairman of the Joint Chiefs of Staff (the same who had expressed puzzlement at the Wake Island meeting between Truman and MacArthur in 1950), was distinctly favourable, but John Foster Dulles, President Eisenhower's Secretary of State, was badly misinformed and until the end was unable to appreciate the issues at stake. Against a shocking background of muddle and machinations, Dulles constantly encouraged the French to fight on beyond their means, while misleading them as to the extent of direct support the United States might be expected to provide *in extremis*. He is reported to have talked wildly about dropping 'one or two atom bombs' on Giap, and, contingent on British acquiescence, a heavy air strike from American carriers was actually planned for the end of April. But Anthony Eden, now Prime Minister and bent on a course of non-intervention, was determined that Indo-China was to go to the negotiating table at the Geneva Conference the following month, and had made this clear to the Americans all along.

On 4 May morale at Dien Bien Phu received a bitter shock when a group of Moroccan colonial troops cut a hole through the barbed-wire defences and defected. The Viet Minh were swift to prevent the hole being plugged by the defenders, and kept it open. Two days later, Giap brought up Russian Katyusha rockets to administer the *coup de grâce*. As a final illusion, the embattled defenders at first took the noise of the rockets to be that of a French relief column. Typical of the persistent French heroism in the last hours was that of a tank commander who had plaster casts removed from both arms, broken earlier in the battle, so that he could man the one remaining operational tank. The last survivor of the Chaffee light tanks that had been flown in and laboriously reassembled, poignantly christened *Douaumont* after the great fort at Verdun, was knocked out at the end of April. All its crew were killed by a direct hit from a 105mm gun.

On 7 May, with men dying at their posts from the effects of fifty-five days of constant bombardment and little sleep or food, Dien Bien Phu was overwhelmed. A French barrage broke up the first assault wave, but later that night the Viet Minh detonated a mine shaft, blowing up the strongpoint known as Eliane 2. Within a few hours they had overrun what remained of de Castries' defences. Later that same day, Giap ordered an all-out attack against the remaining French units with over 25,000 Viet Minh (their numbers bolstered by new forces emerging from the jungle) against fewer than 3,000 garrison troops. At 1700, de Castries radioed French headquarters in Hanoi and talked with Cogny.

> DE CASTRIES: The Viets are everywhere. The situation is very grave. The combat is confused and goes on all around. I feel the end is approaching, but we will fight to the finish.
> COGNY: Of course you will fight to the end. It is out of the question to run up the white flag after your heroic resistance.

Specifically ordered by Cogny not to fly the white flag, Dien Bien Phu never surrendered. In Paris, a woman deputy was heard sobbing as Laniel announced the fall of the fortress to the National Assembly, adding the pointed note: 'France must remind her allies that for seven years now the Army of the French Union has unceasingly protected a particularly crucial region of Asia, and has alone defended the interests of all ...'

It was the ninth anniversary of VE-Day, the victory over Germany. But unsurprisingly celebrations in France were muted.

The calvary was not yet over, however, for the French survivors of Dien Bien Phu. Allegedly out of fear of their being liberated by a French column, the Viet Minh forced their prisoners into killing marches of several hundred miles. Many of the exhausted French, as well as the badly wounded, could not keep up. They were either despatched arbitrarily by their escorts, or left by the wayside to the rats and ants. Out of the original total of 16,544, and of the 10,863 counted as having survived the siege and been taken prisoner, only 3,290 were officially repatriated four months later. Over 3,000 died in the battle, possibly 400 in the last two days' desperate fighting alone. These casualties amounted to 25 per cent of the total committed, a truly terrible proportion rivalling First World War figures. They also represented roughly one-tenth of all French effectives in the whole of Indo-China. Giap's army suffered 8,000 dead and 15,000 wounded. Instead of the 25,000 shells that French intelligence assessed was all Giap's transport could bring up, 350,000 had fallen on the garrison, including 12,000 accidentally presented to the Viet Minh by inaccurate French air drops.

The day after the fall of Dien Bien Phu, in peaceful Switzerland the agenda of the Geneva Conference turned to Indo-China. In consequence France under Pierre Mendès France (the government of 'poor Joseph' Laniel having been swept away on the backwash) withdrew entirely from Indo-China. Thanks to the conference, partition created the communist state of North Vietnam, triumphant and strong in victory, and the weak independent fragments of South Vietnam, Cambodia and Laos. It was the end, with brutal swiftness, of the French dream of *l'Indochine*. Six months later, the standard of revolt against France was hoisted in Algeria, many of whose troops had fought at Dien Bien Phu and had seen France humbled by an army of Asiatic peasants. Dien Bien Phu was to cost France not only Indo-China but the rest of its empire as well.

The imbalance left behind in Vietnam was to lead directly to American intervention. Together with the Korean War, Dien Bien Phu might well be rated one of the most decisive events since 1945. They both demonstrated the superiority of an underdeveloped but impassioned irregular force over a conventional army – a superiority which has still not been overcome today.

The collapse of the hubristic notions of the French foreshadowed any number of historic developments. It would bring about, inevitably, the involvement of the United States claiming to be a supporter of democratic regimes confronting aggressive, expansionist communism, though the left might regard it as another form of colonialism. Despite the destruction of the idealism displayed by the French 'Centurions',[*] the French soldiers who had fought so bravely and resolutely at Dien Bien Phu did not regard it as a battle lost in vain. To them it was just one round in the war against international communism. Soon, the battleground would shift to Algeria. The same French names, such as Yves Godard and Marcel Bigeard, heroes of the one-more-lost battle, would reappear. Confusing enemies, the Paras arrived in Algeria still speaking of '*les Viets*' and convinced that the Algerian uprising too was communist-inspired. They were deceived; it was in fact a display of Arab nationalism, pure and simple, of a variety with which the West would soon become acquainted. As much as in Indo-China, the Paras arrived determined, idiosyncratically, that here was a battle that could not be lost, that had to be won.

Hard as the French fought there, defeat in Algeria led to the downfall of the Fourth Republic and the advent of de Gaulle. Then came revolt against de Gaulle himself, led by disillusioned Paras, which terminated in 1961 with the highly dangerous Revolt of the Generals, headed by Raoul Salan. The abortive Suez operation of 1956,[†] strongly supported by the French Paras, was one more factor, engendered at Dien Bien Phu, that persuaded Frenchmen across the board of the *perfidie* of their Anglo-Saxon allies, who had so markedly let them down in Indo-China. Breaking away from NATO, France progressively decided to do its own thing, a course that would continue through to its resolute opposition to the Iraq War of 2003. Such is the knock-on effect of history.

---

[*] Eponymous title of an outstandingly realistic novel of the era by Jean Larteguy.
[†] Operation Musketeer, an Anglo-French-Israeli plan to recapture the Suez Canal after it had been nationalised by Egyptian President Gamal Abdel Nasser.

EPILOGUE

The French humiliation, and for all the desperate courage shown at Dien Bien Phu it was a deep humiliation, together with the Korean War, marked roughly the end of the first half of the twentieth century. It was a half-century that would leave its mark on world history as the nastiest, cruellest and most brutal ever recorded: and it was the first half of the century of hubris. But, with the detonation of the US bombs at Hiroshima and Nagasaki, and the Soviet Union's acquisition of the same technology, the name of the game changed completely. The superpowers accepted that they could not win a total victory in the style of Napoleon or Hitler. It was altogether too dangerous, if not suicidal. Instead wars were fought with a long reach, by proxy. The US and NATO allies would never allow themselves to come close to direct conflict with the Soviets. Instead wars were fought in Vietnam, Africa and other distant parts of the world by lesser allies, client states, with the great powers in the background. The same could be said of the various Middle Eastern flare-ups. So to a certain extent battles would revert to the style of the eighteenth century, with limited objectives, such as America's war in Vietnam, or President Anwar Sadat's Yom Kippur assault on Israel in 1973.

But the French defeat at Dien Bien Phu did not mark the end of the conflicts of the twentieth century that were scarred by hubris. This book has largely been concerned with conflicts, up to the mid-century, emerging from the Pacific area or Hitler's aggression in Europe. To leap now to the Middle East threatens contextual problems, as it does indeed raise a whole new series of issues. Yet it is impossible to leave the subject of hubris without brief reference to the Six Day War between Israel and its Arab neighbours, followed by a second round with the Yom Kippur War in 1973. No cycle of war described in this book could have displayed hubris, followed by its natural consequence of peripeteia, better than this two-part contest in the Middle East. I have already written about this conflict elsewhere,* but it is essential to make a brief detour here.

By any measure, the Six Day War of June 1967 was one of history's most outstanding campaigns, even if the sunshine has subsequently been dimmed by the realization that it was, from the Israeli side, something of a pre-emptive, lightning strike. The Israelis, however, had made it quite plain that if Egypt's President Nasser blockaded the Straits of Tehran, which would have closed sea access through to Israel's port of Eilat, a red line would be crossed. On 23 May that year the Egyptians did just that. A nation that holds a red line to be a red line, Israel attacked first with an airstrike on the morning of 5 June that destroyed on the ground almost the whole of the Egyptian Air Force. The Israelis then set to destroying the air forces of both Syria and Jordan. The fighting that ensued was a veritable Old Testament victory – Samson and the jawbone of an ass, or Joshua and the walls of Jericho. The Arab armies were shattered, and unfortunate Jordan found itself shorn of all its territories, and responsibilities, on the West Bank.

The resulting sudden transformation of Israel was remarkable and, in the long term, questionable. In those six days it metamorphosed from being an underdog, under constant threat of destruction, to being a power which demanded to be taken into account. Many problems surfaced with victory – one of them the re-emergence of the Palestinian problem. But what was most injurious was the effect it had on the Israelis' mindset, from top to bottom. One eminent Israeli historian, Anita Shapira, in *Israel: A History* (2014) aptly labels the period 1967–73 'The Age of Euphoria' and goes on to quote the Psalms: 'We were like unto them that dream.' Euphoria, or hubris?

Unfortunately for Israel, the brilliant victory in 1967, decisive though it was, did not bring about the dream of peace the country longed for. I was in Israel a couple of years later, and found the whole country still on a high. In Tel Aviv I had an extraordinary encounter with one of the architects of the victory, General Ezer Weizman (later President of Israel). He asked me, as a British historian, for my view of what Israel's next move might be. I said, perhaps incautiously, that I thought Israel

---

* In *Kissinger's Year* (2009) and *But What Do You Actually Do?* (2011).

had one year to make a good peace. This provoked an explosion from Weizman who, launching into an astonishingly racist diatribe about the martial inadequacies of the Egyptians, declared: 'After the victory we have just won we can lick any combination of Arabs that comes against us.'

Weizman, through tragic personal circumstances – his son was gravely wounded in the 1973 war – later swung from being an ultra hawk to being an ultra dove, but in 1969 he represented a very wide cross-section of Israeli opinion, still exultant over the Six Day War. Shapira succinctly sums up the mood I had heard expressed by General Weizman: 'Complacency reigned in Israel due to the scale of the 1967 victory ... The military leadership considered the Egyptian Army inferior and incapable of sacrifice and perseverance.' For the first time a sense almost of invulnerability took over in Israel, a nation that had felt insecure since its creation in 1948. The standard of living soared, particularly among the new rich who thrived on construction projects funded by military contracts. The disease of hubris infected the nation from top to bottom, with the High Command assessing, by 1973, that there would be at least a forty-eight-hour warning if war were to break out again, which would guarantee enough time to mobilize Israeli reserves.

In fact, when Egypt and Syria attacked on Yom Kippur in October 1973, the Arabs astonished the world. In particular it was surprised by Egypt's attack across the Suez Canal. Israel suffered heavy casualties, notably to its vital air force thanks to the careful deployment of Russian anti-aircraft missiles. There was near panic among the Israeli generalship. Moshe Dayan, the charismatic one-eyed Minister of Defence, who had earlier been heard to boast, 'The Americans offer us money and advice; we accept the money and reject the advice,' suffered a nervous breakdown. In private he was talking about the destruction of 'the Third Temple', a metaphor for the State of Israel. There was also talk of using the Jericho weapon, the atomic bomb. Israel came very close to suffering the ultimate penalty of peripeteia. Its armies were defeated at both ends of the country: in the Golan Heights in the north, and in Sinai in the south. It would almost certainly have suffered crushing defeat but for the rushing of American arms to the front, backed up by the remarkable shuttle diplomacy of US Secretary of State Henry Kissinger. Eventually, Israel scored another notable victory. But only just.

All in all the two campaigns showed every ingredient of a classical disaster, a demonstration of the pitfalls that follow the development of hubris. One could enlarge on the consequences of the 1973 Yom Kippur War at length. They are still with us: internationalization of the war in the Middle East, with the attendant danger of its spreading. One might even judge that this second defeat of the Arab armies led – as necessity in war often does – to the invention of a new secret weapon: the human suicide bomber.

In the course of these studies I have pointed out how seldom it is that successful warlords know when to stop. A related observation, and perhaps an obvious one, is how little leaders ever seem capable of learning from history. But the real lesson, I think, is how deep-seated these failings are. The Middle Eastern case study is instructive. All nations have security concerns – they wouldn't be nations if they didn't – and it is fair to say that no nation has felt less secure than Israel. Yet the Israelis, of all people, plainly gave way to hubris in the triumphant wake of the Six-Day War, even though for them it represented an existential threat – the destruction of the Third Temple.

It is easy to condemn all the follies we have been looking at, but Israel's experience shows very clearly that we humans find it difficult to resist infection by hubris. Perhaps we are most vulnerable to it at the moment of our greatest success. Yet it is more insidious than that, because the infection lingers: the heroics of Verdun led to the peripeteia of Dien Bien Phu a full thirty-eight years later, and those of Tsushima to the miscalculations of the Kwantung hotheads at Nomonhan and of Yamamoto at Midway several decades later.

And it is insidious not just over time but in its reach, as can be seen by how thoroughly it pervaded Israel after 1967 – it was not just the High Command, let alone just one man, who succumbed. Mac-Arthur's spectacular downfall happened because, seduced by his record of success, his political and military superiors allowed him, invited him, to venture beyond the 38th Parallel. In other words it was not just the Generalissimo's Caesarism that brought about his misjudgements. The *Führerprinzip* that allowed Hitler to create disaster before Moscow (and elsewhere) was given life not just by his own act of will but by the connivance of millions of Germans. And the mystical nationalism that proved fatal for Japan was a political and cultural phenomenon embraced throughout the Land of the Rising Sun.

If hubris is part of the human condition – deep-seated, lingering, pervasive and potentially lethal – what can we do to avoid it? If it is not just our leaders who ignore history and their own experience, as these chapters have shown, we might conclude that we all have something to learn.

We can go back to where we started in the Prologue, with the ancient Greeks. For Aristotle, *arete* (virtue or excellence) was something that falls between two extremes, between excess on the one hand and defect on the other. It is to be judged according to the circumstances – there is no advance prescription that tells us what to do. But we can be guided by recognizing the two extremes and looking for the mean. Hubris is plainly always the extreme of excess, and by accepting that it lies in wait for us – whether we are a warlord or a simple citizen – we are better equipped to avoid it.

That is not to say that we should always be cautious, or that acts of daring are wrong. Far from it. What we and our leaders need to understand is that the exuberance that follows victory all too easily leads to the wrong decision. Perhaps there are other clues that hubris is creeping up on us. As I have pointed out in these pages, a racist contempt for the enemy has often been a symptom indicating that a leader and even his people are in the grip of hubris – and heading for trouble.

While completing this book, I reread that eloquent and wise writer Albert Camus. His novel *The Plague* describes a mythical pandemic which devastates the North African town of Oran, and which is generally accepted to be an allegory for war or fascism, or some other universal, unspecified evil. The plague is defeated, and Oran celebrates its victory with a firework display witnessed by the novel's hero Dr Rieux. The novel concludes with this passage:

> as he listened to the cries of joy arising from the town, Rieux remembered that such joy is always imperilled. He knew what those jubilant crowds did not know, but could have learned from books: that the plague bacillus never dies or disappears for good; that it can lie dormant for years and years in furniture and linen-chests; that it

bides its time in bedrooms, cellars, trunks and bookshelves; and that perhaps the day would come when, for the bane and the enlightening of men, it would rouse up its rats again and send them forth to die in a happy city.

With the world facing ever more menacing dangers from ambitious leaders, from gangs of warlords and from terrorists, we should note – as the ancient Greeks did – the terrible penalties which befall those who release from Pandora's box the dormant bacillus of hubris.

ACKNOWLEDGEMENTS

After Ruskin castigated Whistler for charging 200 guineas for the labour of two days, Whistler replied crushingly, 'No, I ask you for the knowledge I have gained in the work of a lifetime.' Attempting to express the depth of appreciation I owe over *Hubris* somewhat echoes Whistler – at least in terms of *gestation*. Should my acknowledgments cover only the three years in which *Hubris* actually took to write, or should it go back further?

I was born a few years after the First World War, surrounded by its poignant memories; so most of my childhood life perforce consisted of thinking about war. As a teenage schoolboy in the Second World War, I was given the task of keeping up the school's 'Operation Map', moving small flags backwards and forwards. While the actual battles were raging on the plains of Russia and in the Pacific, it was all very immediate. Most of the time the flags bearing the sinister swastika and the rising sun seemed to move remorselessly forward. After I joined up in 1943, aged seventeen, life evolved seamlessly into active education for warfare.

I began writing my first book on war, *The Price of Glory*, in 1960. Should this date, in fact, be a marker on the road to acknowledgments? If so, I remain indebted to the guru of Medmenham, the late Sir Basil Liddell Hart, whose teaching may have lost some credibility over the passage of time, but who taught one to *think* about war. Then, in succession to him, came the 'Captain Professor', Sir Michael Howard. To him I owe a continuing gratitude for his (to use his favourite word) 'judicious' analysis of history. There followed in his wake the new wave of 'young lions' of military historians, headed by the illustrious Sir John Keegan who, in his seminal *The Face of Battle*, made us all look at warfare in a different dimension.

I have drawn the most enormous – and often unquantifiable

287

– benefit from my association with St Antony's College, Oxford, for over forty years. This particularly applies to all the help I have received over *Hubris* from the Nissan, Russian and Middle East centres. My last book of purely military history, *How Far from Austerlitz?*, was published nearly twenty years ago, but it left me with an enduring indebtedness to David Mynett, who accompanied me to the field of Austerlitz, and sketched most of the illustrations. David was as talented a historian as he was an artist, and he helped me to see a great battlescape in terms of paint and perspective – particularly, in *Hubris*, the grim scenes before Moscow, 1941.

For specific items of research, I am indebted to Alistair Berven of Princeton University, for his the work on Japan between the wars.

Among publishers I owe thanks to Alan Samson and the indefatigable George Weidenfeld for their initial enthusiasm for the *Hubris* project. I have been blessed with two of the brightest editors any author could ask for, Bea Hemming at Weidenfeld & Nicolson and Jonathan Jao of HarperCollins in New York. Then there is this mystical and magical figure, the copy-editor. Peter James, supreme in his calling, has that rare capacity to put himself inside the author's psyche: you disobey him at your peril. In seven books of what he calls 'Horneana', which Peter has edited, I have tried hard not to. If any error should nevertheless have eluded these editorial eagle eyes it is, of course, with the author where the buck stops.

I am beholden to my literary agents, Michael Sissons and Fiona Petherham of PFD in London and Peter Matson in New York; all of whom have provided constant support. For picture and map collation, my gratitude extends to Holly Harley. The toilsome task of marshalling my research notes, and typing out chapters, has fallen to Liz Longley; I am particularly grateful for her ineffable good humour.

I owe warm appreciation in a different coin, notably to two dedicated South African carers, Zelda and Cathy, who brought me back from the dark abyss of a stroke, just in time to complete *Hubris*.

Finally, a tribute to my patient wife, Sheelin. Though she says she hates war, she has put up with it, sacrificing many an hour at her precious painting to read displeasingly martial manuscripts. Her support alone makes this book worthwhile – at least to me.

SELECT BIBLIOGRAPHY

Part One: Tsushima, 1905

Beasley, W.G., *The Modern History of Japan* (London, 1963)
—— *Japanese Imperialism, 1894–1945* (Oxford, 1987)
Buruma, Ian, *Inventing Japan, 1853–1964* (New York, 2003)
Falk, E.A., *Togo and the Rise of Japanese Sea Power* (New York, 1936)
Forczyk, Robert, *Russian Battleship vs Japanese Battleship: Yellow Sea, 1904–1905* (Oxford, 2009)
Hough, Richard Alexander, *The Fleet That Had to Die* (New York, 1960)
Jukes, Geoffrey, *The Russo-Japanese War 1904–1905* (Oxford, 2002)
Kennedy, Paul, *The Rise and Fall of the Great Powers: Economic Change and Military Conflict from 1500 to 2000* (New York, 1987)
Koenig, William, *Epic Sea Battles* (London, 1977; rev. edn, 2004)
Mahan, Alfred T., *The Influence of Sea Power Upon History, 1660–1783* (New York, 1890)
Morris, Edmund, *Theodore Rex* (New York, 2012)
Nish, Ian, *The Origins of the Russo-Japanese War* (London, 1985)
Pleshakov, Constantine, *The Tsar's Last Armada: The Epic Voyage to the Battle of Tsushima* (New York, 2002)
Seager, Robert, *Alfred Thayer Mahan: The Man and His Letters* (Annapolis, 1975)
Semenov, Vladimir Ivanovich, *The Battle of Tsu-Shima* (London, 1906)
—— *Rasplata, or the Price of Blood* (London, 1909)
Sondhaus, Lawrence, *Naval Warfare, 1815–1914* (New York, 2001)
Warner, Denis and Peggy, *The Tide at Sunrise: A History of the Russo-Japanese War 1904–1905* (New York, 1975)
Westwood, J.N., *Russia Against Japan, 1904–1905* (Albany, 1986)

Part Two: Nomonhan, 1939

Colvin, John, *Nomonhan* (London, 1999)
Coox, Alvin D., *Nomonhan: Japan Against Russia, 1939* (Stanford, 1985)
Deakin, F.W., and G.R. Storry, *The Case of Richard Sorge* (London, 1966)
Drea, Edward, *Nomonhan: Japanese-Soviet Tactical Combat, 1939* (Kansas, 1981)

Erickson, John, *The Soviet High Command: A Military-Political History, 1918–1941* (London, 2001)

Zhukov, Georgy, *G. Zhukov, Marshal of the Soviet Union: Reminiscences and Reflections* (Moscow, 1974)

Part Three: Moscow, 1941

Beevor, Anthony, *Stalingrad* (London, 2007)

Billington, J.H., *Fire in the Minds of Men* (New York, 1980)

Braithwaite, Rodric, *Moscow 1941: A City and its People at War* (London, 2006)

Cohen, Eliot and John Gooch, *Military Misfortunes: The Anatomy of Failure in War* (New York, 1990)

Deakin, F.W. and G.R. Storry, *The Case of Richard Sorge* (London, 1966)

Downing, D., *The Moscow Option: An Alternative Second World War* (London, 2001)

Erickson, John, *The Road to Stalingrad: Stalin's War with Germany*, vol. i (London, 1983)

Erickson, John and David Dilks, *Barbarossa: The Axis and the Allies* (Edinburgh, 1994)

Glantz, David, *Barbarossa: Hitler's Invasion of Russia 1941* (Stroud, 2001)

—— *Colossus Reborn: The Red Army at War 1941–1943* (Kansas, 2005)

—— *The Initial Period of War on the Eastern Front 22 June–August 1941* (London, 1993)

—— *Stumbling Colossus: The Red Army on the Eve of World War* (Kansas, 1998)

Glantz, David and Jonathan House, *When Titans Clashed: How the Red Army Stopped Hitler* (Edinburgh, 2000)

Gorodetsky, G., *Grand Delusion: Stalin and the German Invasion of Russia* (New Haven, 1999)

Grossman, Vasily, *Road to Victory: Twelve Tales of the Red Army* (London, 1945)

—— *A Writer at War: Vasily Grossman with the Red Army, 1941–1945*, eds. and trs. Antony Beevor and Luba Vinogradova (London, 2005)

Jukes, G., *The Defence of Moscow* (London, 1969)

Krivosheev, G.F., *Soviet Casualties and Combat Losses in the Twentieth Century* (London, 1997)

Larionov, V., *World War II: Decisive Battles of the Soviet Army* (Moscow, 1984)

Lucas, J., *War on the Eastern Front: The German Soldier in Russia, 1941–1945* (London, 1998)

Overy, Richard, *Russia's War, 1941–1945* (London, 2010)

Pipes, R., *The Russian Revolution, 1899–1919* (London, 1990)

Pleshakov, C., *Stalin's Folly: The Secret History of the German Invasion of Russia, June 1941* (Boston, 2005)

Sakharov, Andrei D., *Memoirs*, tr. R. Lourie (London, 1990)

Sebag Montefiore, Simon, *Stalin: The Court of the Red Tsar* (London, 2003)
Sella, A., *The Value of Life in Soviet Warfare* (London, 1992)
Shukman, Harold, *Stalin's Generals* (London, 1993)
Stolfi, R., *Hitler's Panzers East: World War II Reinterpreted* (Oklahoma, 1992)
Volkogonov, Dmitri, *Triumph and Tragedy*, tr. Harold Shukman, 2 vols (Moscow, 1989; tr. edn, London, 1991)
Werth, A., *Moscow War Diary* (New York, 1942)
—— *Russia at War, 1941–1945* (London, 1964)
Zhukov, Georgy, *G. Zhukov, Marshal of the Soviet Union: Reminiscences and Reflections* (Moscow, 1974)

Part Four: Midway, 1942

Agawa, Hiroyuki, *The Reluctant Admiral* (Tokyo, 1979)
Cook, Theodore F., Jr., 'Our Midway Disaster', in Robert Cowley, ed., *What If? The World's Foremost Military Historians Imagine What Might Have Been* (New York, 1999)
Dowler, John W., *War Without Mercy: Race and Power in the Pacific War* (New York, 1987)
Edgerton, Robert, *Warriors of the Rising Sun: A History of the Japanese Military* (Boulder, 1997)
Fuchida, Mitsuo and Masatake Okumiya, *Midway: The Battle That Doomed Japan* (Annapolis, 1955)
Hastings, Max, *Nemesis: The Battle for Japan 1944–45* (London, 2007)
Healy, Mark and David Chandler, eds., *Campaign Series, Midway 1942: Turning Point in the Pacific* (London, 1993)
Hughes, Wayne, *Fleet Tactics: Theory and Practice* (Annapolis, 1986)
Kahn, David, 'Codebreaking in World Wars I and II: the major successes and failures, their causes and their effects', *The Historical Journal*, 23/3 (1980), 617–39
Keegan, John, *The Price of Admiralty* (London, 1988)
—— *The Second World War* (London, 1997)
Lord, Walter, *Incredible Victory* (New York, 1967)
Marder, Arthur, *Old Friends, New Enemies: The Royal Navy and the Imperial Japanese Navy*, ii: *The Pacific War, 1942–1945* (Oxford, 1990)
Morison, Samuel Eliot, *History of United States Naval Operations in World War II*, vol. iv: *Coral Sea, Midway and Submarine Actions, May 1942–August 1942* (Edison, 2001)
—— *The Two-Ocean War: A Short History of the United States Navy in the Second World War* (Boston, 1963)
Nish, Ian, *Anglo-Japanese Alienation 1919–1952: Papers of the Anglo-Japanese Conference on the History of the Second World War* (Cambridge, 1982)

Overy, Richard, *Why the Allies Won* (New York, 1995)

Parshall, Jonathan and Anthony Tully, *Shattered Sword: The Untold Story of the Battle of Midway* (Dulles, 2005)

Prange, Gordon W., Donald Goldstein and Katherine Dillon, *Miracle at Midway* (New York, 1982)

Schlesinger, James R., *Midway in Retrospect: The Still Under-Appreciated Victory* (Washington D.C., 2005)

Toland, John, *The Rising Sun: The Decline and Fall of the Japanese Empire, 1936–1945* (New York, 1961)

Willmott, H.P., *The Barrier and the Javelin: Japanese and Allied Pacific Strategies, February to June 1942* (Annapolis, 1982)

Part Five: Korea and Dien Bien Phu, 1950–1954

Fall, Bernard B., *Hell in a Very Small Place: The Siege of Dien Bien Phu* (Philadelphia, 1966)

Grauwin, Paul-Henri, *Doctor at Dien-Bien-Phu* (tr. edn, London, 1955)

Greene, Graham, *The Quiet American* (New York, 1956)

Halberstam, David, *The Coldest Winter: America and the Korean War* (New York, 2007)

Halliday, John, and Bruce Cumings, *Korea: The Unknown War* (London, 1990)

Hastings, Max, *The Korean War* (London, 1987)

Horne, Alistair, *The Price of Glory, Verdun 1916* (London, 1962)

——*A Savage War of Peace: Algeria 1954–1962* (London, 1971)

Karnow, Stanley, *Vietnam: A History* (2nd edn, New York, 1997)

Logevall, Fredrik, *Choosing War: The Lost Chance for Peace and the Escalation of War in Vietnam* (Berkeley, 1999)

Morgan, Ted, *Valley of Death: The Tragedy at Dien Bien Phu That Led America into the Vietnam War* (New York, 2010)

O'Ballance, Edgar, *The Indo-China War, 1945–1954* (London, 1964)

Porch, Douglas, *The French Foreign Legion: A Complete History of the Legendary Fighting Force* (New York, 1991)

Rees, David, *Korea the Limited War* (New York, 1964)

Roy, Jules, *The Battle of Dienbienphu*, tr. Robert Baldick (New York, 1965)

Sheehan, Neil, *A Bright Shining Lie: John Paul Vann and America in Vietnam* (New York, 1988)

Stueck, William W., *Rethinking the Korean War: A New Diplomatic and Strategic History* (Princeton, 2002)

Toland, John, *In Mortal Combat: Korea, 1950–1953* (New York, 1991)

Epilogue

Ashrawi, Hanan, *This Side of Peace: A Personal Account* (London, 1995)

SELECT BIBLIOGRAPHY

Bregman, Ahron, *Israel's Wars: A History Since 1947* (2nd edn, London, 2002)

Carey, Roane, ed., *The New Intifada: Resisting Israel's Apartheid* (London, 2001)

Donovan, R., *Israel's Fight for Survival* (New York, 1967)

Eban, A., *Abba Eban: An Autobiography* (London, 1977)

Heikal, M., *The Road to Ramadan* (London, 1975)

Herzog, Chaim, *The Arab-Israeli Wars, War and Peace in the Middle East* (London, 2010)

—— *War of Atonement* (Boston, 1974)

Horne, Alistair, *Macmillan, 1894–1956* (London, 1988)

—— *Kissinger's Year: 1973* (London, 2009)

Kissinger, Henry, *White House Years* (Boston, 1979)

Meir, Golda, *My Life* (London, 1975)

O'Ballance, Edgar, *The Arab-Israeli War, 1948* (London, 1956)

—— *The Third Arab-Israeli War* (London, 1972)

Oren, Michael, *Six Days of War: June 1967 and the Making of the Modern Middle East* (Oxford, 2002)

Ovendale, Ritchie, *The Origins of the Arab-Israeli Wars* (4th edn, Oxford, 2004)

Rogan, Eugene, *The Arabs–A History* (London, 2011)

Safran, N., *From War to War: The Arab-Israeli Confrontation, 1948–1967* (New York, 1969)

Shlaim, Avi, *The Iron Wall: Israel and the Arab World* (London, 2000)

Weizman, E., *On Eagles' Wings* (Tel Aviv, 1975)

INDEX